Peace Politics

Peace Politics

The United States Between the Old and New World Orders

PAUL JOSEPH

TEMPLE UNIVERSITY PRESS

Philadelphia

Temple University Press, Philadelphia 19122

Published 1993
Printed in the United States of America

The paper used in this publication meets the minimum requirements of American National Standard for Information Sciences—Permanence of Paper for Printed Library Materials, ANSI Z39.48-1984 ♾

Library of Congress Cataloging-in-Publication Data

Joseph, Paul, 1948–
Peace politics : the United States between the old and new world orders / Paul Joseph.
p. cm.
Includes bibliographical references and index.
ISBN 1-56639-022-2 (cloth : alk. paper). — ISBN 1-56639-023-0 (pbk. : alk. paper)
1. Peace. 2. World politics—1989– 3. Security, International. 4. United States—Foreign relations—1989– I. Title.
JX1952.J75 1993
327.73–dc20 92-1775

For Linda

Contents

Acknowledgments

Peace Politics explores the need to redefine national security for U.S. citizens and to engage in a cooperative project with other nations in creating a genuine new world order. I draw attention to growing domestic problems in the United States and link global peace issues to the prospect of political realigment at home. The end of the cold war and the slow erosion of the strengths of the United States has brought the need for new departures. In both international and domestic conditions, everyone knows that things are not what they should be. But inertia characterizes our political system, and presidential politics as currently practiced has not produced a full exploration of how we could build a more secure and just foundation for our future. We need to look more deeply. I will be gratified if this book contributes to that project.

Peace Politics is an interdisciplinary work that draws from many features of our academic and political topography. I have often felt the need for guidance through the broad range of issues that are explored in this book. The following friends and colleagues, many themselves interested in interdisciplinary studies, have reviewed parts of the book, offered valuable advice, and saved me from mistakes: Ken Conca (Environmental Studies/Brazil), David Cortright (Peace Movements), Jim Ennis (Sociology/Social Movements), Sergio Fabbrini (Political Science/American Studies), Lou Ferleger (Political Economy), David Guss (Anthropology/Latin America), Ann Helweg (Economics/Latin America), Bill Hoynes (Sociology/Media Studies), Mark Lindeman (Political Science/Public Opinion), Lou Kriesberg (Sociology/

Conflict Resolution), John MacDougall (Sociology/Peace Studies), and Thomas Risse-Kappen (Political Science/Public Opinion). In diverse ways, the following individuals were also extremely helpful: Lisa Brandes, Dale Bryan, Scott Crawford, Margery Davies, Michael Denning, Richard Eichenberg, Gerald Gill, Lois Grossman, Kathy Hoffman, Sandra Lewis, Alfie Kohn, Steve Marrone, James Robbins, Rosalind Shaw, Tony Smith, and Howard Woolf. Chris Williams provided invaluable research assistance toward the end of the writing process. I also owe a special debt to David Meyer, who read every chapter and always offered detailed and useful comments. Whenever we talked, I came away with a sharper focus on what I had drafted and new ideas about how to proceed.

In a more general way, the faculty of Tufts University and my own department of sociology and anthropology provided a supportive atmosphere. Members of the Tufts Environmental Literacy Institute gave me valuable advice on an early draft of one chapter. I also found the annual meetings of the Peace Studies Association and various exchanges with the student executive board members of the Tufts Peace and Justice Studies Program very useful. The William Joiner Center of the University of Massachusetts, Boston, supported a very early stage of this project. Dean Mary Ella Feinleib helped out at the very end.

Peggy Bruno, Peg McCarthy, and Wendy Mayerson provided wonderful secretarial assistance. Work-study students Lesly Adkins-Shellie, Lauren Caputo, and Erica Hoffa helped track down some of the details with skill and a sense of humor.

An impression I often receive from other academic authors is that the craft of preparing a book for publication has become lost. Many feel that their work is slighted by the constant citation of financial and time pressures by their publishers. If true for the industry as a whole, I'm happy to report that Temple University Press is an important exception. Michael Ames offered valuable editorial advice while Debby Stuart supervised the production process with great competence. Both paid prompt attention to my questions. The copy editor, Suzanne Schafer, did an extraordinary job. I'm not sure whether the large number of marginal comments and yellow post-its she fixed to my manuscript reflects more my limitations or her diligence, but I am very grateful for her skill.

As always, my father and stepmother, Joe and Leepee Joseph, and mother, Eva Kelley, took pride in their son, sent clippings of articles, and were supportive in ways that only parents can be.

Loving my three kids—Ian, Sara, and Danny—has delayed this

project, with the serendipitous result of forcing me to confront a transformed world and a different set of issues than when I started. Their contribution to a slower schedule helped make *Peace Politics* more interesting.

Finally, I owe a huge debt to my wife, Linda Schiffman. She understood the importance of this project to me and was the person who helped me defuse the more difficult moments. Linda made it possible, particularly during the last three-month frenzy, for me to devote myself to writing in the way I thought would bring the best results. Her love and caring for our family gave me the happiness I needed.

INTRODUCTION

National Security in the Old and New World Orders

TWO POWERFUL symbols now dominate the debate over national security. The dismantling of the Berlin Wall in the fall of 1989 symbolizes a world in which peace prevails between nations and greater freedom exists within them. The end of Stalinism and the spread of democracy brought widespread celebration. Within the United States, the increasingly rapid transformation of the Eastern bloc also led to an important debate. Critical issues began to be discussed with new urgency: With the Cold War almost certainly over, what external threats did the United States now face, and what policies should be developed to confront those threats? Did we need all of the weapons in our military arsenal? How large should be the defense budget? Could that budget be cut by as much as half during the 1990s? To what uses should the resulting "peace dividend" be applied? Lowering taxes? Reducing the federal deficit? Or remedying weaknesses in the public infrastructure? What about the quality of public education, the state of the environment, access to health care, and public transportation? Could we create more employment opportunities in inner-city neighborhoods besieged by poverty, drugs, and hopelessness? Different people suggested different answers. But the essential fact is that the questions themselves emerged with new urgency. It was almost as though the collapse of the Berlin Wall "over there" allowed us to confront the need for internal reform "over here."

Then, in August 1990, Iraq invaded Kuwait. The cultural and political trappings surrounding Operation Desert Shield, the military build-up in the Persian Gulf, submerged the close look at ourselves.

The critical questions were once again tucked under the rug. In early 1991, a military coalition led by the United States fought the Gulf War. Operation Desert Storm seemed successful. Not only was Iraqi dictator Saddam Hussein kicked out of Kuwait, but President Bush found a new enemy to replace the Kremlin. Washington claimed that offensive military force was still needed to confront external threats. Many Americans were fascinated by the war, particularly with the antiseptic image of high-tech combat without significant casualties. Many felt good about the country. But the United States continued its dependency on foreign oil while ignoring multiple dangers to the global environment. The concept of an independent press went by the wayside. Domestic opposition—whether public opinion, the organized antiwar movement, or Congress—was blunted. And George Bush emerged from the war as the most popular president in U.S. history.

The Berlin Wall and the Gulf War are very different symbols, both literally and in the implication that each carries for U.S. politics. The end of the Cold War is an opportunity for domestic renewal; the Gulf War by and large sustains current foreign and domestic policies. *Peace Politics* examines the relative influence of these two images. By recasting our relationships with other countries, and by defining our security more broadly, we can follow a path of peace and begin the process of establishing a more equitable and stable society at home. The end of the Cold War opens the door to a possible political realignment of the United States. I argue not only that creating a new global system is a better way to meet U.S. security needs but also that it is possible to nurture the already existing tendencies that support such a shift. A coalition of social movements and a presidential campaign can strengthen these "peace elements," or harbingers of a new world order during the 1990s. I do not, however, regard the adoption of alternative approaches to international security and domestic renewal to be inevitable. I present evidence to support the need for a new direction and analysis to assess the possibilities of moving in that direction. But I predict no particular outcome.

Peace Politics focuses on global issues but does not honor the classic boundary between foreign and domestic affairs. I begin, and end, with the United States. The country faces significant problems that must be confronted by policies and priorities that depart from those of the last fifty years. While domestic decay is not a "threat" as traditionally conceived by political scientists, current trends demonstrate a slow erosion of our quality of life in many spheres. A defense policy is supposed to protect us. Thus, we should ask ourselves two questions: First, exactly what are the domestic conditions that are being protected? And second, is it possible that the defense policies chosen during the Cold War are in fact active contributors to the ongoing processes of decline?

Domestic Decay

As measured by official figures, the poverty rate in the United States remains close to 15 percent. In the most powerful country in the world, more than one-fifth of the children grow up in poverty. Think about the implications of this statement. One is tempted to stop and say: "See, the need for a new set of national priorities is already demonstrated." Unfortunately, there is more.

Once inflation is taken into account, overall income levels have remained roughly level for the past fifteen years. The typical wage earner makes just about as much as in the mid-1970s. Family breadwinners have worked longer hours and more members of the family have gone to work. When adjustments for this extra work are taken into account, four-fifths of families had a reduced standard of living (Joint Economic Committee of Congress in Moberg 1992). In many respects, we are also becoming a more polarized society. In the 1980s, the nation's income became much less equally distributed (after a century in which the pattern of inequality remained very stable). The top 20 percent, which received 41.6 percent of the total income in 1980, received 44 percent in 1988. The bottom 20 percent, which received 5.1 percent of the income in 1980, received only 4.6 percent eight years later (U.S. Census Bureau in Phillips 1990). The distribution of wealth is even more uneven, with the top .5 percent of U.S. households holding approximately one-quarter of the total wealth (Joint Economic Committee of Congress in Phillips 1990:241). Between 1977 and 1988, real income declined for almost every income decile, or tenth, save for the two highest groups. After adjustments for inflation, the middle-income groups earned about 5 percent less over this period, and the income of the lowest tenth of the population fell almost 15 percent. Meanwhile, the average income of the top 5 percent went from $134,543 to $166,016, and that of the top 1 percent went from $270,053 to $404,566 (measured in constant 1987 dollars) (Urban Institute in Phillips 1990).

The pattern of increasing inequality extends beyond income and wealth. Our tax codes have become more biased as well. According to a study produced by the Citizens for Tax Justice that used 1978 as a base year, the taxes of the wealthiest one million families fell during the 1980s by 30 percent while the bill for middle-class Americans rose by $5.8 billion (Frisby 1991). Our society creates many jobs that provide high pay and enable the occupants to exercise skill. But many more positions are concentrated at the other end of the spectrum. There is even a generic term describing the routine, structured, deadening, and dead-end quality of so many new employment opportunities: "McJob." Custodians, security guards, and waitresses are the fastest growing occupational categories in the United States today. Many of these new jobs do not pay enough to support a family. Over the 1980s, the number of impoverished *working* Americans rose by about two million, or 23 percent (Reich 1989c).

These economic and work patterns underscore widespread social and cultural inequalities. For example, the persistence of institutional gender and ethnic discrimination is explained in part by the types of jobs that are being created. It is especially difficult to reduce the large earning gaps between men and women, and between whites and many ethnic groups, while employment opportunities lying at the middle of the wage spectrum are being lost. The economic dichotomization of the United States is also partly responsible for the pervasiveness of violence. More than thirty thousand citizens are shot to death each year. Among young African-American men, homicide is the leading cause of death. Handguns are used in twelve thousand suicides each year (Canham-Clyne 1991).

Economists warn that we are not investing enough in public infrastructure such as our transportation system. Our future vitality is also undermined by inadequate private investment in plant and equipment and research and development. As a result, productivity has stagnated. Between 1948 and 1973, for example, the value of output per hour in the nonfarm sector of the economy grew at an average rate of 2.51 percent a year. At that pace of productivity increase, the gross national product would double every twenty-eight years. In fact, the rapid improvement in living conditions during the 1950s and 1960s rested on this dramatic gain in economic performance. Between 1973 and 1982, however, the rate of productivity growth declined to almost zero. The last few years have seen some improvement, but the time it takes for the GNP to double at the overall productivity rate achieved after 1973 is more than a half century (Heilbroner 1991). This slower rate corresponds to the level income earnings of the typical family since the early 1970s. If we do not make a more determined commitment to protect our future, our standard of living will remain stagnant. Except for some types of high technology, the categories of U.S. commodities for which demand exists in other countries are becoming limited to public relations techniques, entertainment symbols, and other components of the service sector. In the export market, steel, cars, and heavy machinery are being replaced by advertising executives, financial wizards, and Madonna. Whether this represents a sufficient base for the United States to compete globally is not at all clear.

Access to decent health care, quality education, and housing is also becoming less equitable. The infant mortality rate in the United States in 1989 was 10 per thousand, leaving us ranked twentieth in the world in this key health indicator. Primarily because of poverty, the black infant mortality rate was 17.6, more than twice the average for whites and higher than the rate achieved by thirty-one other countries including Hungary, Poland, and Cuba (Children's Defense Fund 1991). Recently, health care has become even more expensive and many employers are reducing their contribution to this form of work benefit. Currently, 33 million people or more than 15 percent of the population are without health insurance of any kind (National Center for Health Care Statistics 1990). In cities and towns, quality public education, the last hope of any society based on equal opportunity, is under siege. For most school systems, the issue has become how best to stem the loss of teachers and programs, rather than how to improve curriculum or introduce other measures of educational reform. A recent report by the Carnegie Foundation for the Advancement of Teaching found significantly less satisfaction and control over professional life among teachers than a similar survey conducted as recently as 1987 (Cohen 1990). Finally, home ownership rates for those between 25 and 44 years of age declined during the 1980s, while the cost of owning a home relative to income increased significantly. We have even created a curious term, "affordable housing." Its usual application to low- and low-to-middle-income projects, signals our awareness that, for most, the cost of a place to live has moved well beyond the comfort zone.

Environmentally, the total emission of greenhouse gases and their proportion in the atmosphere continues to increase. So does the prospect for record high temperatures. Air quality has reached health-threatening levels in hundreds of cities. Frequently, the air we breathe is literally poison. Our health is also threatened by toxic waste dumps, too many of which are located in precisely those urban and rural areas where poor people live. Meanwhile, the world's forests continue to decline annually by an area roughly comparable to Austria. Clean drinking water is becoming a scarce commodity. And continued soil erosion threatens future agricultural productivity (Mathews 1989; Renner 1989).

Our consumer society has created many opportunities to enjoy life. And a large part of the public is favored with a high standard of living. At the same time, the treatment of too many of our citizens is a disgrace. Child abuse and violence against women are epidemic. The search for a cure for AIDS does not receive the attention it requires. Too many people live on streets instead of in homes, and we remain indifferent to a slow erosion of human decency in our day-to-day treatment of one another. In many respects, the quality of our political democracy has suffered as well. Voter participation rates have declined, and the dominance of candidate image and campaign finances in electoral campaigns is dismaying. Our concept of citizenship has become more limited (I discuss this point below in the context of military preparations during the Cold War). These circumstances do not represent a secure domestic base for our future.

National Security in the Old and New World Order

In a world dominated by competing nation-states, the end of the Cold War presents an opportunity to transform both the meaning of national security and the mechanisms we employ to achieve it. In what follows, I offer a systematic comparison of security as conceived in the "old" (Cold War) and "new" world orders. Each perspective identifies a different set of principal enemies or threats to security and proposes alternative methods of coping with these threats. Each looks at peace, and the economic and social impact of preparing for war in a different way. The old and new world orders are informed by alternative intellectual paradigms, and each proposes a different set of policies to confront the problems that have been identified. Table I-1 summarizes the differences between the old and new world order approaches to national security.[1]

1. Several comments on the development of this comparison are necessary. First, the stark contrast between the "old" and "new" may convey the mistaken impression that the security discussion during the Cold War was homogeneous. While that was clearly not the case, the new world order described in this book offers an entirely different paradigm. Developing a comparison of the two perspectives through an "ideal type" methodology that focuses

TABLE I-1
Old and New World Order Concepts of National Security

	Old	*New*
Principal threats to national security	Soviet Union Third World revolutionary forces	Dictatorship Environmental degradation Global economic problems (domestic decay)
Principal applications of military force	Extended deterrence Conventional defense of Europe Interventionary capability	Basic deterrance → nuclear disarmament Peacekeeping forces under U.N. Non-offensive defense
Democracy and the role of the public	Formal rights of citizenship	Citizen education Social activism Strong democracy
Cultural attitudes toward war and peace	"Spectator militarism"	Civic culture of peace
Political and economic relations with developing countries	Maintaining access to markets	Encourage genuine development; sense of "shared fate"
Concept of peace	Negative peace/absence of war	Positive peace/reduction of structural violence
Military spending and the economy	Minimal impact	Peace dividend and economic conversion
Intellectual and policy paradigm	Realism	Common security

on essential features is justified. Second, recent changes in global politics have been so profound that few participants in the security debate now discuss their position in terms of the "the old world order." Everyone, at some level, recognizes that something "new" is on the horizon. Rhetoric aside, the versions of the new world order discussed by public officials in Washington, most electoral candidates, the mainstream of both political parties, and even most academics have more in common with the "old" conceptions than with an approach to national security that is genuinely new. Third, the two perspectives would disagree on the very organization of the table itself. In the traditional approach, foreign and domestic affairs are separated. For proponents of the new world order, integration of global and domestic issues is fundamental. For the traditional approach, the individual cells in the table remain distinct from each other. For the new world order, the topics run together. From the new perspective, for example, it is difficult to discuss peace without posing questions about economic and cultural development.

Enemies, Threats, and Responses

The enemies that present themselves and the external enemies we choose help to define domestic politics, since we close ranks when confronted with a clear military threat. We cannot afford the "luxury" of internal reform when an external challenger is trying to knock down the gates. A world where enemies pose a military threat narrows the domestic agenda. But a world that requires global cooperation to overcome common threats enables us to entertain new possibilities at home. We need to ponder the full implications of a world without enemies capable of posing a military challenge. General Colin Powell, chairman of the Joint Chiefs of Staff, observed, a month after the defeat of Iraq in the Gulf War: "I'm running out of villains. I'm down to Castro and Kim Il Sung" (quoted in Kaplan 1991). The implications of Powell's statement extend well beyond the size of the military budget and the question of which weapons should be procured.

Since the end of World War II, our government and most of the population has identified the Soviet Union as our principal enemy. According to the traditional concept of security—protecting our sovereignty, our territory, our core values, and our basic institutions—Moscow was identified as *the* threat. Our response affected not only our economy and our technical priorities but domestic legislation, our culture, and even the language we employ when thinking about the past, present, and future of our society. It has been difficult to be imaginative about social change while confronting the Kremlin. Reformers have been severely constrained by the perceived need to confront the Soviets with overwhelming military force. National security abroad has meant national security at home. On occasion, social movements have succeeded in modifying the prevailing orientations of the Democratic and Republican parties. But proponents of domestic reform generally have labored under the ideological shadow of Stalinism and the cultural and military edifice of the rivalry with the Soviet Union. Some political and economic projects were deemed too expensive—things we just could not afford because military preparations came first. In their time, social security, Medicaid, collective bargaining, and national health insurance have all been labeled "communist." Putting up our guard against the "outside world" has made it more difficult to be flexible in considering alternatives for our "inside world."

By most accounts, the Cold War was rooted in a fundamental antagonism between the Soviet Union and the United States. Two very different economic, political, and cultural systems underscored the competition between the countries. Washington and Moscow saw each other as enemies, and each shared a stake in preserving the conflict. In each country, powerful economic and political organizations, strongholds of bureaucratic power, and huge military forces benefited from the Cold War. These interests shared such a strong commitment to the superpower antagonism that they actually drew attention to the strengths of their opponents. Each year during the 1980s, the Pentagon published a slick, colorful pamphlet called "The Soviet Threat." Ominous pictures of heavy missiles, tank squadrons, and submarines filled its pages. The Kremlin replied in kind, titling their version, "Whence the Threat to Peace?" Pictures of fighter planes and the MX missile, and maps of far-flung U.S. military bases filled its pages. Stalinists had an interest in portraying the United States as the embodiment of expansionary imperialism and the possessor of a strong military machine. The Pentagon and U.S. defense contractors had an interest in preserving an image of the Soviet Union as dominated by hard-line ideologists bent on exporting revolution. As a result, the Cold War contained both antagonism and a peculiar form of cooperation.[2] According to Deputy Secretary of State Lawrence Eagleburger, the Cold War was "characterized by a remarkably stable and predictable set of relations among the great powers" (in Thompson 1990). Both the Pentagon and the Kremlin recently discontinued their respective publications.

As well as creating militarized Eastern and Western blocs, the Cold War defined the very terms "East" and "West" (Kaldor 1990; Migone 1989). The preservation of spheres of influence for each side among developing nations is perhaps the best example of superpower cooperation. But the use of nuclear weapons to bind Eastern Europe to the Warsaw Pact under Soviet leadership, and Western Europe to NATO under U.S. leadership, is another important example of how the seeming antagonism was regulated in a way that met mutual interests. As

2. Mann (1987) has codified a set of six "conventions" that existed between the two superpowers during the Cold War: (*a*) nuclear weapons may be developed and deployed but never used; (*b*) each superpower has its own sphere of influence in Europe and the "Third World"; (*c*) no direct clashes between NATO and Warsaw Pact troops may be permitted; (*d*) client states that are not part of either of the two principal military blocs may fight each other; (*e*) conventions (*a*) through (*d*) may be tested and amended by actions of client states (Cuba, for example, may test the U.S. sphere of influence but will be left on its own if the U.S. responds); and (*f*) a "contest convention" can be conducted using the nuclear arsenal during periods of crisis to clarify ambiguous intentions and aims regarding spheres of influence.

U.S. Senator David Boren observed: "It may sound like an odd thing to say but I don't think that we fully understand [that] the decline of the Soviet Union might lead to our decline as well. As long as there was an external Soviet threat, as long as there was a threat from the Warsaw Pact, as long as we were providing the shield of military protection for them . . . they [Europe and Japan] needed the United States" (quoted in Klare 1991a:416). Extending the "nuclear umbrella" over Europe enabled the United States to consolidate economic and cultural patterns that helped maintain social stability in the West after 1945. The capacity to project all forms of offensive military force helped create an inclusive consumerist culture—an economy based primarily on private enterprise but with a prime role for government that was exercised through a high level of military spending and the social institutions necessary for regulating and reproducing a particular type of "capitalism." According to Kaldor (1990), "Instead of preventing war, [deterrence] actually turns out to be a way of keeping the idea of war and the idea of conflict alive, either to legitimize the growth of military forces or for domestic or intra-bloc purposes." The psychological discipline of confrontation facilitated the internal cohesion of each bloc. The Cold War narrowed the boundaries of permissible politics in inter-state relations among Western nations and within the United States itself. Of course, the impact of the Cold War in securing the ideological center was at least as great among the Warsaw Pact nations and within the Soviet Union. The old world order thrived on external threats.

From the perspective of the old world order, revolutionary movements—in the Third World—were also identified as important threats to national security. To block the alleged expansionism of the Eastern bloc, Washington relied on a combination of nuclear weapons and conventional military force. To counter revolutionary movements in developing countries, an interventionary or counterrevolutionary capability was created. Far more money was spent on the military equipment and personnel to fight "low-intensity wars" than on nuclear weapons. During the Cold War the United States used this capability and intervened militarily in the Third World on many occasions. Such actions helped fix in the minds of many Americans the concept of a world filled with hostile "others." To protect our security, a strong military, consisting of the ability to project many different types of offensive force, was needed.[3]

3. To preserve the concept of a world with continued threats to the United States, the

The range of threats identified by proponents of a new world order is quite different. Dictatorship and other forms of repressive government, global militarism, environmental decay, poverty, and underdevelopment are threats to the world as a whole and to the United States. Security must be conceived over a longer time frame, as something for our grandchildren as well as for our immediate future. Genuine military, environmental, economic, and psychological security is not something that one country can accomplish on its own. Cooperation between countries and consistent standards for human rights must replace the push and pull of competitive diplomacy and military threats. For the United States, the new world order implies a shift in nuclear weapons policy and a dramatic reduction in the number of nuclear warheads. The role of military force will not entirely evaporate. New threats to democracy may appear. But the employment of and capacity for a military response would be regulated more strongly by international authority, principally the United Nations. In other areas of acute tension throughout the world, the configuration of military forces would move towards "non-offensive defense," or maintaining the capacity to blunt conventional attack without creating for oneself the ability to conduct an offensive. A broad range of international mechanisms for conflict resolution would be strengthened. *Peace Politics* will explore many dimensions of this perspective on security.

Culture, Democracy, and Citizenship

The military aspects of the old world order include specific weapons systems, personnel, economic and bureaucratic interests, and an attitude toward war called "spectator militarism" (Shaw 1988). Spectator militarism is the infatuation of the public with the prowess of the armed forces, and the identification of the nation's strength and influence in world affairs with military preparedness. Since World War II, the relationship of most U.S. citizens toward war has changed. War is now more remote: The chances that an individual will spend a substantial portion of his or her career serving in the defense sector

---

Pentagon's first post–Cold War era document envisions seven scenarios for potential foreign conflict. Still classified documents "indicate that the leadership of the Defense Department has instructed the military chiefs to request forces and weapons sufficient to fight at least two large regional wars simultaneously, one against Iraq in the Persian Gulf and one against North Korea, while also being ready to conduct a major military campaign in Europe to prevent a resurgent Russia from pursuing expansionist aims" (Tyler 1992). The document also says Washington should be prepared to respond to contingencies such as a military coup in the Philippines, or a "narco-terrorist" plot in Panama that threatens access to the Panama Canal.

are much lower. Professional armed forces control nuclear weapons, and a specialized work force operates military production plants. A war has not been fought on U.S. territory, and relatively few have engaged in combat. There have been important exceptions, such as the intense fighting in Vietnam and the worries of millions of families for their loved ones during the Gulf War. By and large, however, we have been very fortunate in our lack of direct experience with war.

At the same time, the expectation that we will have to fight a war somewhere, at some time, is nearly universal. The population shares the cultural perception that the threat of war is omnipresent.[4] Endorsing the expenditure of vast sums to build weapons becomes entirely natural. We have to be prepared. Support for the military is still the most powerful mechanism for defining citizenship, the nation, and even the "we" of community life. The public is mobilized through ideological means, without authentic democratic participation, and without a significant opportunity to affect political outcomes in the manner of other historical instances of mobilization, such as the civil rights movement or the struggle to establish the right for collective bargaining. Spectator militarism is, in fact, connected to the broader processes of decay now eroding our democratic institutions.

Ritual, or the constant reenactment of important moral and social bonds, is necessary to secure spectator militarism. The public has little firsthand knowledge of specific weapons systems and military doc-

---

4. A prime illustration of spectator militarism is the principal Cold War document, National Security Memorandum 68 (Etzold and Gaddis 1979). NSC-68 was signed by President Truman in April 1950 and clearly links the urgent need to respond to an external threat, U.S. national identity, and the struggle between good and evil. For Paul Nitze, the author, the problem facing the postwar United States was not the Soviet Union as a whole but the Kremlin, which is "inescapably militant" because it is "possessed by a worldwide revolutionary movement, because it inherits the traditional Russian drive for imperialism and because it is a totalitarian dictatorship." The fundamental design of the Kremlin is to gain the "complete subversion or forcible destruction of the machinery of government and structure of societies of the non-Soviet world." In this view, the conflict between the United States and the Soviet Union is total; no compromise or "peaceful coexistence" is possible. At stake is civilization itself. In this battle, the Soviet Union enjoys two organizational sources of strength: the Communist Party and the secret police. Each is capable of imposing "ideological uniformity" at home and "propaganda, subversion, and espionage" abroad. The Soviet Union's ideological "pretensions," or promises of a society with equal justice and a fairer distribution of resources, form another asset. So, too, is an "utterly amoral and opportunistic conduct of foreign policy" that gives the Kremlin great tactical flexibility. By contrast, the goals of the United States are completely benign. According to the authors of NSC-68 they are ". . . to form a more perfect union, establish Justice, insure domestic tranquility, provide for the common defense, promote the general Welfare, and secure the Blessings of Liberty to ourselves and our Posterity." This sense of the perfect "we" counterposed to the evil "them" is characteristic of the old world order.

trines. We are different from the citizens of Lebanon, Yugoslavia, or Cambodia who are, unfortunately, well educated in these areas. We are well-informed about military superficialities and fascinated with the high-tech performance of weapons. The prospect of people dying also seems to capture our attention. But we do not know much about the history and social context of foreign policy events. We are like sports fans. The game is important, and we certainly want to win. But the events come and go as we watch others do the hard work. The media plays an important role as well, primarily by portraying war in terms befitting the Olympic Games. During Operation Desert Shield, for example, the television networks framed the impending war in simplistic terms that nonetheless carried enormous political weight. Complexities were reduced to the most basic terms. "Bush vs. Saddam: Showdown in the Gulf" was a typical handle. Television would cut away from football games at halftime to interview troops in the Saudi sands: fifteen minutes for citizen identification and consolidation of national loyalties, a few advertisements, and then back to the third quarter. The public could support (root for) the troops sent to the Gulf. But for most of us there was no need to make a significant personal commitment. In this way, the mechanisms for insuring citizen acceptance of the inevitability of war and of the cultural props of the old world order were renewed. (My emphasis here is on most of the citizens living in the United States. Certainly, these comments do not apply to those who are in the armed forces and may actually have to fight. For them, the prospect of combat is all too real.)

The concept of spectator militarism encompasses another key point: the public's support for war policies is not total. Acceptance of military policy can drop away when the prospect of a real or potential sacrifice is raised. Many of the values held by Americans are opposed to war. Much of the public does not identify national security and collective identity with military force. While acceptance can be secured under the right circumstances, public support for a war policy is usually shallow and volatile. The public is also aware of the costs of armed conflict and feels strongly that, in the end, not too many of our people can actually die. Spectator militarism exists alongside another set of attitudes consistent with the development of a new world order.

Is there an alternative culture that could be developed as part of the transition to a new world order? In the sense of creating a more active sense of citizenship and political symbols that are conducive to peace, the answer is yes. A key step is the development of what Boulding calls a global civic culture, or "the patterning of how we share a common space, common resources, and common opportunities and how we manage interdependence in that 'company of strangers' which we call the public. It has to do with the interactions that create the sense of a common public interest" (1988:xvii). A civic culture is not a substitute for personal and family life. But it does recognize that our private lives are affected by the surrounding physical and social space of our communities and cities, our nation and our planet. Developing a sense of the complexity of the globe's physical and social dynamics, and how these affect our personal choices, does not have as its goal the elimination of all forms of national identification. A nonbelligerent form of patriotism is to be celebrated. Nor does the development of a civic culture mean eradication of the tremendous cultural diversity that exists on the planet. On the contrary, the richness ethnicity brings could be appreciated more fully in a less competitive environment. But a civic culture of peace does imply that our future security must be sought in concert with other nations.

A civic culture would extend the interpersonal skills that we use every day, in work settings, among friends, and within our families, into the public sphere. We already value the ability to see another person's point of view and to negotiate differences so that both parties can feel that their needs are being met. We also value reconciliation mechanisms in personal and community affairs. But we do not expect to see our nation's leaders employ the same techniques when they conduct foreign affairs. We do not demand from them an ability to mediate or resolve conflict. At a deeper level, a civic culture of peace would expand our sense of time so that we would feel ourselves in the midst of a more complex history and part of an unfolding future (Boulding speaks of a need to appreciate "the present" as encompassing two hundred years). Our knowledge of language and cultural diversity would grow, as would our capacity to recognize common themes of humanity that link us together. We would appreciate still more the costs of violence and the options available to avoid it. Finally, we would become more adept at locating ourselves more precisely in the whirl of developments and processes that shape the globe. This sense of civic culture is tied to the concept of "strong democracy" that "rests on the idea of a self-governing community of citizens who are united less by homogeneous interests than by civic education and who are made capable of common purpose and mutual action by virtue of their civic attitudes and participatory institutions rather than their altruism or their good nature" (Barber 1984:117). At bottom, the new world order is about shared fate, about recapturing a sense of moral obligation to others without thinking that we are sacrificing ourselves in the process.

Paradigms

Realism, the dominant academic paradigm for interpreting the international system, is another bulwark of the old world order. Realism also corresponds to the assumptions about global politics held by most decisionmakers. In this view, the international system consists of competing nation-states, each looking out foremost for itself (Morgenthau 1967; Waltz 1967, 1979). The pursuit of political and military security by each state precedes the attainment of other possible goals such as global economic justice, environmental protection, and a common commitment to a human rights standard. Before attempting to pursue any of these more idealist goals, statesmen must respect the logic of power itself. This means achieving a balance of power that will prevent any country from seeking more than its "legitimate" share, acknowledging that relatively few countries—perhaps only one—have the main responsibility for orchestrating the balancing act among nations, and avoiding unwarranted domestic influence in the conduct of foreign affairs. In its classical form, realism treats each state as though it were a "black box," that is, as a unified actor with no significant internal cleavages. Power is "zero-sum." A country can get more only at the expense of another. Although inter-state competition is a constant for realists, the outbreak of war itself can be prevented by recognizing the inevitability of the resulting tension and managing it through political alliances and a balance of military power achieved through a combination of arms sales and arms control. Foreign policy is the search for equilibrium, for a system where one country does not threaten the political and military security of another. This equilibrium is defined by those ultimately responsible for the international system. In the realist viewpoint, a foreign policy that attempts more ambitious projects such as the advancement of democracy or the promotion of greater economic justice or protection of the environment is dangerous and can even produce destabilization and war itself. A good foreign policy is a morally neutral foreign policy. On a fundamental level, security is still based on military power.[5]

---

5. A recent Pentagon report to Congress on the future role of the U.S. military in the Pacific provides a striking example of the logic of realism: "US presence in the region . . .," the report notes, "is not solely Soviet-oriented." Instead, the U.S. military is to serve as "re-

Realism does not preclude attention to economics, especially where it is self-interested. Alan Tonelson believes the United States should follow an "interest-based foreign policy" that "would confine itself to securing certain specific objectives that are intrinsically important to America's security and welfare—for example, the protection of regions that are important sources of raw materials or critical manufactured goods, those that are major loci of investment or prime markets, and those that by virtue of their location are strategically vital" (1991). While realism does not stress economic relations, it dovetails nicely with the old world order emphasis on maintaining global access to markets, labor, and raw materials. For a powerful country like the United States, which bears responsibility for the management of global tensions, a strong military is essential. Yet, according to the tenets of realism, proper fiscal management can prevent military spending from having a significant impact on the economy. At times, technical spin-offs and other assets provided by the defense effort can even stimulate the civilian sector.

The realist perspective can be compared with two other approaches to international relations and the possibilities of future peace. Both have been labeled "idealist", although they are quite different from each other. The first, an "economic globalist" paradigm, focuses on the role of market forces and the importance of reducing the barriers to international economic trade (Levy 1989:260–62). In turn, the extension of capitalist economic relations is supposed to strengthen political democracy and create a mutual interest in peace. Nations sharing similar economic and political institutions, linked by trade and by underlying respect for the legitimacy of each other's democratic practices, will not go to war with each other. Peace is a consequence of gradual convergence based upon liberal principles.

The recent end of the Cold War and the possible spread of liberal democracies and market relations throughout Europe and the former Soviet Union call new attention to this possible route to world peace (Fukuyama 1989; Kaysen 1990; Mueller 1989; Russett 1990). According to proponents of the economic globalist paradigm, the modern era is witnessing the gradual delegitimation of war. As a consequence of industrialization, countries have far more to lose by war's destructiveness than they have to gain by acquiring whatever is left of another country's infrastructure. Raw materials are of relatively less impor-

---

gional balancer, honest broker . . . ultimate security guarantor" and "irreplaceable balancing wheel" (in Kaplan 1991c).

tance and can be secured far more cheaply through trade than by forced acquisition. Technical advances accompanying the industrial revolution have also made the prospect of war more horrific. The disruption of civilian life and the destruction of economic life that result from bombing are considerable. Even those who are not direct combatants are vulnerable. Recognition of the costs of war is reinforced by the nuclear revolution. It is no longer possible for anyone, even the most protected leader, to be guaranteed safety. In liberal democracies, leaders and populations see enough of themselves in other liberal democracies that they are extremely reluctant to move beyond quarreling to actual combat.

Belligerence among democracies is further tempered by the widely shared norm of seeking to resolve disputes without resort to force, and by the slow but significant development of international institutions and law. Democracies thus assume and are reassured by the existence of various conflict resolution mechanisms in other democracies. In the culmination of this process, the reluctance to engage in armed conflict changes from a rational calculation that no true benefit can accrue from war to an even more powerful subconscious conviction. War is not an option because it is not even considered by political leaders. It is now obsolete. Security is based on the spread of market forces, the continued growth of trade, and the institutionalization of political democracy. Relations between the United States and Canada serve as a benchmark for the future.[6]

On one level, the argument that market forces and political democracy in the United States, Europe, Japan, and (probably) the former Eastern bloc are making the world more peaceful seems peculiarly myopic. In recent years, we have been confronted with numerous wars fought between developing states, civil wars within developing states, and proxy wars in which the East-West conflict was superimposed on local and regional wars. In addition, there have been a significant number of wars of intervention in which liberal democracies (as well as the Soviet Union) fought, not each other, but other, mostly Third World countries. Statistically, in fact, democracies are as prone to war as are non-democracies. (There is, however, strong empirical support for the thesis that liberal democracies do not fight *each other*.) The Cold War era was not peaceful; over its duration more than 125 wars occurred, resulting in an estimated 25 million deaths (Sivard

6. A critique of the thesis that the world is becoming more peaceful is provided by Mearsheimer (1990).

1989). Many of those instances of armed conflict do not correspond to the formal definitions of war used by political scientists. But people still died.[7] From this standpoint, the "long peace" of the Cold War can hardly be considered free from war. Moreover, the social, cultural, and economic consequences of preparing for war became considerable in both democracies and non-democracies, even where actual military engagement did not occur. Global arms production is now valued at one trillion dollars a year, a sum roughly equal to the total income of the lower half of the world's population of five billion. This process of militarization, at home as well as abroad, has made it difficult to speak of a generic peace process over the course of the twentieth century, since the end of World War II, or through any other specific period.

Instead, the end of the Cold War has uncovered long-seething instabilities and conflicts. Much attention has been focused on increased ethnic and nationalist rivalries, particularly in Yugoslavia and the former Soviet Union. But Ireland, southern Africa, the Middle East, and parts of the Indian subcontinent contain other examples of "subnational" warfare that could easily intensify during the remainder of the decade (Tirman 1991). These conflicts revolve around grievances between minorities and dominant groups, and even between secondary minorities holding grievances against the "first" minority. In many instances, such as the Iran-Iraq war, ethnic and national antagonisms have been further complicated by overlapping religious and cultural boundaries. When blended with competing economic interests and fractious political leadership, interethnic rivalries have created a caldron of conflict. Washington has largely turned its back on the prospect of using its influence to help put out the fire beneath it.

Moreover, the already alarming level of poverty found in developing countries may deepen, leading to still further marginalization and intensification of "technological apartheid" whereby the lowest paying, most toxic, least secure, and most exploitive work is performed as far away from the industrial nations as possible. But the developed countries are not fully isolated from these trends. Economic refugees have already moved into Europe and the United States, spawning new hatreds in Italy, Germany, Austria, and France. Multinational corporations have used the poor working conditions and low wages typical in

7. Academic studies often define war as conflict involving 1,000 combat deaths and fought between two or more nation-states. Civilian deaths and armed conflict involving non-state parties would be excluded by this definition.

the free trade zones established on the border with Mexico and throughout the Pacific Rim either to undercut income levels and benefits paid to workers within the United States, or to eliminate jobs entirely. Poverty overseas has hurt local communities at home.

Mounting environmental pressures may also exacerbate the problems of population growth, famine, flooding, and deforestation, and produce further dislocations for millions of poor people. We may see new forms of "eco-conflict" and wars over scarce resources such as water in the Middle East. Even changes in the climate that disrupt the atmosphere and hence local agriculture can add to the mounting number of environmental refugees (Homer-Dixon 1991). These tensions are further fueled by the still uncontrolled trade in military arms and the acquisition of large arsenals throughout the world, both by governments and by various subnational units (*Bulletin of the Atomic Scientists* 1990; Hartung 1991, Klare 1991b). Another possibility is that increased economic rivalries will lead to new tensions between industrialized nation-states. In this scenario, increased economic interdependence may create not peace but intensified competition. Disagreements over import barriers, for example, may crystallize, resulting in trade blocs and eventual political and military conflict (Wallerstein 1989).

Market relations and political democracy (as well as changing public attitudes and the active mobilization of tens of millions of people) are probably making war obsolete as far as the major industrial states are concerned. Unfortunately, this still leaves the rest of the world far from peaceful, with the possibility of U.S. military intervention remaining. Peace as the absence of war does not address other threats to global and national security. While peace researchers are generally critical of so-called negative peace, security from the outbreak of nuclear and conventional war remains essential. Modern war, even without the employment of atomic, biological, or chemical weapons, is so destructive that the preservation of negative peace is almost always an important if not overriding goal. Nonetheless, we cannot be content simply because we are in the zone that by a limited definition is considered "peaceful." The alternative concept of positive peace (Galtung 1969) as the reduction of structural violence brings us to the perspective of "common security," which provides the second alternative to realism. Policies predicated on common security serve as the concrete building-blocks of the "new world order." Proponents of common security are critical of the inequities and inconsistencies of market-based peace systems. While the market is not rejected, emphasis is instead placed on developing a coordinated global attack against a broad range of shared threats, on strengthening transnational institutions and international law, and on adopting a common human rights code as better methods of creating a more genuine peace.

Developing the specific policies that would fulfill the common security vision of the new world order, and nurturing the political will to carry them out, are mammoth tasks. And yet the beginnings are already in place. The first premise is that all nations and people have a right to security—security from the threat of war and nuclear devastation, from infringements on national sovereignty, from poverty and despair, from environmental threats, and from politically repressive governments. Security means meeting human needs, present and future. National security cannot be achieved through unilateral action. True security derives not from military force but from economic prosperity and justice, a vital social and cultural life, a broad affirmation of human, civil, and political rights, and ecological safety. Common security is also comprehensive security. An end to global militarization and the conversion of military facilities to civilian use are prerequisites for creating a new world order. According to the Commission on Disarmament chaired by Olof Palme of Sweden: "War is losing its meaning as an instrument of national policy, becoming instead an engine of senseless destruction that leaves the root causes of conflict unresolved" (1982). Massive spending for military forces drains societies of needed financial, technical and human resources. The World Commission on Environment and Development headed by Gro Brundtland of Norway concludes that "the arms race—in all parts of the world—preempts resources that might be used more productively to diminish the security threats created by environmental conflict and the resentments that are fueled by widespread poverty" (1987:7). Military force is not a legitimate instrument for resolving disputes among nations or promoting national interests. Restraint should be the underlying tenor of all international relations. The U.S.–based Institute for Peace and International Security notes that Washington's relations with the Third World must rest upon respect for different paths of political and economic development, and support for global efforts to transcend pervasive poverty, repression, and environmental degradation (1988). International security leadership must derive more and more from transnational institutions devoted to conflict resolution, international law, peacekeeping, verification and monitoring of military forces and agreements, and the development of international standards of economic, social, and political rights (Karns and Mingst 1991).

Johansen (1991) has proposed five principles or guidelines of common security: reciprocity, or evaluating one's own actions by the same standards by which one judges the behavior of other nations; equity, especially in encouraging a more equitable distribution of economic assets and the elimination of poverty; sustainable development, or meeting present needs without compromising the ability of future generations to meet their own needs as well; democratization, or increased government accountability both within and between nations; and demilitarization, including not only the reduction of arms but the reduction of the role of military power in international affairs.

To achieve this vision would be a tall order. And yet it can be done. But the political will necessary to enact these global policies cannot be separated from domestic renewal. In the pages that follow, I use the term *progressive politics* as the shorthand reference to the set of policies that serve as stepping stones to the new world order and a new political agenda at home. Progressive politics are defined as follows: for international affairs, cutting the defense budget in half, developing a foreign policy committed to a consistent standard of human rights, and using U.S. political and economic leadership to encourage global development and environmental protection in a manner that preserves our self-interest and enhances the living conditions of the rest of the world; for domestic issues, making public education, access to health care, and affordable housing stronger priorities, applying a "peace dividend" to build a stronger economy for our future, and redressing the many forms of inequality that continue to afflict our society. These policies would not eliminate market forces or material incentives. The goal is to blend efficiency, accountability, and performance within a stronger commitment to meeting a broader range of human needs. These goals are not idealist, although many readers may find them so. My argument does not call for self-sacrifice in the name of others; it calls for development of a strategy that best meets our security. True realism lies in programs of common security for the planet and domestic renewal for the United States.

1

The Bomb and the Rain Forest

EACH YEAR, about 250 species, or two-thirds of the bird species that nest in the forests of the eastern United States, fly thousands of miles to spend their winters in locales such as Costa Rica, the Greater Antilles, Belize, Mexico, and Peru. Recently, ornithologists have become concerned about the possibility that the number of migrating songbirds is declining. Careful compilation of census figures in several well-known study sites has indicated a decline of close to 50 percent over the past forty years. The Breeding Bird Survey, organized by the U.S. Fish and Wildlife Service, found statistically significant declines in twenty species of songbirds over the last ten years. Furthermore, a comparison of radar images from weather stations in the 1960s and the late 1980s showed that the number of migrating birds crossing the Gulf of Mexico had dropped by half (Dumanoski 1990).

The voyages of the migrating songbirds serve as a metaphor in the following attempt to link the war system in the United States with environmental decay in the Amazonian rain forest. Their migrations are a concrete reminder of the interconnections between habitats on this planet and of the shared fate of humans and other species that live within them. The links to be established between the consequences of preparations in the United States to fight wars and environmental decay in the Amazon may be less tangible than the flight of the birds across the Gulf of Mexico. But the ties are no less real. The aesthetic value of the birds is significant. But beyond this lie other vital issues: pesticide use, agricultural and forestry practices, Third World poverty, Third World external debt, and patterns of commercial development in both the First and the Third World. An attempt to protect migrating birds forces us to look beyond the limitations of immediate geographic space and scientific specialization. Security for songbirds raises the broader issue of overall environmental security and its relationship to economic, social, and other institutional forces.

My basic argument is simple: we need a concept of security that recognizes a broad range of threats stemming from environmental degradation, global poverty, human rights abuses, and the international drug economy, as well as the more traditional threats deriving from the distribution of political and military power. Redefining national security in this broader way necessitates a transformation in our thinking about world politics (Porter 1990). The end of the Cold War provides an opportunity to discard our prevailing images of the enemy and to think about how we might achieve national security in common with other nations (Brundtland 1987; Palme 1982).[1] We now, finally, have a chance to appreciate, both popularly and politically, how our fate is shared with the rest of the world.

My argument comprises four steps. First, the social processes created by the priority in the old (Cold War) world order of projecting offensive military force, particularly through nuclear weapons, have been counterproductive. Security has been undermined by the attempt to achieve military superiority and to use military strength to achieve foreign policy objectives. Second, the commitment to develop military force has been a principal drain on domestic investment, especially in manufacturing and public infrastructure. Among the results are a net loss of employment, a more polarized distribution of income, and growing problems with a broad range of public services such as education and health care. Third, military spending and the decline in manufacturing are linked to three distinct public deficits: the budget of the federal government, the balance of trade, and the rate of public investment. Over the 1980s, in addition to exacerbating domestic problems, these deficits helped make financial entrepreneur-

---

1. The Palme Commission defined the principles of common security as follows: All nations have a legitimate right to security; military force is not a legitimate instrument for resolving disputes between nations; restraint is necessary in expressions of national policy; security cannot be obtained through military superiority; reductions and qualitative limitations of armaments are necessary; and "linkages" between arms negotiations and political events should be avoided (1982:8–11). More recent common security perspectives have focused on the need to confront a broad range of security threats that include environmental and economic as well as military tensions. They also stress the impossibility of confronting these threats adequately through unilateral action (Solo, Sasson, and Leavitt 1989).

ship a more important priority than genuine productive activity. Among the results were higher interest rates and the rapid growth of debt held by both the United States and developing countries. Last, externally held debt was a principal factor in the transformation of the internal social structure of many developing countries. Government subsidies declined. Poverty and social marginalization increased. International debt also led to pressures on the environment, exemplified in this chapter by the rapid deforestation of the Amazon.

These four steps form the top tier of Figure 1-1. The main features and consequences of each step, as well as the reinforcing mechanisms, are contained in the second tier of the chart. Feedback loops, depicted in boldface, convey the generally negative impact of this global system on the overall security of U.S. citizens. The figure shows not only that domestic reform is needed, but that we have a common interest with most inhabitants of developing countries in transforming this social system and thereby changing U.S. relations with the rest of the globe.[2]

Some caveats are necessary. Before introducing them, let us return briefly to the metaphor of the migrating songbirds. While some scientists feel certain that the numbers are declining, others are not quite as pessimistic. Consider the reports indicating huge differences in the number of birds crossing the Gulf of Mexico. The cautious viewpoint is that it is difficult to separate normal fluctuations in population, which in the case of birds can be quite dramatic, from longer trends. Do we really face a significant problem, or are we merely seeing the bottom of the normal distribution curve? Moreover, populations of some bird species, particularly in the southeastern United States, seem to be stable or even to be increasing slightly. Beyond the question of whether the number of songbirds is declining lie other contentious issues involving the reasons for the presumed decline. The most respected student of migrating birds estimates that changes in the North American habitat have reduced songbirds to one-quarter of their precolonial level (Terbough 1989). Our forests have become fragmented, full of predators, and contaminated with toxins and pesticides. Studies presented at a recent symposium organized by the Manomet

---

2. I make no apologies for using the self-interest of U.S. citizens as a reference point. It would be nice if the social behavior of the human species was fully altruistic. But the political will necessary to support significant changes in policy continues to rest upon national self-interest, albeit reconceptualized to no longer embody exploitative global relations. My purpose is to demonstrate that self-interest and recognition of shared fate with the rest of the planet are not in contradiction.

FIG 1-1 The Bomb and the Rainforest

Bird Observatory show that birds in forests interlaced with roads and housing developments are more vulnerable to skunks and raccoons. In the Caribbean and South and Central America, where migrating birds spend the winter months, tropical rain forests are being cut down or burned in order to create pastureland for cattle raising or new agricultural areas of marginal value for the desperately poor. Some ornithologists point to drastic shifts in bird diets and local habitats as evidence that the principal problem is in the tropics. They fear that losses in the wintering habitat may tip a precarious balance and lead to a rapid decline in populations.

The issues raised by the prospect of a reduced number of songbirds are typical of a number of environmental problems such as global warming, low-level radiation and chemical toxins, and loss of species diversity. The evidence is either inconclusive or short of the proof required by conventional standards. Scientists disagree in their judgments concerning the severity and causes of the problem. Yet, each year, a growing number feel that the situation is sufficiently urgent that they must go beyond the traditional definition of their professional roles and directly enter the political arena. For these scientists, to research a problem until all areas of ambiguity are resolved is to risk permitting the actual dangers to mount untreated. For the most threatened species of songbirds, scientific proof may come too late to preserve their habitat.

The goal of preserving songbirds thus challenges our intellectual horizons. Does their status represent an early warning sign that we are in danger of missing? Are the songbirds analogous to the canaries that miners used to bring with them beneath the surface to determine if the air was safe to breathe? The impressive journey of birds between continents, as well as their exposure to several threats at each habitat, raises the need for a multidisciplinary and global approach to address the question of how best to preserve their security.

Before proceeding with my argument, I raise several points to guard against misinterpretation. First, the framework about to be outlined that links the manufacture of the nuclear bomb and other war preparations in the United States to the destruction of the rainforest in Brazil is not reductionist. Perceptions of the Soviet threat during the Cold War, population growth, the policies and selfishness exhibited by some Third World elites, the development of "post-industrial" society, and a materialistic culture have all helped shape the social system I am about to describe. Obviously, the judgment that the Soviet Union represented a military threat to the United States fueled the desire to maintain a strong military posture. Population pressures in many developing countries have had generally negative influences on the prospects for adopting ecologically sound policies. In many cases, the political, economic, and military elites of developing countries did not make wise use of the loans granted by international lending agencies and privately owned Western banks. Funds designated for development projects became ensnared in corruption or diverted for the personal benefit of local elites.[3] In the United States, the decline in manufacturing, lower real wages and salaries, increased income disparities, and loss of employment in many regions are not fully explained by the impact of military spending. Many features of post-industrialism, including the larger role played by communications, informational and financial services, and public relations, also contribute to the deindustrialization of the United States. Finally, a materialist culture that stresses the short-term acquisition of products over intergenerational equity molds our habits and our attitudes toward the environment.

Second, important controversies accompany each step in the argument. For example, I will argue that military spending adversely affects domestic manufacturing. Not everyone agrees. Space and editorial considerations dictate a strategy of acknowledging the existence of these disputes, but avoiding excessive rebuttals. At the same time, I do not want to be too equivocal in my presentation. The war system and the destruction of the rain forest *are* part of the same social system as defined by Talcott Parsons: "both a complex of interdependencies between parts, components, and processes that involves discernible regularities of relationship, and a similar type of interdependency between such a complex and its surrounding environment" (1968:458).

Third, this is not a linear argument but a description of mutually reinforcing patterns. I do not offer a precise formula along the lines of "so many bombs have been responsible for the destruction of so many hectares of forest." This exercise develops a flow chart but not multiple-

3. Still, adherents of the view that the cause of the current plight of developing nations with regard to debt lies mainly in the selfish greed and poor accounting practices of their elites should keep in mind comparable activities within the United States. Donald Trump's capacity for acquisition and display rivals that of Zaire's President Mobutu or any other Third World contender. In size, the U.S. savings and loans disaster outdistances any of the frauds perpetrated on Third World people who are so clearly unprotected in comparison to the people of the United States, where more rigorous regulation, careful scrutiny, and concern for human needs always characterize financial decisions.

regression equations or other efforts to measure causality in quantitative terms.[4]

Preparations to Use Offensive Military Force

Since the end of World War II, United States policymakers have considered the ability to project superior military force to be an essential component of national security. As applied to nuclear weapons, however, the doctrine of extended deterrence that prevailed throughout the Cold War and continues to exist today actually threatens our own security. Extended deterrence would prevent military attacks not only against ourselves but against our allies as well, and rests ultimately upon the threat to use nuclear weapons first (an argument developed further in Chapter 6). During the Cold War, government officials made public statements that refused to rule out the first use of atomic bombs. They also built the actual weapons designed to reinforce that possibility. These actions also appeared to military planners in Moscow, in a worst case scenario, as an effort to create a first-strike capability. The United States produced more than 10,000 nuclear warheads for strategic use against the Soviet Union, and even more than that for use in a variety of battlefield and regional conflicts. The Pentagon placed these bombs upon a broad variety of technically sophisticated delivery systems. Moscow responded in kind. Actions that increased the credibility of United States first use only encouraged the Soviets to move closer to first use for fear that their retaliatory force would be wiped out. Many U.S. professional strategists began to worry that the existence of numerous Soviet land-based missiles with improved accuracy reflected a possible intent to strike first. Privately, leading U.S. policymakers might have thought the chance that they would actually use nuclear weapons was quite remote. But their decisions to develop counterforce and other war-fighting systems sustained those in the Pentagon who actually believed in the possibility of winning a nuclear war (Joseph 1985). The reciprocity of the situation was such that each side could muster a scenario showing that the other side was preparing to fight and win a war with atomic weapons.

4. My approach avoids two common mistakes. The first would be to focus only upon developments within the territorial boundaries of the nation-state. The world is interconnected and global conditions affect political and economic circumstances within the United States. The second would be to collapse national characteristics into an all-encompassing global system. Despite the influence of the international system, the nation remains the principal unit in economic, political, and cultural life. The challenge is to incorporate the global perspective without ignoring the continued salience of the national system.

Washington's commitment to extended deterrence produced a chain of actions culminating in the development of Soviet nuclear war-fighting systems aimed at the United States. Meanwhile, political leaders in other countries, watching the superpowers behave as though nuclear weapons carried political and military influence, decided that their own ability to control events would be enhanced if they acquired an atomic arsenal. Washington and Moscow thought that nuclear weapons carried clout, so they would get some, too. Extended deterrence sustained nuclear proliferation, thus threatening U.S. security from another direction. To end this dilemma, Washington should sever any connection between nuclear weapons and global politics and adopt explicitly the more modest position of basic deterrence, which would seek only to deter a nuclear attack against the U.S.

In addition to creating a self-threatening condition in terms of military security, nuclear weapons also contributed to a state of psychological insecurity, pessimism, and repressed fear known as "nuclearism" (Lifton and Falk 1982; Kovel 1983; Mack 1983). Research carried out among adolescents indicates that growing up under the shadow of the bomb exerts a corrosive influence on the socialization process (Carlsson-Paige and Levin 1987; Yudkin 1984). The prospect of a nuclear war, which, until recently, was considered likely by a staggering one-third of the population, creates a generalized uncertainty about the future, with malignant results. The feelings of unease, powerlessness and isolation that accompany the culture of nuclear weapons leads to what Lifton has termed a "sense of radical futurelessness." In his view, repression of these fears creates "psychic numbing." Higher divorce rates, ideological rigidity, religious fundamentalism, patterns of violence, impulsive behavior, a decline in ethically grounded behavior, and more tenuous parent-child bonding have all been ascribed, in part, to the fear of nuclear war. In this critique, atomic weapons may form a critical element in a process of dehumanization, even without a single warhead being detonated.[5]

Nuclear weapons production in the United States is also an envi-

---

5. Skepticism arises on two issues. First, not all psychologists believe that awareness of nuclear weapons has had such a significant psychological effect (Coles 1985b). Second, even if large nuclear arsenals continue to exist, recent global changes may reduce nuclear fears and anxieties. A researcher in this field who has carried out comparative studies on the fear of war and the threat of violence finds 10- to 15-year-old Germans now drawing pictures of aerosol cans, mountains of garbage, polluting automobiles and other symbols of ecological damage. Five years ago, the same age group sketched missiles, bombs, and smoking ruins (Petra Hesse, personal conversation, 1990).

ronmental disaster. Making credible the doctrine of extended deterrence has required stockpiling tens of thousands of warheads, which threaten environmental security. Whatever military security benefits may have been derived from that nuclear arsenal are now far outweighed by the impact of the nuclear wastes that have been produced by the manufacture of weapons-grade plutonium and the tritium used to boost the yield of atomic warheads. The Department of Energy annually produces hundreds of millions of gallons of waste from nuclear weapons production. An estimated 99 percent of all high-level nuclear waste and 75 percent of low-level nuclear waste in the United States comes from the nuclear reactions produced for military purposes (Center for Defense Information 1989).

Public fears of nuclear waste are mounting, and no technically viable, politically acceptable disposal solution has emerged (Carter 1987). Much of the concern has focused on groundwater, uranium dust, and the emission of radon gas into the atmosphere. Radioactive iodine, for example, was secretly released from the Hanford Nuclear Reservation in Washington, which is now permanently closed (Steele 1989). At Rocky Flats Nuclear Munitions Plant near Denver, the possibility of contaminated groundwater is the leading concern. While conducting "Operation Desert Glow," the FBI searched for evidence of deliberate violation of environmental laws. The weapons plant at Savannah River, South Carolina, is also closed (turtles in the surrounding area are radioactive). The private contractors who run these plants and the government agencies responsible for their supervision have not stressed safety and environmental protection. Over the nuclear era, capital investment for maintenance of key components of the entire nuclear weapons complex has averaged less than 2 percent of the operating budget, compared with the 4 to 7 percent normally associated with industrial facilities. No compelling case for reopening these nuclear weapons facilities to produce still more warheads has yet been made (Albright, Zamora, and Lewis 1990). Meanwhile, the date for opening a permanent site for disposal of nuclear wastes in Nevada's Yucca Mountain has been postponed from 1998 to 2010. Many questions have been raised about the long-term safety of the site (Broad 1990). Estimates of the total cost of cleaning up and modernizing the nuclear weapons complex have been placed as high as $150 billion to $200 billion over thirty years (Peach 1989).[6]

6. The estimate by the Department of Energy is $66–110 billion, while the General Ac-

In a pattern that has been called "radioactive colonialism," several native American cultures have been particularly affected by uranium mining for nuclear weapons. Of the 150 Navajo miners who worked underground at Kerr-McGee's uranium deposits near Ship Rock, New Mexico, during the 1950s, 18 had died of radiation-induced lung cancer by 1975. Five years later, twenty more were dead, and another 95 had contracted respiratory ailments and cancers (Churchill and LaDuke 1985:103). Elsewhere, the water runoff from a uranium mill near Church Rock, New Mexico, has hurt the livestock of Navajos (Gault 1989). In both cases, raw uranium tailings had been deposited adjacent to rivers that provided the only significant source of surface water in the immediate area. Similarly, uranium mill tailings have been washed into the Cheyenne River in the Black Hills region, homeland of the Greater Sioux Nation. From 1952 until 1981, the Anaconda Corporation leased seven thousand acres of Laguna Pueblo land that at one point was the world's largest open pit uranium mine. Under an agreement negotiated by the Tribal Council, the work force rose from 350 in 1952 to 650 in 1979. Economic conditions were quite good compared to those on other reservations. But when the extractable ore ran out, Anaconda left. In its wake, the company left radioactive slag and massive unemployment. Then, the Environmental Protection Agency discovered contamination in the local Paguate River and received reports of both increased death rates from radioactive cancer

---

counting Office's projected cost is $100–155 billion, or roughly two million dollars for every nuclear warhead ever produced by the United States. More recent assessments have reached $200 billion. The GAO Report on modernizing and cleaning up the nuclear weapons complex is quite sober regarding costs: "Funding for environmental compliance and safety and health activities has been increased by $383 million to almost $1.4 billion, and funding for environmental cleanup was increased by $242 million to $401 million. In the fiscal year 1990 budget request, radioactive waste management funding was decreased by $21 million to $575 million. While DOE is requesting increased funding for many problem areas, it is important to note that the funds represent only a small down payment on resolving the problems of the complex. This is particularly true in the environmental cleanup area, where DOE plans to spend $401 million on a problem estimated to cost from $40 billion to $70 billion" (Peach 1989:14).

The environmental impact of the military appears in many other ways. In fiscal 1988, for example, the U.S. Defense Fuel Supply Center purchased 206 billion barrels of petroleum, or enough to run the entire public transit system of the United States for 22 years. A single U.S. carrier group (aircraft carrier plus supporting flotilla) requires almost 10,000 barrels of fuel for a single day's operations (Center for Defense Information 1989). Added to the vast consumption of oil under normal operating conditions is the environmental impact of toxic wastes on military bases (Renner 1991; Shulman 1990). Here, the estimated price tag on the cleanup is between $20 and $40 billion.

and a rise in congenital birth defects. The costs of the cleanup may well exceed all the royalties ever received from Anaconda.

Economic Impact of Military Spending

Besides producing nuclear weapons, the United States spends considerable sums on its conventional military arsenal. In fact, expenditures on atomic weapons account for less than a quarter of the total defense budget. The remainder is spent on the weapons and troops dedicated to the mission of protecting Europe from conventional attack, and on maintaining the ability to deploy military force virtually anywhere in the Third World. During the Cold War, the United States prepared for conventional war with the Warsaw Pact, and for a range of other possibilities including both conventional war and counterinsurgency outside of Europe. All this was very expensive. The annual cost is now almost $300 billion. What has been the impact of this huge commitment on the economy of the United States?

To answer this question, we must first appreciate that as a form of economic expenditure, military production is unique. It contributes neither to the improvement of the immediate standard of living (as do consumer goods and services) nor to the potential of future production (as does investment in the industrial infrastructure or in human capital). Resources consumed by the military have been siphoned from our present and future standard of living. While military spending may stimulate particular sectors of the economy, its overall impact on manufacturing is negative.[7] Fewer employment opportunities are created within the United States by military than by equivalent nonmilitary spending, and an indirect consequence is greater financial entrepreneurship and rising domestic and international debt. In turn, this debt has catastrophic consequences for living standards in the developing countries, threatens the prosperity of U.S. citizens, and contributes to pressures on the environment.

Toward the end of the 1980s, an important debate emerged over

7. The question of whether military or social spending by the government has a greater macroeconomic effect has produced tremendous disagreement. Some recent simulations conducted by the Congressional Budget Office and Data Resources, Inc., show a roughly equal effect for military and civilian expenditures. For arguments that the macroeconomic impact of military spending either are marginal or can be managed with a series of reforms, see Gansler 1980 and 1989, and Huntington 1988/89. Chan 1985 presents a useful review of the principal controversies. The argument presented here is that military spending has undermined the vitality of the *manufacturing* sector.

the impact of military spending on the foundations of the domestic economy and the shrinking U.S. share of the international market. The most visible figure of the so-called declinist school was Paul Kennedy, whose *Rise and Fall of the Great Powers* (1987) served as the focal point for the debate. Kennedy argued that the United States was losing its competitive position relative to other market countries, especially Japan and Europe; that a decline in economic power affects other aspects of a nation's power; and that an important cause of the decline was an overcommitment to military spending. Manifestations of this deterioration included the poor quality of U.S. primary and secondary education, low test scores, low rates of savings and investment, the training of fewer engineers and scientists, and low funding for research and development in basic public and industrial infrastructure. In these respects, the consequences accompanying U.S. "imperial overreach" and fixation on military power replicate the patterns of decline experienced by countries previously responsible for global management.[8]

While much of the debate has centered on Kennedy's book, in fact many of his arguments concerning the impact of military spending had already been developed by other, generally unacknowledged, critics of military spending. DeGrasse (1983) and Dumas (1982) found U.S. defense expenditures inflationary, in part because the funds spent by the government in the production of military goods bring forth increased demand for consumer and producer goods without a corresponding increase in supply. An increase in military spending, particularly without a compensating increase in taxation, does not allow the government to pay its bills without borrowing heavily. Inflation-induced deficit financing during the Vietnam War is a classic example of this pattern. Another reason military spending is inflationary is that defense contractors have little incentive to hold down costs. Because of the structure of their cost-plus contracts, manufacturers in the defense sector not only can afford to pay more for what they need but may even have an interest in systematically increasing their costs, which are passed on to the Pentagon and the rest of the economy. Military spending thus bids up the price for all buyers of machine tools, computer chips, and certain kinds of labor including engineers, scientists, and skilled production workers. Finally, military spending is inflationary because it contributes to the government deficit. Fed-

8. For counterarguments to Kennedy's contention regarding the impact of military spending, see Friedberg 1989; Huntington 1988/89; and Kupchan 1989.

eral borrowing to compensate for a large defense sector sustains high interest rates that set off further inflationary processes throughout the economy.[9]

Less employment is generated by military spending than by other forms of government spending, such as investment in health care or education (Joseph 1984).[10] In 1981, for example, spending one billion dollars on guided missile production created 9,000 jobs. Spending the same amount on public transit would have created 21,500 jobs, on education 63,000 jobs, and on pollution control 16,500 jobs (Renner 1990:157). Defense spending may also have an adverse impact on productivity in the civilian sector (Melman 1970, 1989). Countries such as West Germany and Japan have registered higher rates of productivity growth while devoting lower proportions of their GNP to defense than the United States.[11]

The amount and impact of military spending within the federal budget is usually underestimated. By official figures, the defense budget varied over the 1980s from 25 to 30 percent of the federal budget. Yet the true proportion was closer to 50 percent.[12] Military spending accounts for two-thirds of federal purchases of goods and services and

---

9. Why did the significant increase in military spending during the first Reagan administration not lead to increased inflation? There are three answers: First, petroleum costs were far lower than expected. Second, real wages and salaries declined, which helped keep other prices down. Third, a massive inflow of foreign capital kept interest rates far lower than otherwise expected given the size of the federal deficit. Fred Bergsten, former assistant secretary of the treasury for international economics, has estimated that foreign capital inflow kept U.S. interest rates 5 percentage points lower than they otherwise would have been (Hart et al. 1986:350). Thus, while there is a tendency for military spending to be inflationary, inflation can be countered by such deflationary influences as the reluctance or inability of OPEC to raise the price of crude, lower wages for many Americans, and the compensating activities of foreign investors.

10. Here, too, the impact of military spending on employment is controversial. For arguments that defense and nondefense spending create roughly the same employment see Congressional Budget Office 1983 and Gold 1990.

11. Claims for an inverse relationship between civilian productivity and percent of GNP devoted to defense are supported by relatively superficial statistical associations (Congressional Budget Office 1983; Sivard 1989). At issue is whether these correlations reflect causality. Besides the impact of defense spending, there are clearly non-military-associated factors that help account for the decline in U.S. productivity performance (Berger et al. 1989).

12. The higher proportion is derived by adding to the official figure given for the Department of Defense the following: expenditures for nuclear warhead production (which are formally part of the budget of the Department of Energy), veterans benefits, a proportion of payments on the national debt which can be attributed to previous military expenditures, and relatively small expenditures by NASA, International Security Assistance programs, and the National Oceanic and Atmospheric Administration which are defense-related. Trust funds such as Social Security are excluded from the federal government budget base.

70 percent of research and development supported by Washington.[13] The military's share of total public and private research and development investment is between 35 and 40 percent, compared to 4 percent in West Germany and 1 percent in Japan. In 1984, the Air Force spent more on research and development of missiles than the entire research budget of General Motors. More than one-third of the nation's scientists and engineers work in the defense sector.[14] One leading economist argues that, aside from the attraction of higher pay, "the best and the brightest among America's engineering and science prospects tend to enter military R and D because it is simply more fun. . . . The large U.S. military establishment handicaps future civilian economic success" (Thurow 1985). Recently, virtually every manufacturing sector, save that of military-related goods, has experienced a trade deficit.[15] Overall manufacturing employment has dropped, real wages have declined, regions specializing in basic manufacturing have experienced long-term stagnation, and the distribution of national income has become more polarized. Claims for trickle-down effects that boost the entire economy, and for the potential of creative "spin-offs" or civilian applications of products originally developed for the military are overstated.[16] Only about 2 percent of the Pentagon's R and D budget goes to basic research. Less than 20 percent is committed to the development of the technologies most likely to produce commodities that would increase U.S. competitiveness (Stowsky 1986:698).

In these respects, military spending actually serves as a implicit or "closet" industrial policy that targets aerospace, electronics, and communications for growth while undermining most other sectors of the

---

13. In 1987, federal research and development expenditures were roughly $60 billion, or roughly half of combined government and private sector spending on research. If directed properly, the same funds spent on civilian research would enhance productivity and encourage the adoption of economic practices that are more environmentally sustainable.

14. One indicator of the consequent weakening of civilian research is the so-called patent balance in which an increasing number of patents filed in the United States are from other countries, while a declining number filed in foreign countries have been awarded to U.S. citizens (Dumas 1982; Ullmann 1989).

15. See Ullmann 1984:166 on the declining export-import ratios of most branches of U.S. industry. For military-related goods, exports went from $10.2 billion in 1980 to $24.4 billion in 1984. An estimated 840,000 U.S. jobs are dependent on foreign arms sales (Markusen 1986).

16. The recent relative improvement of some industries is explained more by the weaker dollar and the consequent lower price of exported goods than by improvements in manufacturing productivity that would signal long-term strength for the economy. Examples of successful commercial applications of military technology do exist. At issue, ultimately, is the overall impact of military-led research and development on the performance of the entire economy.

economy (Markusen 1986). The Defense Department targets specific sectors believed to have long-term potential, supplies substantial research and development funding for these sectors, creates incentives and provides funding for innovation, serves as a large and dependable customer, and provides training assistance and adjustment. Gansler (1989:282) explicitly endorses this economic role for military spending: "It seems highly desirable for the Department of Defense to take the lead in achieving greater integration of military and civilian technology, both in engineering and manufacturing." Gansler supports a "DoD-led initiative to successfully improve the nation's security posture along with its international industrial competitiveness."

Yet the United States may need a broader government role, not in directing each facet of the economy, but in supporting research and innovation, and encouraging necessary long-range projects that the private sector fails to pursue because of short-term market considerations. Many of the advanced industrial sectors that were dominated by the United States during the postwar period are in the process of being transformed by the application of microelectronics-based production equipment. Stowsky argues that in the future:

> Market success will depend not just on the advantages conferred by the nation's factories, labor pool, access to resources, and so on, but also on the ability of that nation's corporations to master the use of the new technologies in complex processes of product design and manufacturing. And because the development of such mastery requires a high level of sustained development in both physical and human resources, government policies toward trade and industry play an increasingly important role in creating and maintaining a nation's comparative advantage in international trade. (Stowsky 1986:699)

Yet it is precisely the commitment to defense spending that prevents the federal government from playing this critical role in our economic future. Even when new technologies are developed in the civilian sector, Japan, Europe, and even other Pacific Rim countries seem to have been best able to exploit the commercial applications. Simon Ramo, a founder of TRW, a company with a range of high-tech products, argues that the greatest need is not for specialized technicians but for personnel skilled in "mundane, grubby engineering—the designing of a product so that it will meet given specifications, cost less to produce, use a minimum of critical materials in short supply, be reliable in performance, and require reasonable maintenance in the hands of a customer" (quoted in Stowsky 1986:718). Of several government attempts to create business consortiums capable of developing products for both the military and the commercial sector, none has yet been successful.

Finally, military spending hurts the overall financial position of the federal government. One part of this process is quite simple: U.S. military expenditures abroad, such as in the construction of military bases, produce a direct outflow of dollars and increase the balance of payments deficit (Dumas 1982). More important, military spending adds to three distinct deficits that are collectively undermining both the strength of the economy and our future security. The first deficit is the huge gap between revenues and expenditures and the consequent accumulation of a huge federal debt. The second deficit is in trade—we import far more than we export. The third deficit is in public investments—the transportation system, water and waste disposal, parts of the communications and energy systems, and education—that make it possible for the rest of the economy to work well (Aschauer 1990; Moberg 1991). Our vast commitment to military spending does not fully account for these deficits, but it has exacerbated the problems associated with each. The consequences include higher interest rates, increased borrowing from abroad, accelerated foreign acquisition of U.S. assets, and the loss of real income for U.S. citizens. For the Third World, the consequences are even more severe. Over the 1980s, loan payments took an ever-increasing proportion of government revenues and even of the gross national product. Most countries saddled with debt attempted to pay off loans by boosting exports and by curbing domestic consumption, lowering still further the living conditions of their populations. Most important, the problems accompanying each deficit cannot be resolved without dramatic cuts in military spending. Let us look more closely at the impact of each deficit.

In 1980, after the first two hundred years of the federal government's existence, its total debt stood at approximately $1 trillion. Over the next ten years, military spending contributed to a federal deficit that ran well over $100 billion a year (and is now over $300 billion). By the end of the decade, the federal debt had tripled to $3.3 trillion. Interest on the debt is now the second largest and most rapidly growing item in the federal budget (after the Department of Defense). The slide of the United States into debtor status has been precipitous. As recently as 1982, the United States was the largest creditor nation in the world, with net overseas assets of almost $200 billion. Now we have surpassed Brazil and Mexico to become the largest debtor nation in the world.[17] Retiring this debt, or even managing it, will be difficult. In effect, we have sent a huge bill to our grandchildren.

To avoid government-induced inflation, foreign capital was needed to purchase U.S. securities. To attract these funds, interest rates were kept high. As a result, federal officials in Washington found themselves with an "undesirable increase in dependency on overseas savings. If either domestic savings were higher or the government deficit were smaller, there would be less need to attract savings from other countries, with the likely result being lower interest rates in the United States" (Ferleger and Mandle 1989). By keeping interest rates high and the dollar strong, Washington, in effect, chose to make its own treasury bills more of a priority than the economy's steel mills. By the mid-1980s, foreign capital inflow reached 3 percent of our GNP, and financed more than half of all new private investment (Hart et al. 1986:350). Most of this money went to finance the government deficit and to underwrite various takeovers, mergers, and leveraged buyouts. Investment in industries that could potentially export goods, or otherwise compete with foreign imports in domestic markets, did not occur. Instead, U.S. consumers and businesses tended to increase their own debt as a way of maintaining their expenditures with stable (or perhaps even declining) incomes and revenues.

As the total debt increased, it became itself a source of speculative investment. More money could be made on the manipulation and resale of existing assets than on creating new productive capital (Pollen 1989). In the words of one economist, "Investment and research took back seats to quick reshufflings of facilities and other assets in a way more suited to arbitragers than to managements with competence in the organization of production" (Ullmann 1989:14).[18] Larger debt also made it difficult for manufacturers to be competitive in the world economy, and actually created incentives to disinvest from basic industry. Instead of using product innovation and productivity increases, manufacturers tried to gain advantages by lowering wages, reducing benefits, and moving jobs to overseas assembly plants. It be-

17. Since our GNP is significantly larger than those Third World countries who also hold large debts, our payments are considered more affordable. Nonetheless, interest payments detract funds from other possible uses such as lowering taxes, restoring needed social programs that were cut during the 1980s, or enabling the government to make the investments needed in our public infrastructure.

18. This is hardly new in American business—as Thorstein Veblen pointed out at the turn of the century. But the reasons are different today, as exemplified by the impact of military spending on manufacturing and government research priorities.

came more profitable to take capital out of manufacturing and to invest it instead in the wave of mergers, acquisitions, and liquidations organized by Wall Street.[19] Loans to developing countries such as Brazil, Mexico, Venezuela, and Argentina were also more attractive because they carried significantly higher interest rates than industrial investments within the developed world (Dornbusch 1987:27).

The second deficit is the balance of trade, currently averaging more than a $100 billion a year. Because the United States imports far more than it exports, dollars accumulate overseas. These funds, located primarily in Europe and Japan, must be then reinvested. For much of the 1980s, this capital was attracted back to the United States by offering government bonds and other securities at high interest rates. Dollars flowing out to purchase automobiles, electronic goods, and other products were balanced by dollars flowing in to purchase treasury notes or even real estate, factories, insurance companies, and other major economic assets. Unfortunately, the higher interest rates necessary to draw these funds back to the United States also tended to weaken the domestic economy. In addition, higher interest rates damaged those developing countries taking out new loans or negotiating extensions of existing debts. Instabilities associated with the U.S. economy were thus exported to other countries, whose payments to international banks often rose dramatically on loans with floating interest rates.

The third government deficit is the relative decline of investment in the public infrastructure; such investment has dropped from an average of a little more than 2 percent of the GNP in the 1950s and 1960s to less than one-half of 1 percent during the 1980s. Among the results have been transportation bottlenecks on the highways and in airports, millions of hours of lost working time, and billions of gallons of wasted gasoline. During the last two decades, U.S. productivity has also dropped to about half the level achieved over the first twenty years after World War II. Countries with greater public investments have enjoyed the largest productivity growth—Japan is the prime example. Public spending on public works creates jobs and stimulates the rest of the economy in many other ways. Besides improving our bridges, highways, and airports, the federal government could play a

---

19. These mergers also hurt the productivity of the economy. A National Science Foundation study of two hundred companies that together account for 90 percent of spending on research and development found an average increase of 5.4 percent in 1986–87. In twenty-four companies involved in mergers and leveraged buyouts, however, research spending was cut by 5.3 percent (in Ullmann 1989:15).

major role in improving education and other "human capital" opportunities, encouraging recycling, and addressing other environmental problems. In fact, such public infrastructure spending may increase overall productivity as much as two to five times as fast as private investments (Aschauer 1990). Thus, military spending preempts tax money that the government could put to more productive use.

What, then, is the cumulative impact of the $300 billion commitment to military spending on the rest of the economy? I have reviewed arguments that military spending has an adverse impact on employment, productivity, inflation, and research and development priorities. Controversy surrounds each contention. Yet, even if these various macroeconomic consequences are relatively small, military spending is still a significant waste because it is a deduction from consumption and investment. Waste in this sense differs from the popular conception that highlights two-hundred-dollar screwdrivers and eight-hundred-dollar toilet seats. Military procurement *is* characterized by exorbitant costs and gross mismanagement. The taxpayer should not have to foot the bill. But even more importantly, unnecessary military spending is a lost opportunity to invest in the nation's future. Our security priorities have become distorted. The defense budget reduces disposable income through added taxation, and makes it more difficult for the government to support a variety of infrastructure rebuilding projects. Military spending also weakens the manufacturing base of the United States, increases the federal deficit, and is an indirect contributor to the increased domination of financial entrepreneurship over productive activities in which people actually make things that other people use. The combination of our balance of trade deficit and the new debtor status of the United States had the effect, over the course of the 1980s, of keeping real interest rates high. The consequences were negative for the economic security of many Americans, for most inhabitants of developing countries, and for the environment. I examine next the principal mechanism by which economic instabilities associated with military spending are conveyed to developing countries, namely, external debt.

Impact of Debt on Developing Countries

The debt of the developing world has now reached more than $1.3 trillion, or almost half of its collective gross national product (Durning 1990; World Bank 1991). In Ferraro's summary: "In 1970, the 17 heavily indebted nations had an external public debt of $17.923 billion—which amounted to 9.8 percent of their GNP. By 1987, these same nations owed $402.171 billion, or 47.5 percent of their GNP. Interest payments owed by these countries went from $2.789 billion in 1970 to $36.252 billion in 1987" (1991:325). While the social utility of the projects funded by international lending agencies has always been questionable, until recently it could at least be said that more capital was flowing into developing countries than was coming out in principal and interest. In the mid-1980s, however, the stream reversed course. By 1988, Third World countries were paying out almost $50 billion more a year than they were receiving (MacNeill, Winsemius, and Yakushiji 1991). Total debt service, the actual repayment of principal plus interest, accounted for a quarter of the total exports of goods and services for the 17 most indebted nations (World Bank in Ferraro 1991:326).[20] The repercussions are enormous. Besides inducing deeper poverty, weakening democracy, and altering economic priorities, international debt has led to severe pressures on the environment. The countries facing the most difficult economic situations are experiencing rapid rates of deforestation (Repetto 1990). Half the Third World external debt and more than two-thirds of global deforestation are concentrated in 14 countries. As one analyst notes, "The massive diversion of resources to the North has taken a toll not only on the people of developing lands, but on the land itself. Forests have been recklessly logged, mineral deposits carelessly mined, and fisheries overexploited, all to pay foreign creditors" (Durning 1990: 144).

---

20. The increased liquidity of international banks and the new desire to loan the capital to developing countries emerged in several steps. Two military buildups, Vietnam and the Reagan programs in the first half of the 1980s, contributed to federal government deficits, currency speculation, and stagnation in manufacturing productivity. But the origins of international debt are located more in the oil price increases of the early 1970s, which created massive amounts of petrodollars in search of profitable outlets. With declining investment opportunities in the developed countries, banks holding Eurodollars, petrodollars, and other forms of offshore holdings began to look elsewhere, particularly to Third World governments and enterprises, for new profit opportunities. From 1973 to 1980, while industrial production in the developed nations increased 2.5 times and trade 4.5 times, international bank loans increased 5.5 times (Frank 1984:729). The 1981–82 global recession reduced demand for Third World exports, and brought declining terms of trade for many commodities. High interest rates in the United States were especially damaging for developing countries. More recently, new loan opportunities in developing nations have dropped off. International financial institutions are now more concerned with the management of existing debt than with further expansion. U.S. defense spending during the 1980s and the accompanying high interest rates thus exacerbated the already existing problem of Third World debt rather than causing it in the first place.

The effort to pay off this debt has transformed the political, economic, and social structure of many developing nations. New loans have been required to settle old ones. As a condition for rolling over or extending already existing loans, the International Monetary Fund sets certain conditions known as "structural adjustment." While IMF financial packages are relatively small, acceptance of their terms becomes the standard used by private lending institutions in offering their much larger loans. The IMF clears the way, and the private banks march behind. For example, a developing country might be required to devalue its currency to make imports more expensive and its own exports more attractive. In theory, some of the resulting gains in the balance of trade can be applied against external debt. Unfortunately, currency devaluation also lowers the public's standard of living, at least in terms of its ability to buy overseas products. The IMF might also require a reduction of government expenditures on social programs or subsidies of transportation or basic foods that ease the burden of the poor. Paying off Western banks becomes a more important government priority than preserving the local safety net. The IMF might also encourage the adoption of lower wages and other forms of austerity in order to reduce domestic consumption and imports. Again, in theory, additional funds are freed for the local government and for the international banks. The IMF defends its policies as necessary medicine against the corruption and economic inefficiency that plagues many developing countries. But its tonic of free trade and capital flow also has systematically suppressed internal demand and enabled local capital that could have been used for domestic investment to simply leave the country. For most such countries, the results have been catastrophic.

Debt service has contributed to the recent decline of incomes in most of Africa, Asia, and Latin America. Per capita public health expenditures in the developing world increased from $4 in 1960 to $7 in 1970 and to $11 in 1980. Over the 1980s, however, there was no increase at all. In education, public expenditures increased from $9 per capita in 1960 to $17 in 1970 and $27 in 1980. Again, there has been no increase since that date. Meanwhile, per capita military expenditures rose from $15 in 1960 to $25 in 1970 and $33 in 1980. Unlike social expenditures, however, military spending continued to increase, to $38 in 1987. (The equivalent figures for the developed countries, in 1986 dollars, were $521 for public health expenditures, $581 for education, and $630 for the military [Sivard 1989: 46].) According to the Inter-American Development Bank: "By 1982, seven countries of the region [South America] saw a full decade of rising incomes wiped out, as their per capita Gross Domestic Product fell to 1972 levels or lower. Estimates indicate that for the region as a whole per capita GDP levels in 1983 were lower than they were in 1977, and in some countries as low as in the 1960s" (Annual Report 1983:2). An early 1980s estimate by the World Bank and the U.N. Food and Agriculture Organization put the number of people living in absolute poverty at between seven hundred million and one billion. Now, in all probability, well over a billion people—more than 20 percent of the world's population—live in abject conditions.[21] Per capita grain production is now declining in more than forty developing countries (even while specialty foods are frequently exported for consumption in industrialized countries) (Brown 1987). This long-term decline in living standards also places added pressures on the environment, in particular on forests which are being cut down for fuel and for new agricultural projects.

Poverty in developing countries is disproportionally focused on specific ethnic groups, those living in rural areas, children, and women. In fact, an immediate consequence of IMF-prompted changes in government subsidies is an increased burden upon women who now face added domestic responsibilities for providing food, caring for children, and maintaining health care as best as they are able. (Women are also often those employed in assembly plants whose products are exported to provide currency.) As agricultural plots are forced into more remote areas, travel time to gather fuel, food, and fodder increases as well. In Nepal, as agricultural plots were forced into steep forested hillsides, food consumption fell and the daily journey of women increased by more than an hour. From village to village, childhood malnutrition rates were closely associated with the speed of deforestation (Durning 1990:145). Furthermore, under conditions of poverty, it seems to make sense to have as many (preferably male) offspring as possible. Poor couples, knowing that some are likely to die, have large families as part of an overall strategy for economic survival. This adds to population pressures and to environmental degradation.

International debt held by developing nations also affects the secu-

21. Within the United States, the poverty rate also increased over the 1980s. About 20 percent of children in this country are now officially defined as poor. The distribution of income has become more polarized, with the gap between the top and bottom 20 percent wider than at any time over the course of the century (Phillips 1990).

rity of U.S. citizens. The most severe consequence would be a wave of defaults from countries unable to pay their debts. The resulting instability could bring down the main international financial pillars and throw the domestic economy into turmoil. However, the debt situation receives close attention from bankers, the federal government, and international institutions, and most experts feel that outright bankruptcy is unlikely to occur. International debt has become a long-term condition—more of a syndrome than an immediate crisis. (From the standpoint of most people living in debtor nations, of course, the situation is already one of crisis.) However, U.S. interests are threatened even if foreign debt is "managed properly." For example, one impact of the IMF strategy of imposing austerity on debtor nations is the loss of employment within the United States itself. Countries saddled with debt experience limited domestic consumption and are not in a position to import products manufactured in the United States. As a result, our own exports decline, and our balance of trade problems become more difficult to resolve. Exports to Latin America, for example, fell by 26 percent between 1981 and 1986, just as the debt burden rose to truly staggering proportions. By 1984, the debt crisis had cost an estimated half-million jobs within the United States (Wood 1988).[22] By the end of the decade, that figure reached almost one million (Ferraro 1991). In fact, there is a clear contradiction between Washington's policies of encouraging U.S. exports on the one hand, and creating conditions that reduce the ability of developing countries to import on the other (Mead 1987). Reduced living standards in developing countries also contribute to employment losses in the United States, simply by tempting corporate decisionmakers to lower their labor costs by moving assembly plants overseas. Even where jobs are not directly lost, unions may decide to renegotiate lower pay scales or offer other "give-backs" in the hope of forestalling the loss of jobs to other countries. Finally, poverty in developing countries threatens U.S. environmental interests. The desperate situation faced by the poor forces them into actions, such as clearing land and burning timber for fuel, that further global warming and endan-

22. Overall, U.S. exports of manufactured goods to less-developed countries dropped 40 percent between 1980–81 and 1983–84 (Blake and Walters 1987:86). While the share of U.S. exports in the entire world market fell from 17.5 percent in 1966 to 14.0 percent in 1984, the share of world trade held by U.S.-based multinationals actually rose from 17.7 percent to 18.1 percent during this same period (MacEwan and Tabb 1989:86). Corporations have not been hurt by the internationalization of production, but U.S. workers have.

gers everyone. Debt, economic deprivation and environmental degradation become mutually reinforcing.

Deforestation

Tropical forests are disappearing at an alarming rate. Each year, 40 to 50 million acres of forest—roughly the area of the state of Washington—vanishes. (Shabecoff 1990). Indeed, each year it has been necessary to revise upwards estimates of the rate of loss. In Brazil, which is often used to illustrate the problems associated with deforestation because it contains 30 percent of the world's tropical forest, an estimated 22 million acres were lost in 1987.[23]

What is the significance of this loss? Perhaps two million species, more than half the world's total, inhabit tropical forests. Approximately two thousand species of fish, more than exist in all of the Atlantic Ocean, live in the Amazon River. Biologists estimate that species are disappearing in tropical forests at a rate between one and ten thousand times faster than the natural rate of extinction (Wolf 1988). At current rates, perhaps as many as 20 percent of all living species may disappear by the end of the century (Mathews 1989:165).

Should we be worried? After all, 80 percent of the species would still be left. Many of those that are being lost do not seem to affect us very much. Is it such a threat if some obscure species of ant whose entire population lives on just one tree, or a strange plant that no one will ever see, dies out? One answer is essentially ethical: We disgrace ourselves as human beings if we stand idly by while so many participants in our common heritage are disappearing. To do nothing would be to forfeit an essential part of ourselves. Another answer is more practical: The Amazon is an important source for naturally occurring pharmaceutical substances. Valuable uses for a significant number of plants from the region have already been discovered, and we will probably identify still more—if it is not too late. Finally, the loss of species at accelerated rates, no matter how obscure they might be, serves as an early warning sign. We are receiving a message: As our social life is now organized, the carrying capacity of the planet has been reached. It is essential that steps to remedy the situation be taken immediately.

---

23. Fearnside (1989) reviews different estimates of the extent of deforestation in Brazil (ranging from a low of 5 percent to as high as 12 percent). For Brazil, 1987 may have been an anomalously high year (World Resources Institute 1990:42).

Together with species loss, shrinking rain forests also threaten the planet's environment. Deforestation in Brazil accounts for more than 15 percent of the world's total emissions of carbon dioxide, the gas that is the major contributor to the greenhouse effect. As noted by Wirth: "Within the next century, average global temperatures may have risen by as much as 5 to 10 degrees F[ahrenheit] compared with preindustrial times. The absolute magnitude of these temperatures, as well as the rapidity of temperature change, will exceed any previously experienced in human history. . . . The most dramatic effects [include] . . . an unprecedented rise in sea level resulting from thermal expansion of the oceans and melting of glaciers and polar ice. The dramatic anticipated increases in global temperatures are virtually certain to cause a wide variety of modifications in regional climates. Parched soils, scorching droughts, and massive heat waves could become commonplace. . . . Tropical humid climates could become hotter and wetter, with an increase in the frequency of tropical storms (1991:386–88). Much of the increase in methane, another greenhouse gas, can also be attributed to deforestation (Speth 1989:1).[24] Evidence of degradation in the rain forest can be quite spectacular. In 1987, 170,000 fires were photographed by a satellite belonging to Brazil's National Space Research Institute; 7,600 were detected in a single day. Added to the loss of timber are the effects of deforestation on soil, water quality, and local climate (Repetto 1990). An increase in soil erosion rates, for example, seems to accompany intensified logging efforts. The soil that does remain appears to lose nutrients more quickly. Erosion increases sedimentation in rivers and has been known to affect fisheries. Rainfall may be reduced as well, thus continuing the cycle of degradation.

The impact of external debt, poverty, and population pressures upon deforestation can be seen clearly in the state of Rondonia, where the population has increased by an average annual rate of 14 percent since 1980. Over a quarter of the new arrivals have come from the state of Parana, where small coffee farms have been displaced by large, mechanized enterprises producing soybeans. Most of the soybeans are exported to Europe for cattle feed, and presumably help to earn reserves that can be applied against Brazil's debt of more than

24. But the industrial states remain the main source of greenhouse gases. Environmental practices in the Amazon are damaging. But our own social organization and personal habits must change as well.

$125 billion.[25] Settlers entering the forest move roughly every other year to clear new land (Hildyard 1989b). Deforested areas rose from 3 percent of Rondonia in 1980 to 24 percent in 1988 (World Resources Institute 1990:43). Much of this devastation is the result of government policies. In Rondonia, most deforested land is not even used for farming. In fact, austerity measures, stemming largely from the necessity to pay back foreign loans, have reduced the credit available for the purchase of fertilizer and other agricultural inputs needed if the land is to be farmed. Instead, the government has extended tax credits to support cattle ranching and other large-scale ventures. Poor settlers actually burn timber and sell the cleared land to large ranchers rather than try to work the land themselves. (Land titles are granted based on evidence of land "improvement," such as clearing it of timber. Low agricultural taxes also make farms and large ranches attractive holdings, even where they generate relatively little income.) Deforestation also serves as an escape valve for those who have lost their smaller farms and for urban populations who either cannot find employment or choose not to live in the crowded cities along the coast. The result is direct economic loss. According to a study conducted by Charles Peters of the Institute of Economic Botany at the New York Botanical Garden, per-hectare revenues from wild rubber and Brazil nuts are approximately twice those earned from cattle ranching (Brooke 1990).

Land-clearing for ranches, timber, and rudimentary agriculture are the most commonly cited reasons for deforestation, but road building, mining, and oil concessions are other important elements affecting the stability of the Amazon region (Thompson and Dudley 1989). These projects have affected indigenous people such as the Yanomami, who have been particularly vulnerable to the spread of malaria throughout the Amazon (the number of reported cases rose from 51,000 in 1970 to more than a million in 1990) (Maxwell 1991a). The proliferation of mosquitos responsible for this epidemic can be traced to alterations in water use stemming from the large dams built throughout the Amazon region, and to gold-mining techniques that leave behind large stagnant pools of water where mosquitos breed.

While environmental decay is linked to external debt, the particular mechanisms are different for each situation. In the case of the Brazilian Amazon, a broad complex of reasons lie behind the clearing of

25. In 1989, Brazil's total long-term debt stood at 33.7 percent of the GNP (up from 12.2 percent in 1970). Debt service (interest plus principal) was 26.7 percent of exports (up from 12.5 percent in 1970) (World Bank, in Ferraro 1991).

thousands of hectares of forest for the purpose of raising cattle. The export of beef to industrialized countries (the so-called hamburger connection) is not the dominant motivation. Cattle raising is not very profitable and Amazonian beef, because it is disease-ridden, is currently barred from entry into U.S. markets (Hecht 1989; Hecht and Cockburn 1989). National tax policies, speculation on land, the status and cultural value of owning cattle, and the importance of livestock as a hedge against inflation provide additional incentives to clear the land. Japanese timber interests also figure prominently. Still another important factor is the influence of the right-wing landowner lobby in Brazil's national politics. This constituency has identified development of the Amazon with national security and national destiny. The "development" of the Amazon basin has produced an intensely concentrated pattern of land distribution, with estates created from millions of hectares of forest which nonetheless fail to provide many jobs.[26] Thus, external debt is not the only pressure fueling tropical deforestation. National culture, the indigenous class structure, and the desire to preserve opportunities for the military and landowners to become wealthy, also come into play. Each has a role in the clearing of the forest.

So how, precisely, does Brazil's external debt contribute to deforestation? First, as mentioned above, the labor force involved in actual land-clearing operations is a product of crop-switching operations along the coast, which are in turn prompted by the need to generate exports which can be applied against loan accounts. Instead of small farmers growing products for local consumption and national markets, the agricultural system now includes larger tracts dedicated to producing crops suitable for export. Farmers excluded from this process flee to the Amazon out of desperation. Once there, they act accordingly. Second, external debt fuels inflation, which in turn has triggered land speculation in the Amazon. For many of the wealthy, acquisition of newly cleared land is a better method of protecting personal assets, or even enhancing them, than investing in the industrialized cities. Third, IMF conditions attached to new loans stipulate reductions in the size of the Brazilian government. These directives

---

26. Maxwell points out that in 1985, "30 percent of rural properties in Brazil were less than ten hectares, yet they occupied only 0.1 percent of farmland; 1.9 percent of properties of over a thousand hectares occupied 57 percent of the agricultural land. The largest 152 Amazonian estates occupied 40 million hectares, equal to the total area of cultivated land in Brazil" (1991a:27).

have been implemented against the newer and weaker government agencies, or precisely those most concerned with environmental protection. Finally, the focus on quick extraction and nonsustainable economic practices in the Amazon is part of an overall cycle of boom or bust that itself reflects the recent explosion of international debt. Western banks made loans to developing countries without regard for social responsibility or adequate supervision. The assumptions underlying the financial choices made by these banks are not very different from those supervising the reckless exploitation of the Amazon basin. In each case, the ideology of freedom of the marketplace has dominated. While external debt does not account for every tree that is chopped down, it does help secure an overall economic environment and a system of political control that prevents the adoption of socially equitable and environmentally responsible policies. The Amazon is being "developed" in a way that preserves the power of the military and other elites in national politics—or precisely those who will make sure that the international banks will get their money and that internal reform will be blocked.

Debt and deforestation also undermine political democracy. For the Amazon, the clearest example is the assassination of Brazilian labor leader Chico Mendes by cattle ranchers in December 1988 (Maxwell 1991b). Mendes had helped build a union of rubber tappers and nut gatherers, which had succeeded in creating four reserves in the Amazon state of Acre to be managed by rubber-tapper communities. While his death was unique for the international attention it attracted, shootings are not uncommon. Mining projects in the Amazon have led to confrontations between indigenous peoples on the one hand, and miners and the Brazilian military on the other (Treece 1989). The Union for Rural Democracy (UDR), set up by landowners in response to the prospect of significant land reform, has hired lawyers to fight the government in the courts and teams of gunmen to terrorize peasants seeking land. Arbitrary detention, torture, and "disappearances" have been used to deter reform efforts. According to Amnesty International, a thousand peasants, rubber tappers, indigenous people, union officials, and their supporters have been killed in the Amazon since 1980 (World Resources Institute 1990:110).

Debt and deforestation are linked to the active role played by the military in the national and regional politics of developing countries. Repaying external debt requires a reduction in government subsidies and in the standard of living of most of the population, and thus increases the likelihood of internal political violence. In fact, austerity measures imposed by the IMF have led to protests in several countries in which more than three thousand people have been killed. Even where a large-scale popular response does not occur, the potential for antigovernment actions against IMF-sponsored policies is constantly present. Without the threat of state violence, the populist response to the frequently onerous terms would be stronger still. The problem has been posed well: "Will it be politically feasible, on a sustained basis, for the governments of the debtor countries to enforce the measures that would be required to achieve even the payment of interest? To say, as some do, that there is no need for the capital to be repaid is no comfort because that would mean paying interest on the debt for all eternity. Can it be seriously expected that hundreds of millions of the world's poorest populations would be content to toil away in order to transfer resources to their rich rentier creditors?" (Lever in Ferraro 1991:334). External debt thus favors a more permanent military role in securing domestic political control.

Besides political repression, economic authoritarianism may be reinforced as well. The IMF and other banking institutions pride themselves on developing the market forces that they identify with political freedoms. But the priority of reducing living standards to pay off external debt has required extensive economic control by the state. For example, Brazil's President Fernando Collor de Mello froze bank accounts and other assets in an effort to combat inflation. The market as decisionmaker no longer operates. Only the federal government can decide when these funds are to be released. The result, even without direct military rule, is neither political nor market democracy but a more authoritarian form of state capitalism.

At this point, we must reach all the way back to the United States to identify an entirely different connection between military force and developing nations laboring under the burden of external debt. In the United States, extensive preparations for "low-intensity conflict," or wars of intervention, dovetail with the efforts of established elites in developing countries to maintain control over their own populations (Lopez 1990; Klare 1988). A substantial portion of government revenues may be devoted to the purchase of military equipment from the United States and other arms suppliers.[27] Military spending also has a

27. Brazil has not been a large arms importer. But a military government in power between 1964 and 1985 accumulated much of the current national debt through "security and development" schemes focused on nuclear power and large-scale energy projects such as dams.

significant impact on the economies of the developing countries, primarily by reducing rates of capital savings and by competing for public funds with rural development, social programs and environmental protection (Ball 1988; Grobar and Porter 1989). Finally, the military is the ultimate enforcer of the terms that accompany renegotiation of the externally held debt. The armed forces strengthen administrative centralization, corruption, and bureaucratization, and limit the possibilities of participatory democracy. The U.S. military sustains its counterparts in developing countries either directly through training programs and the supply of arms and equipment, or indirectly by propping up a social system that rests on intensive exploitation and the subsequent need for social control. With military contractors no longer supplying weapons for the Cold War, it may be possible that new markets in the Third World will become an outlet for dumping surplus armaments. Michael Klare has identified five other "functional components" of the superpower arms race that may find their way to developing countries: the proliferation of missiles, a new array of conventional weapons (especially in the aftermath of the Gulf War), the application of modern managerial techniques to the control of armed forces, command and control equipment, and military infrastructures such as air bases (in Strong 1991).

The international drug trade is another consequence of the social system structured by foreign debt, Third World poverty, militarism, and environmental decay. Where local agricultural opportunities plummet and poverty becomes endemic, cocaine production emerges as a tempting alternative. Traditionally grown on hillsides in subtropical forests, a new variety of coca plant called *epadu* has been found suitable for lowland rainforests. Peru, Bolivia, and Colombia lead in production, but recently portions of Brazil are becoming active as well. Without making a conscious choice to do so, governments in the region are becoming dependent upon drug trafficking to assist with their debt payments and with other economic problems such as unemployment. Drug cartels purchase coca paste from farmers with U.S. dollars which are then converted into local currency through the official banking system. The accumulation of these dollars, which in Peru has reached up to $13 million a day, can be applied later against external debt (Serrano 1991/92). In Bolivia, coca production accounts for one out of every three jobs, and the value of the crop leaving the country exceeds all legal exports combined. Peru's illegal trade is estimated to be worth more than a third of its official exports.

Coca farming has become a threat to local democratic institutions and to the local environment. National parks have been taken over in Peru and Colombia, and large stretches of forest have been cut down. The chemicals used to covert coca leaves into paste and then cocaine, including sulfuric acid, kerosene, acetone, toluene, carbide, and lime, have entered the headwaters of the Amazon (Brooke 1989). Growers sometimes use paraquat, and even Agent Orange, the defoliant used by the U.S. military in Vietnam, to clear the ground for coca bushes.

Officially, Washington has been very concerned about the international drug trade. Its main efforts at control have been attempts to interdict supply routes and to destroy the coca fields themselves. Under the Andean Initiative, for example, the United States offers military aid to the region to help combat the drug trade. In Colombia, the Bush administration provided helicopters to improve the mobility of the forces engaged in antidrug efforts, and aircraft to monitor drug trafficking along the coast. The idea of a naval blockade has also been discussed (but thus far rejected by Colombian authorities). In Peru, the United States is spending $35 million to assist Lima in its war against a particularly vicious guerrilla group known as the Sendero Luminoso, or Shining Path. In this effort, Washington has also helped establish the Santa Lucia police base in Peru's Upper Huallaga Valley, which is used to launch raids against coca cultivators (Constable 1990). Unfortunately, these means of attempting to control the drug trade are working at cross purposes with the goal of limiting the influence of the Sendero. By attempting to eradicate coca farming without providing an viable alternative, Washington is actually driving the resentful peasantry into the hands of the very organization whose influence it wants to counter. The repression of the peasantry carried out by Lima's special security forces has led to an escalating pattern of human rights abuses and "disappearances" in the zones where coca plants are grown. Despite the advice of local and international experts to find other methods of curbing trafficking, no economic alternative to coca production is being offered. Washington is making no effort to purchase the crop directly or to provide other forms of assistance that could relieve the poverty that underlies the initial decision to enter coca farming. Certainly, a decline in real GNP in Peru of between 15 and 25 percent from September 1988 to September 1989 has been partially responsible for the increase in drug-related activities of the Sendero Luminoso (Ferraro 1991). But alternative development projects such as crop substitution are not on Washington's agenda. Instead, the United States is sponsoring, literally, a "drug war."

Critics have been quick to point out that the additional U.S. military presence will strengthen the influence of the already powerful and often brutal security forces, reinforce entrenched problems of military corruption, and raise long-standing sensitivities regarding Washington's role in the region. Human rights groups, including Amnesty International and Americas Watch, have also raised concerns that the loosening of restrictions on antidrug personnel may create a larger role for the military in national politics. But in U.S. official thinking, coca growing and drug trafficking have become fused with international terrorism, which is best confronted with military force. This process only consolidates old world order thinking about security threats: traditional "enemy images" are reinforced (Kirk 1991), efforts to eradicate the drug trade are subsumed within prevailing doctrines of national security (Morales 1989), and the U.S. military becomes the principal protective barrier against external threats (Klare 1991a).

Individuals use drugs and push drugs on others primarily because of surrounding circumstances, not because they are "bad" people. Yet we tend to blame individual users in the United States and criminal cartels in South America for the security threat presented by international trafficking, rather than to focus on the social system that created each. Former U.S. attorney general Richard Thornburgh, for example, argues that "every cocaine sniffer and crack smoker in this country shares some of the responsibility [for assassinations of government officials in Colombia], as well as for the deadly cross fire that erupts in many of our violent inner-city drug marts. Without the enormous appetite of American drug users there would be no Colombia cocaine cartel" (in Dowd 1989). Thornburgh fails to recognize that in some areas of the United States, a decision to participate in some facet of the drug trade is often driven by the absence of other opportunities. In Third World countries where poverty is endemic, growing coca leaves is one of the few opportunities for survival. The devastation of many neighborhoods in the United States was well under way before the latest influx of drugs, and the factors causing this decay are connected to those undermining the Amazon. The impact of the "Bomb and the Rain Forest" social system is felt disproportionately by women and peoples of color. Within the United States, the plutonium cycle and mineral extraction has affected native Americans. Weaker manufacturing is one of the factors underlying a more polarized distribution of income to the detriment of racial minorities. In the Amazon, the prevailing pattern of development has disrupted the lives of indigenous peoples. An important trickle-down consequence of external debt is an intensification of domestic work for women. And the drug trade is but the grossest expression of the transnational connections that threaten national and global security. But it is difficult to see and to act on these complex interrelationships. The communities stand thousands of miles apart, and the individuals in each place have little means to communicate with each other. Yet the ties between them are strong. Each participates in and is victimized by a system of drug trafficking that is itself a consequence of poverty, militarism, and external financial pressure. Each has become a dumping ground for a variety of toxic chemicals. Each is kept in place by a system of organized violence and physical threats. Each now faces a sense of hopelessness and despair that will continue to deepen unless dramatic steps to reverse community deterioration are taken. The particulars differ for each situation. But in general outline the necessary reforms are similar: creation of genuine employment, an end to environmental savaging, restoration of public health, and resolution of long-festering conflicts. In developing alternative policies, each community can draw upon a history of strong, cohesive social bonds. Each must develop political allies, and actively engage the pieces of the "Bomb and Rain Forest" social system that most directly affect them. The fate of those in Dorchester, Massachusetts, El Barrio, New York, and Washington, D.C., is shared with those living in Xapuri in the Brazilian state of Acre, the Parque Nacional do Xingu, and the Yanomami Indian reservation in Roraima.

Reversing Environmental Decay

Militarism lies at the core of the social system that connects preparations for the use of military force with environmental destruction. Military spending has accelerated several alarming economic trends, including deindustrialization, a more polarized income distribution, and historically high interest rates. For developing countries, mounting external debt, linked to but not fully explained by military spending, has produced a series of adverse effects that threaten both Third World populations and the interests of most U.S. citizens. Economic stagnation overseas has reduced demand for exports and cost jobs at home. Multinational corporations have seized upon austerity and poverty in developing countries to undercut wage levels and employment levels within the United States. External debt also fuels several forms of environmental destruction which respect no national boundaries. Carbon dioxide, for example, stemming from deforestation in the Amazon contributes to global warming everywhere. Chlorofluorocarbons emitted in the Third World deplete the ozone layer and elevate skin cancer in the First. The international traffic in drugs, consistently listed by Americans as one of the leading security threats, is in some way a "logical" response to the experiences of hopelessness, despair, and lack of opportunity that exist throughout the system. Yet the trade remains immune to military interdiction or other solutions emanating from the traditional national security paradigm. No significant reform of this system will take place without a much lower profile both for military expenditures and for militarism as a way of thinking.

This chapter began with the strong possibility that the number of migrating songbirds crossing the Gulf of Mexico is declining, and that the fate of the birds serves as an early warning sign of deteriorating conditions in our own environment. In broad terms, preserving the future security of human beings may not be very different from preserving the security of migrating birds. Enhancing the future for both will require an interdisciplinary perspective that is sensitive to a range of threats and capable of crossing national boundaries. Defense policy, foreign policy, trade policy, and environmental policy are best formulated in the context of each other. An adequate global environmental policy must address the impact of international debt and rampant poverty on fragile resources. Environmental problems may actually fuel new forms of acute global conflict that would be difficult for the United States to ignore (Homer-Dixon 1991). An adequate trade policy must consider the impact of military establishments on the productivity of industrial enterprises and on interest rates. An adequate foreign policy should encourage the spread of the democratic institutions and redistributive policies that are prerequisites for population control and protection of the environment. And an adequate defense policy must redefine threats to U.S. security to include the environmental decay to which the military is itself an important contributor, as well as the desperation that stems from unemployment, poverty and social frustration. A defense policy that seeks merely to repress or counter the social movements that stem from these conditions costs a considerable amount of money and does not provide long-term security for U.S. citizens.

Given the intricacies of the linkages described above, as well as the interests that are served by their continued existence, the most committed effort at environmental reform will take ten to twenty years before we make significant progress toward a sustainable planet. One modest estimate of the expenditures required to produce a coordinated effort to reduce the international debt of developing nations, carry out restructuring of industrial practices in the developed world, support research and monitoring programs, develop renewable forms of energy, and provide a fund to finance environmentally sound development is $150 billion through the rest of the century (Worldwatch 1988). Current annual military expenditures are close to $1 trillion. Some of the necessary funds may come from a CFC tax or a carbon tax (Speth 1989). But in the United States, cuts in the military budget are the most important potential source of funding to support the global environmental effort and restore the strength of the public infrastructure.[28] A more ambitious (and realistic) estimate of costs for a global program of sustainable development comes from the June 1992 meeting of the United Nations Conference on Environment and Development (UNCED) held at Rio de Janeiro. That "Earth Summit" established Agenda 21, a nonbinding, eight-hundred-page series of proposals that would counter environmental destruction while simultaneously encouraging development that would protect future generations. Conference organizers placed the annual cost of meeting these goals at $125 billion (Johnstone 1992). At the moment there is little evidence on the part of the more developed nations to make a significant contribution to fund Agenda 21, or to otherwise establish a system of financing that would meet these goals. Indeed, the gap between specific proposals and financing grows each year. Yet funds could be raised through a concerted effort to reform global practices revolving around militarism, wasteful production, environmental abuse, and poverty. According to the *Green Agenda*, money could be raised from three sources: (1) a system of taxes on nonrenewable energy resources and on carbon emissions in the more developed countries, (2) a renewed commitment from the richer countries to provide development assistance at the UN goal of 0.7 percent of gross national product,[29] and (3) a shift of 10 percent of military expenditures toward a UN global fund that

28. As noted by *Business Week*: "spending cuts of the magnitude that the Pentagon is examining would, at the very least, put a dent in the intractable $150 billion budget deficit—and pull down interest rates and inflation. That, in turn, should enhance investment and boost housing activity. Part of the budget savings, meanwhile, would almost certainly be diverted to spending on infrastructure and education, which could help to enhance lagging U.S. productivity. By the end of the century, U.S. GNP could be growing nearly 20 percent faster than it would be without the cutbacks" (1989a:51).

29. Currently Norway contributes 1.17 percent of its GNP, while the Netherlands, Denmark, and Sweden all contribute more than 0.9 percent. In contrast, the United States contributes only 0.21 percent, followed by the United Kingdom with 0.27 percent and Japan with 0.31 percent (Johnstone 1992).

would sponsor socially and ecologically sustainable projects (cited by Johnstone 1992). Unfortunately, political leadership in the United States currently shows little interest in participating with other countries in this effort, let alone in establishing a global leadership role. At the Earth Summit, Washington weakened the language of a Global Warming Convention, a legally binding treaty that seeks to curb emissions of carbon dioxide and other gases that can cause global warming. Only then did it sign. Alone among the more developed nations, the Bush administration refused to sign a biodiversity convention, another legally binding treaty that would encourage protection of plants and wildlife.

Otherwise, an effort to negotiate a fair payment on international loans would be another useful step in avoiding financial ruin to Western banks while permitting the adoption of more equitable and sustainable policies. Land reform is necessary. Strengthening of local markets and a return to agricultural practices oriented more toward meeting the needs of the internal population than toward growth in exports are also required. Some interesting experiments in preserving the rain forest, particularly in Colombia, have taken place. These projects return the land to those who know how to use it without disrupting the ecosystem, namely the local cultures (Bunyard 1989; Schwartz 1989). Preservation of the cultural identity of indigenous people in the region not only is a valuable goal in itself but also may provide us with an opportunity, through ethnobiology, to learn more about sustainable methods of preserving flora and fauna (Posey 1989).

The most destructive practices of the industrialized countries must be reversed. Our own current exorbitant per capita energy use, for example, must be reduced if appeals to developing countries to use their environmental resources more wisely are to be taken seriously. Likewise, arguments for saving the rain forest on behalf of the entire planet will not be effective unless the developed countries simultaneously reduce their contributions to the worldwide release of greenhouse gases. In these respects, the recent record of international efforts to reduce such emissions, including the provisions to share technologies with developing countries, represents a useful first step (Moomaw 1990). Another positive sign is growing sensitivity on the part of international lending institutions, particularly the World Bank, to the environmental consequences of the projects they fund.[30] The

30. The recent decision of the World Bank, taken under pressure from Indians, environ-

environmental impact of our economic practices should be systematically measured and incorporated into the standards that we use to judge national and international performance (Repetto et al. 1989). Finally, it may be possible to develop "debt-for-nature" swaps such as those recently negotiated in Bolivia, Costa Rica, Ecuador, and the Philippines, whereby part of a country's external debt is exchanged for stronger environmental control over rain forest preserves. Unfortunately, the debt that has been retired by these arrangements is very small (about $100 million compared to the total burden in the developing world of $1.3 trillion) (MacNeill, Winsemius and Yakushiji 1991:103). Without a corresponding commitment to provide more genuine economic security for the inhabitants of developing countries, debt-for-nature swaps may be only a more subtle form of continued control by the North over the resources of the South.

From the perspective of common security, U.S. peace policies must extend beyond arms control to exert stronger controls over proliferation, strengthen mechanisms of conflict resolution, and even to secure a peace dividend that can be applied to domestic renewal. But a renewed commitment to global development is also essential. The existing record of economic development efforts is unimpressive, and foreign aid is not popular among the electorate. In 1989, the United States devoted only $7.66 billion in developmental assistance (Organization for Economic Cooperation and Development in Postel and Flavin 1991). This sum is less than 3 percent of what the United States spends on its military forces. Much of this aid is clearly politically motivated and has little to do with fostering more sustainable forms of development. Israel, Egypt, and El Salvador, which together have 1.2 percent of the world's population, receive 39 percent of U.S. nonmilitary assistance. What is required is not just more aid but a reconceptualization of its direction and purpose. Fortunately, development models that incorporate a long-term perspective on the environment and human development do exist (James 1988; Panayotou 1990; Smuckler and Berg 1988; United Nations Development Program 1991). But economic activity does not occur apart from politics and culture. For true gains to be realized, changes in land distribution and political leadership will be needed as well. Put bluntly, policies that favor the

---

mentalists, and human rights groups, to withdraw its previously announced support for the Xingu Hydroelectric Project serves as an example (Hildyard 1989a). Rich (1989), however, remains skeptical of the reform tendencies displayed recently by the major developmental banks.

interests of the rich will only encourage land speculation and other environmental pressures (Southgate 1990). Projects that genuinely respect environmental considerations frequently call upon the knowledge and social relationships of the local population rather than expertise from the developed world. Development projects that attend to environmental impact also place other critical issues on the agenda: gender relations, deep-seated inequalities, political freedoms, and human rights. Achieving success in terms of the environment often depends upon achieving success in strengthening democracy.

I will return to the issue of U.S. support for global development and its connection to a new world order. But first we must examine more directly the principal obstacle to such a commitment, namely, the role of military force in world politics. The recent Gulf War will serve as the focal point for my analysis.

2

Old and New World Orders in Operation Desert Storm

ON JANUARY 16, 1991, a United States–led military coalition launched Operation Desert Storm by bombing targets in Baghdad and elsewhere in Iraq. Six weeks later, a ground war to oust Iraq from occupied Kuwait was started. The Iraqi military was routed in less than four days. From the standpoint of the Bush administration, the military and political success of Operation Desert Storm was virtually total. Saddam Hussein's army suffered enormously while U.S. and other coalition casualties were comparatively light. The military action enjoyed explicit international and congressional support, and the coalition of diverse nations fighting in the Gulf held together reasonably well. The performance of the latest military equipment seemed to be very good and perhaps even excellent. The war was popular with the people and the press. President Bush gathered record-breaking performance ratings in the polls, and much of the public seemed to take comfort in this demonstration of U.S. strength.

Beyond the war itself, there were additional benefits for the administration. President Bush told U.S. troops after the cease-fire: "We promised this would not be another Vietnam. And we kept that promise. The specter of Vietnam has been buried forever in the desert sands of the Arabian Peninsula" (*Boston Globe* March 19, 1991:1). Despite the end of the Cold War and the dawn of a new era of peace with the Soviet Union and Eastern Europe, weapons modernization now seemed necessary. Military force would continue to be a useful instrument of policy in Washington's version of the new world order. Domestic opposition to the administration's policies seemed to slip away. In contrast with a year earlier, no one spoke of a "peace dividend," an issue that potentially favored the Democratic party over the Republicans. The public, the press, and even the Democrats seemed to lose interest, at least temporarily, in discussing needed reforms in such areas as education, health, and housing. The comments of Michael Novak, director of social and political studies for the American Enterprise Institute, offer a striking example of how the Gulf War seemed to suppress social critics in the United States. "This is the end of the decline," he asserted. "This is the decline of the declinists. The mother of all battles turned into the daughter of disasters for the declinists. For years, people are going to cite the lessons of the Persian Gulf" (in Applebome 1991). Note that the target singled out by Novak was not the Iraqis or Saddam Hussein but the thesis that the United States is in decline and that domestic restructuring is necessary. The victory for the Bush administration seemed complete, not only in the military and foreign policy realms, but also in the domestic arena, where post–World War II priorities were reinforced. No new departures, certainly not those embodying peace and political realignment with an explicitly progressive political agenda, could be forthcoming.

In fact, the political, military, and social consequences of the Gulf war are more complex. Elements that support peaceful policies exist alongside those that support the continued need to prepare for war. This chapter balances the peace elements, or embryonic components of a genuinely new world order, that are embedded in the military drive to oust Saddam Hussein from Kuwait with the elements of Operation Desert Storm that sustain the old world order. As the war recedes more evidence appears linking the Reagan and Bush administration to Saddam's drive for internal and regional power. Questions surrounding the continued utility of military force in the post–Cold War era are of particular concern.

Despite its trappings of success, the Gulf War is a powerful illustration of the counterproductive aspects of military force as an instrument of national policy. We are in the midst of a long contradictory process in which war as an instrument of policy is becoming outmoded. United States intervention in Vietnam and Soviet intervention in Afghanistan are critical events in this process. But the ill-fated military involvement of the U.S. Marines in Beirut, the widespread destruction that accompanied the invasion of Panama, and the failure to find a military solution in Cambodia are also key experiences in this delegitimation of war. The pace of the evolution is uneven and its visible expressions are contradictory. As a result, the growing influence of peace elements can be overwhelmed by concerted efforts to reinforce what peace researchers call the "war system"—that is, the structure of state policies, organized interests, and cultural values that sustain armed conflict in the international system. After all, Operation Desert Storm *was* a war. People died. But even in that war, we can detect elements upon which a more durable structure of peace and the new world order can be built.

On one level, the perception that war is increasingly irrational (that is, incapable of achieving stated foreign policy goals or enhancing the security of U.S. citizens) is already reflected in the decisions of U.S. policymakers who would otherwise disavow such a view. The Bush administration was forced to acknowledge, however indirectly, the limited capacity of armed force to achieve foreign policy goals. Operation Desert Storm did not remove a dictator from power, nor did it enhance democracy in the Middle East. Postwar instability forced reintervention to save the Kurds and the war left environmental devastation in its wake. In various ways, Washington had to accommodate itself to untidy legacies of battle.

On another level, it is now possible for a new set of political leaders to articulate the self-defeating aspects of military action more forcefully and thereby begin to carve out a new identity for the United States in its relations with the rest of the world. If the deepening irrationality of military force is acknowledged, the necessary departure from our current dependency on armed force can be carried out more quickly and with greater intelligence. Ironically, the counterproductive nature of war can be detected in the midst of what would seem to be an overwhelming case for the utility of military force: the forced reversal of an illegitimate occupation of Kuwait by the Iraqi military and Saddam Hussein.

The Gulf War and the Old World Order

The Bush administration committed U.S. troops to the Gulf and then used them against Saddam Hussein to preserve the old world order. The main purpose of Operation Desert Storm was not to defend democracy but to preserve the status of the United States as a superpower whose influence is based primarily on military power, and to perpetuate a dynamic of world politics that revolves around competing political and military power rather than economic and environmental cooperation. Five aspects of the old world order outlined in the Introduction were reinforced by U.S. policy in the Persian Gulf. The first is the premise that the world consists primarily of enemies who pose threats to U.S. security. Some of these threats are genuine, others are magnified or wholly manufactured to fulfill the role of enemies in sustaining the war system. Second is the premise that these real and imagined threats are best confronted with offensive military force. Thus, even where threats emanating from enemies are successfully deterred, the international system is still premised on a system of competition backed by armed force. Projection of force is more important than diplomacy. Third is the assumption of privileged access to the physical and human resources in developing countries that are central to the Western economies, and fourth the existence of a cultural system securing public support for the need to prepare for war. Finally, there is the "realist" perspective, which provides the intellectual underpinning of the traditional definition of security, and which sustained the policy-making instincts of decisionmakers with respect to Iraq. The development of peace politics in the United States rests on the thesis that end of the Cold War with the Soviet Union permits the replacement of these five elements. The consequence of the Gulf War is to make it more difficult to do so.

The Need for Enemies

The end of the Cold War posed a threat, not to the security of the United States as a whole, but to the parties that benefited from the continuation of managed opposition to an external enemy. Operation Desert Storm provided a rationale for projecting military force even as the centers of power in the Soviet Union that had previously sustained the need for military force were disappearing. At the Fifth Annual Defense Contracting Workshop, sponsored by the Aspen Procurement Institute, for example, co-chairman Jim Roberts opened the proceedings with the words: "Thank you, Saddam Hussein." His audience cheered (*In These Times*, November 21–December 4, 1990:5). Enemy images characterized both the official pronouncements of the Bush administration and the coverage by the press and media. President Bush's State of the Union Address, delivered in the midst of the war, invoked the essential goodness of the United States: 'We are a nation of rock-solid realism and clear-eyed idealism. We are Americans. We are the nation that believes in the future. We are the nation that can shape the future" (*New York Times*, January 30, 1991). On the other hand, the motivations of Saddam Hussein and the Arab world in general are presented as being much more difficult to understand. Writing in the *New York Times*, Judith Miller offered the assessment that Saddam's refusal to withdraw from Kuwait "demonstrates a messianic streak. . . . His recalcitrance, however, does not necessarily imply that he is irrational. Rather it demonstrates that he has, in an Arab context, a strong sense of destiny and mission. . . . What may appear irrational to a Western audience may not only be rational from a certain Arab perspective, but also touch a deep nerve in the Arab psyche" (February 25, 1991). The military expulsion of Iraq from Kuwait thus helped maintain the mental set associated with existing policies toward the external world, especially in creating and then fixing an "other" readily susceptible to demonization. It would continue to appear that the only rational set of policies would be premised on maintaining the capability to go to war.

Force Projection

The principal basis of U.S. influence in the old world order was military force, of which there were three types: first, a powerful strategic arsenal guided by the doctrine of extended deterrence (see Chapter 6); second, the large commitment of U.S. troops to NATO and the defense of Europe; and third, interventionary capability in the Third World. The first and second types of military power are now threatened by the transformation of Eastern Europe and the former Soviet Union. Operation Desert Storm secures the need for the third military pillar of political influence. To preserve the old world order, the Bush administration had to demonstrate that military force still produces results. Diplomacy could not be permitted to succeed. The solution had to be achieved by military means.

The decision to commit U.S. troops in response to the Iraqi occupation of Kuwait came from President Bush himself, British Prime Minister Margaret Thatcher, Defense Secretary Richard Cheney, and National Security Advisor Brent Scowcroft.[1] Three days after the invasion, Bush was encouraging Saudi King Fahd to accept a planning

1. According to Woodward (1991), Bush's initial reaction to the invasion was tentative. No immediate decision to send troops was made. However, after meeting with Thatcher in Colorado, the President declared that Iraq's invasion of Kuwait could "not stand." Thatcher may have recalled her own lessons of the 1982 Falklands war, and the political and military success it brought her then unpopular government. An interview with Jordan's King Hussein (1991) also supports this picture of Thatcher's hawkish role. Besides Thatcher, the Saudi Ambassador to the United States, Prince Bandar bin Sultan, played a significant role in securing a military commitment from Washington.

team of high-level experts and a plan to deploy U.S. troops on Saudi territory. Once Saudi acceptance was secured, the scale of the U.S. effort was overwhelming. The Pentagon deployed over 100,000 troops in the initial stage, and shortly thereafter, 200,000. Some preliminary intelligence reports supported those inclined to see an Iraqi threat to Saudi Arabia. But most evidence indicates that Saddam did not seriously consider an invasion of Saudi Arabia. At any rate, as an action to block a possible Iraqi invasion of Saudi Arabia and its oil fields, many experts found Operation Desert Shield excessive (Ball 1990). Edward Luttwak, a military strategist at the Center for Strategic and International Studies and a frequent consultant to the Pentagon, claims that "Saudi Arabia could have been defended with 20,000 Air Force personnel and 16,000 ground troops" (in Massing 1991:17).[2] The size of the initial U.S. deployment made the alternative policy of economic sanctions and negotiations less likely to succeed. Sanctions take time. Yet the Bush administration could not have left that many troops out in the desert for months, or even more than a year, with the attendant disruptions to their families and careers. In this respect, the decision to go to war might have been made when Bush committed such a large initial force.

Possible negotiated solutions were never entertained. When, in early October, JCS Chairman Colin Powell discussed the "option" of economic strangulation, Bush responded, "I don't think there's time politically for that strategy" (Woodward 1991). Bush could have meant that the more protracted strategy was risky for his own chances for reelection, or that the international coalition lined up against Saddam was not strong enough to withstand a year of ever-widening fault lines. At any rate, Bush went on to request a briefing on possible offensive options against Iraqi troops in Kuwait. By the end of October, plans to ship the troops and equipment necessary to carry out a high-speed mobile assault had been approved. Bush's mind had been made up. On November 8, the day after the midterm elections, Bush ordered an additional 150,000 troops to the Gulf to provide "an offensive military option."[3]

---

2. Washington's initial reaction was also shaped by the pre-existing contingency Operation Plan 90-1002, which provided for a force of between 100,000 and 200,000 (Woodward 1991).

3. In one respect, Bush's application of overwhelming military force reflects the influence of the criteria for committing U.S. military force overseas elucidated by former Secretary of Defense Casper Weinberger in 1984. With Vietnam serving as his reference point, Weinberger called for avoiding "the danger of this gradualist, incremental approach, which almost

It is impossible to say definitively that a diplomatic solution could have been secured, but the possibility did exist. Jordan's King Hussein has said that Saddam had agreed to send a representative to discuss Iraqi withdrawal from Kuwait at an emergency Arab summit meeting to be held August 5 in Jidda, Saudi Arabia. These plans fell through when Egypt led the drive to denounce Saddam in terms that precluded his participation. One diplomat said "there was general knowledge that the Americans and the British were behind the Egyptian actions" (Viorst 1991a). King Hussein also insisted that Saddam Hussein did not lie to Egyptian president Hosni Mubarak about not wanting to invade Kuwait in late July, that Iraq was provoked into the invasion by the failure of the al-Sabah family to make good on its promises to pay $10 billion to Iraq, and that Iraqi troops never intended to enter Saudi Arabia (Hussein 1991). The outlines of a negotiated settlement were always apparent: resolution of financial disagreements between Iraq and Kuwait over the pricing of oil and of the issue of how to manage jointly the Rumaila oil field, assurance of Iraqi naval access to the Gulf, and establishment of a payment schedule for the money that Kuwait agreed that it owed Iraq. While a settlement along these lines would not have addressed the significant damage, human and physical, that Iraq had inflicted on Kuwait following the August occupation, Baghdad's stance in the fall of 1990 was described by negotiating experts as "a serious prenegotiation position." But the United States did not want a diplomatic solution.

Besides Powell, the other administration official who favored consideration of a possible negotiated solution was Secretary of State James Baker. Baker developed extensive measures of cooperation with the Soviet Union in an effort to achieve an Iraqi withdrawal from Kuwait.[4] The most visible sign of U.S. diplomacy, Bush's promise to

---

always means the use of insufficient force." In applying the "doctrine of invincible force," Bush apparently agreed with Weinberger's emphasis on attacking "wholeheartedly and with the clear intention of winning." Bush also followed Weinberger's requirement of securing "reasonable assurances from the American people and their elected representatives in Congress." But Bush also ignored two of Weinberger's other criteria: first, that military force should be committed only "as a last resort . . . only after other means have failed (it was not clear that a combination of economic sanctions and diplomacy would have failed); and second, that such force establish "clearly defined political and military objectives" (the military and political purposes of Operational Desert Storm were at times limited to the removal of Iraqi troops from Kuwait, and at other times defined more ambitiously to include the removal of Saddam from power and the destruction of Iraqi military capability).

4. On January 29, Baker and Soviet Foreign Minister Aleksandr Bessmertnykh issued a joint statement calling on Iraq to withdraw from Kuwait. The statement also noted that the

send Baker to Baghdad to meet with Saddam or to welcome Iraqi Foreign Minister Tariq Aziz to meet with him in Washington, was later described by administration officials as "primarily for domestic considerations," or an effort to convince Congress and the American people that the president was doing everything possible to avert a war.

Meanwhile, internal administration reviews found that economic sanctions were working well and, in combination with negotiations, may have had the desired impact, especially if the withdrawal were permitted to take place in stages. In October, CIA director William Webster told the Senate that sanctions had reduced Iraq's imports by 90 percent and its exports by 97 percent, bringing about a 40 to 50 percent drop in GNP. Unfortunately, Bush had no intention of making "concessions," even where such action could have been a step toward regional peace. (Approval of something your opponent desires is not a concession as long as it also meets your own interests and those of outside parties.) But the U.S. position and the U.N. resolutions were carefully constructed to minimize the possibility of a negotiated settlement. In particular, the requirement that an unconditional withdrawal from Kuwait precede any negotiation deprived both sides of room for political maneuver. In this context, it made sense for Saddam Hussein to think that the U.S. objective was not only the removal of Iraqi troops from Kuwait but also his own removal from office. (For example, Washington steadfastly refused to provide a guarantee of nonaggression even after an Iraqi withdrawal from Kuwait.) Saddam realized that an unconditional withdrawal from Kuwait would be a defeat; he also feared that such an action would serve only as a prelude to further defeats.

In this context, Roger Fisher of the Harvard Negotiation Project constructed a table depicting his estimate of Saddam's options regarding the acceptance of the U.N. resolutions that included the unconditional withdrawal from Kuwait as these might be perceived in Iraq. These choices, as of January 23, after the initiation of the bombing but before the ground war, appear in Table 2-1. Given this construction of options, it made more sense for Saddam to remain in Kuwait and fight rather than withdraw (Fisher 1991; Fisher, Kupfer, and Stone 1991).

---

coalition was seeking "the liberation of Kuwait, not the destruction of Iraq," that "a cessation of hostilities would be possible if Iraq would make an unequivocal commitment to withdrawal from Kuwait," and pledged "mutual U.S.–Soviet efforts" to confront "the causes of instability and the course of conflict, including the Arab-Israeli conflict." Many considered the statement a departure from policy, and Baker was criticized from within the administration itself.

TABLE 2-1
Saddam Hussein's Currently Perceived Choice

QUESTION: *Shall I now say that I will withdraw from Kuwait?*

If I say yes

- – The bombing may not stop.
- – The threat will remain.
- – The blockade will continue.
- – I yield to U.S. ultimatum.
- – By yielding to military threats I encourage more.
- – Israel may attack at any time as "retaliation"
- – I look weak.
- – I "lose."
- – I lose credibility in Arab world.
- – Military morale will fall.
- – U.S. will make new demands:
  - – compensate Kuwait
  - – compensate hostages
  - – destroy Iraqi military
  - – resign from office
  - – war crimes trials
- – I may get hung as criminal.

If I say no

- + I stand up to the U.S.
- + I am a hero to many Arabs.
- + I look strong.

But:

- – The war and blockade will continue.
- – I may get killed.

However:

- + I keep my options open:
- + OPTION A
  - + Ceasefire on some U.N. terms more favorable than U.S. terms, such as:
    - – We withdraw from Kuwait
    - + I say "For Palestinians"
    - + I stay in office
    - + We negotiate the rest
- + OPTION B
  - + Fight on and on and on
  - + Hunker down in bunkers
  - + We tolerate casualties better than U.S. does
  - + If we last longer we win (as happened in Vietnam)
  - + Fighting for our country, we will last longer than U.S. soldiers not knowing their purpose
  - + Political differences in U.S. and Europe will undercut the war
  - + Good chance of outlasting the U.S. If not, go to:
- + OPTION C
  - + Martyrdom!
  - + Set all oil fields on fire
  - + Pollute the Gulf with unending oil
  - + Alienate Arabs toward the West for a hundred years

Note: Reprinted, by permission of the author, from Fisher 1991.

The United Nations resolutions did not reflect the framework of collective security or an attempt by the international community to restore the status quo ante. Instead, the U.N. acted largely as a temporary political and military alliance, and Operation Desert Shield became more an *American* response. The military command structure was determined by the Pentagon. Washington conducted the nation-by-nation arrangements to create the military coalition. And the United States, rather than the Security Council, was responsible for soliciting funds. (The coalition itself included Syrian President Hafez al-Assad, who has been condemned by the U.S. government for his support of terrorism and involvement in drug trafficking. Bush also managed to secure an abstention rather than a veto from China at the U.N., even while that country repressed political dissent and continued its own illegitimate occupation of Tibet.) The atmosphere prior to President Bush's withdrawal deadline, instead of encouraging multilateral negotiations over the price of oil, management of specific oil fields, and access to ports, became one that negotiating experts call a "total conflict syndrome." Territorial claims, regional needs, frontier corrections, raw materials, political power, dispossessed peoples, power, glory, and the distribution of wealth became intertwined with cultural and religious values, all in the absence of a clear commitment to obtaining a peaceful resolution (Kriesberg and Thorson 1991).

From the standpoint of the Bush administration, the worst-case scenario in the days immediately preceding the expiration of the January 15 deadline would have been a partial Iraqi military withdrawal, perhaps to the Rumaila oil field and the islands of Bubiyan and Warbah. That move, in combination with acceptance of the less onerous U.N. resolutions, would have put considerable pressure on the United States to avoid the initiation of war. Another possible problem was that Moscow might have actually succeeded in convincing Saddam to withdraw from Kuwait. The prospect that the Soviet Union could pull a negotiated solution out of the fire was the explicit fear voiced by U.S. conservatives. Former national security council staffer Richard Pipes, for example, called last-minute Soviet efforts "a spoiling action, and I hope we don't allow them to spoil what could be a clear-cut military victory" (Constable 1991). It was precisely at this point that George Bush issued his call to overthrow Saddam Hussein, an action not likely to improve the negotiating atmosphere or to make Saddam think that there was some way to alleviate the pressure against him. Bush issued and stuck by an ultimatum to avoid a solution that would have enhanced Moscow's role as peacekeeper in the post–Cold War world, gained sympathy for the USSR among the European and American publics, and denied the lesson that Bush wanted most to demonstrate, namely, that military strength continues to be important. Successful Soviet diplomacy would have placed even greater constraints on the unilateral use of U.S. military force in the future. In fact, any diplomatic solution would have threatened the goal of preserving the old world order.

Access to Resources

While it is fashionable to dismiss economic interests, especially with regard to oil, as motivating factors in U.S. decision making, preserving privileged access to resources played a critical role in the Gulf War and the maintenance of the old world order. The U.S. response to the Iraqi invasion of Kuwait did produce an immediate jump in the price of crude, and windfall profits for many of the largest oil companies. But profit in this most immediate sense was not an important factor in Washington's decision making. The Bush administration did not set out to provide more profits for oil companies, for Raytheon—the manufacturer of the Patriot missile, or for other defense contractors whose circumstances were improved by Operation Desert Storm. Although Raytheon received additional orders for the Patriot missile (partly because Congress, not the Pentagon, insisted on it), most weapons contractors did not directly benefit from the Gulf War, because the Pentagon chose to deplete some of its excess inventory rather than issue new orders.[5] But present in the economic calculus that led to the Bush administration's determination to restore the positions of Kuwaiti emir Sheikh Jaber al-Ahmad al-Sabah and the rest of the royal family *was* a commitment to support Middle East producers who would continue to price their oil and use their profits in ways consistent with the financial stability of the West (Ferguson 1991; Friedman 1990a). In this respect, Bush's initial motivation for sending troops to Saudi Arabia to protect oil reserves is a straightforward demonstration of old world order decision making (Woodward 1991).

Cultural Support for the Efficacy of Military Force

In the United States, the military aspects of the old world order include specific weapons systems, personnel, and economic and bureaucratic interests, as well as a set of attitudes toward war called "spectator militarism" (outlined in the introduction). This form of cul-

---

5. However, eight of the leading defense contractors did see their stock value rise by a total of $5.3 billion in the month after the war began (Kotz and Larudee 1991).

tural adhesion to the war system socializes individuals to the expectation that war is universal, that significant investments in weapons and personnel must to be made, and that a nation's strength is measured by its military capabilities. Media, press, film, sports, and prevailing definitions of masculinity reinforce the seeming "naturalness" of war. The strength of the United States and our identity as a nation are linked closely with the preparation for war. At the same time, under spectator militarism, few citizens actually experience war firsthand. The expectation of war is counterbalanced by the awareness that war is hell, by the feeling that the other avenues of recourse must be exhausted before combat is initiated, and by the expectation that the sacrifices should not be too great. Popular support for a war may be secured, but this support is shallow and volatile. In the end, not too many of our people should actually die.

In terms of the rituals that preserve spectator militarism, the actions of the Bush administration in prosecuting the Gulf War had much in common with the military response of the British government following the Argentine invasion of the Falkland/Malvinas islands in 1982. The parallels are remarkable. Neither the Bush administration nor the Thatcher government took actions to block the invasion to which it eventually responded, although each had available adequate information about the likelihood of invasion. The Pentagon ignored two CIA intelligence warnings that Iraq was about to invade Kuwait, and Defense Secretary Richard Cheney did not follow Colin Powell's pre-August advice to warn Saddam Hussein to stay out of Kuwait. Both wars favored administrations whose domestic popularity was fading and the press and media generally complied with concerted efforts to control the information available to the public. Sources not fully conforming to the government point of view—CNN in the United States, the BBC in Great Britain—came under attack. In each instance, the enemy was likened to Hitler. The *London Times*, for example, argued that "Argentina's seizure of the Falkland Islands is as perfect an example of unprovoked military expansion as the world has had to witness since the end of Adolf Hitler" (April 5, 1982, in Smith 1991:115). Official sources of information, including government, media, and mainstream experts, depicted Argentineans (the "Latin personality") and Iraqis (the "Arab personality") alike as irrational, emotive, and without respect for the law. In contrast, "we" were found rational, reasonable, and law-abiding.[6] Both publics be-

6. Smith (1991:117) identifies the following code in the press underlying the ritual

lieved that the war made "people prouder to be American (British)," and yet both publics perceived significant problems within their respective countries.[7] The Bush and Thatcher administrations enjoyed strong public support, yet most of the public did not participate in hysterical forms of patriotism. The prevailing tone of the debate conducted by the legislative branch was not jingoistic. In each instance, the initiation of military force was delayed until diplomacy was perceived to be a failure. The United States built up its military strength in the Saudi desert. The British loaded their troops on a naval task force which then spent some time steaming through the Atlantic. Negotiations had to be tried, and it had to be shown that they could not reach an acceptable solution, before the war could begin.

In each war, a military incident occurred that seemed in gross violation of the existing moral code—the U.S. bombed of hundreds of civilians in a shelter in the Amariya district of Baghdad; the British sank an Argentine ship, the *General Belgrano*, outside the "Exclusion Zone," causing the loss of hundreds of lives. Both publics found these actions unacceptable. Both governments scrambled to explain the actions as exceptions to normal practice in a fight for a legitimate cause. In both countries, many people opposed the wars. At the same time, each administration appeared to hold the "moral high ground," which made it difficult for the opposition to attract further support.

The Falklands war has been called "a festival of rationality, a celebration of modernity, and a rite of democracy" (Smith 1991:113). The same can be said for the Gulf War, especially in reference to the celebration of technology through favorable media coverage and a public

---

content of the Falklands/Malvinas war, according to which the following pairs are labeled sacred/profane: British/Argentineans; moral/immoral; democracy/dictatorship; free/unfree; liberators/aggressors; law abiding/law breaking; law enforcing/criminals; rational/irrational; strategic/emotive.

7. In Britain, "at the beginning of April [1982], 33 percent of the population said they would vote Conservative if there was an election. By May 2nd, this figure had risen to 43 percent, and by June 20th, 52 percent. This 'Falklands factor' was to culminate in a landslide General Election victory in June 1983. The increase in solidarity can also be traced to greater public acceptance of the war. The May 2nd poll showed that although 71 percent of the population were 'satisfied' with the government's handling of the crisis, only 40 percent were prepared to see a single serviceman die in order to regain the islands. On June 20th, although over 250 British soldiers and sailors had died, 81 percent said that the decision to send the task force was correct" (Smith 1991:131).

The U.S. data is similar. Public support for President Bush's decisions rose during the war and in the immediate aftermath of hostilities. Bush received record performance ratings and many Americans found the Gulf War good for the country's sense of confidence. By the summer of 1991, however, a significant reduction of public support for the Gulf War could be detected. (Public opinion is explored in more depth in the next chapter.)

impressed by carefully chosen demonstrations of high-tech wizardry. Neither war would have received public support without invoking the values considered pillars of society as a whole. The Gulf War seemed to reassure many of the fundamental strength of our society. In Vietnam, technology had seemed to be of little use. In Operation Desert Storm, technology seemed to bring an easy victory. Perhaps things were not as bad as they seemed.

In fact, the technical virtuosity allegedly displayed during the war has been exaggerated. First, only 7.4 percent of the 88,500 tons of bombs dropped during Operation Desert Storm were precision-guided ordnance. Less discriminating weapons were used far more extensively, including cluster bomb units containing hundreds of bomblets with a large kill radius, fuel-air explosives, and the BLU-82 or "Daisy Cutter," a 15,000-pound bomb that can be launched only by rolling it out the back door of a MC-130 Hercules cargo plane. Second, a full 70 percent of the smart bombs, whose successes were so impressive when shown on television, failed to destroy their targets.[8] Even the contribution of the much-praised Patriot missile is open to reexamination.[9] In some cases, Patriots prevented damage from Scud attacks; in others, the Raytheon missile actually caused roughly as much damage as could be expected from an incoming Scud.[10] In the defense of more populated areas in Israel, the performance of the Patriot was even more problematic. The Israeli newspaper *Maariv* reported, "Before the Patriots came 13 Scuds exploded in Israel. No one was killed; 115

---

8. In an interview with CNN, former secretary of the navy John Lehman said friends in the Pentagon gave a 60 percent success rate for laser-guided bombs "which are consistent with test performances" (Kaplan 1991a). In this case, "success" means that the weapon hit the ground within a specific radius. It does not mean that the target was destroyed.

9. Raytheon and the army claim that Patriots intercepted 45 out of 47 Scud missiles. The problem is that the term "intercept" is used when the Patriot gets within theoretical lethal range and the fuse explodes. It does not mean that the Patriot actually destroyed the Scud. Sometimes Patriots hit a Scud but only succeeded in causing it to break up into smaller pieces which, together with the still intact warhead, caused damage. Other Scuds were hit at such low altitudes that debris from both the Patriot and Scud rained down near the target area. On still other occasions, Patriots were fired against Scuds, missed their targets and fell back to earth, at times in residential neighborhoods. Scuds that broke up into many pieces as they worked their way through the atmosphere caused especially difficult problems, as radar and killing systems are taxed when they encounter multiple targets. On January 25, for example, in Riyadh, a Scud broke into fourteen pieces. Since the Patriot command system was programmed to fire two missiles at each target, a total of twenty-eight Patriots, costing $700,000 each or a total of $19.6 million, were fired in response.

10. At a classified conference of weapons scientists, held less than two months after the conflict ended, a Raytheon engineer could not answer the question of whether Scud missiles would have caused less damage if the Patriots had not been used (Kaplan 1991b:1).

persons were wounded and 2,698 apartments were damaged. After the Patriots came, 11 Scuds were engaged. Four persons were killed, 174 wounded and 9,029 apartments damaged. In all, there were 15 percent fewer Scuds after the Patriots arrived, yet 55 percent higher casualties and over three times as much damage" (Kaplan 1991b:22). According to MIT Professor Theodore Postol, "The limited data publicly available suggests that the Patriot did not, in fact, significantly reduce ground damage from Scud attacks against Israeli cities." In opposition to those arguing that the Patriot demonstrated the feasibility of SDI, Postol drew the following lessons: "that realizable ballistic missile defenses can easily be pushed to the limit, even when they are facing a technologically primitive adversary who inadvertently introduces design flaws in its missiles; that even a relatively well-tested system like Patriot can malfunction when it is deployed and used for the first time; that the unexpected can and will happen; and that even a relatively simple system like Patriot, which is managed by a relatively modest several-million-line computer code, can have software errors that result in a complete failure of the system to perform its basic function" (Postol 1991/92:121). The Army and Raytheon initially claimed a success rate of 96 percent (45 hits out of 47 Scuds engaged). That rate was later revised downward when Les Aspin, chairman of the House Armed Services Committee, stated that more than half of the Scud warheads were missed by Patriot, and Israeli Defense Forces assessments put the unintercepted rate at 80 percent or more (in Postol 1991/92:135). The assumption that the Patriot and the other examples of high technology enabled Washington to fight with effectiveness and discrimination seems premature at best.

Beyond the ritualist endorsement of technology, spectator militarism invoked an image of the United States as a unified community. At first, wearing a yellow ribbon signified, not blanket support for U.S. government policy, but an opportunity to (finally) feel that we were together as one people. According to sociologist David Reisman, "The Gulf War ribbons were a coming together of cultural segments and all classes, for once showing that we were Americans and humane" (in Nolan 1991:18). Many Americans felt better about themselves after the war—at least temporarily. Eventually, yellow ribbons became fused with the national flag in a more intense form of support that blocked out oppositional voices. As an expression of spectator militarism, the act of wearing the yellow ribbon raised the question of why we so desperately felt the need for a win in the first place.

The Realist Paradigm of International Relations and the Old World Order

In the "realist" view, the international system consists of competing nation-states, each looking out primarily for itself. Political and military security precede other global concerns such as economic interdependence, environmental protection, and a common commitment to human rights. In this view, Washington can best play its role of global leader by recognizing the inevitability of conflict and by managing it through a combination of political alliances, arms sales, and limited forms of arms control. Realists do not believe in the possibility of normative or ethically grounded foreign policies such as the attempt to uphold a human rights standard. Washington should be guided instead by self-interest and the need to maintain a balance of power on favorable terms.

United States support for Saddam Hussein prior to the August invasion of Kuwait is an almost perfect example of the application of the realist perspective (and of the thinking of the old world order). By applying a balance of power policy without regard for morality, Washington aided Saddam Hussein's acquisition of power, strengthened his military, and then advanced a confusing set of signals that encouraged the Iraqi leader to think that he could invade Kuwait without suffering retribution. U.S. support for Saddam's political ambitions dates back to the early 1970s when Washington encouraged a revolt of the Kurds against Baghdad to serve the interests of then U.S. ally, the Shah of Iran, who favored destabilization measures against his neighbor. When Saddam Hussein, then the second-most powerful political leader of the Baath party, reached a border settlement with Iran, Washington terminated aid to the Kurds—with disastrous consequences for the ethnic minority. After the 1979 overthrow of the Shah and the acquisition of power in Tehran by Islamic fundamentalists, the United States "tilted" toward Iraq in the hope of providing a counterweight. During its war with Iran, Iraq purchased almost $50 billion of military equipment with help from the United States, the Soviet Union, France, China, Germany, and the United Kingdom (Klare 1991b). Satellite data was provided to Saddam, now the leader of Iraq, through third party Arab governments. Aid in the form of U.S. agricultural credits and government-backed Import-Export Bank loans totaled $1 billion between 1986 and 1990. Despite a ban on the direct export of military equipment to Iraq, companies in the United States offered substantial assistance. The Bush administration knew these credits were being used illegally to acquire weapons of mass destruction (Farrell 1992a; Sciolino and Wines 1992). U.S. companies were encouraged to offer Iraq "advanced electronics for its missile program, technology useful for its chemical weapons factories, feasibility studies of how to marry fuel-air explosives to ballistic missiles, and technology to test the flight of these missiles and find targets in neighboring countries such as Saudi Arabia and Israel" (Kurkjian 1991:12). U.S. sales to Iraq of sensitive technology reached $500 million over the second half of the 1980s (Draper 1992a). Pentagon concerns about building up Saddam's military strength were dismissed by the commerce and state departments. The Bush administration may have been instrumental in delaying an indictment against the Atlanta branch of the Banca Nazionale del Lavoro, accused of channeling $2 billion in support of Saddam Hussein's arms network (Farrell 1992b). Two weeks before Saddam ordered troops into Kuwait, Washington approved a $5 million sale of computers to the agencies running Baghdad's military industrialization program.

Despite the State Department's human rights reports, one of which found Iraq's record "abysmal," the Reagan and Bush administrations followed a consistent policy of "constructive engagement." In addition to offering military assistance, government officials extended agricultural credits, shared intelligence information during the Iraq-Iran war, and lobbied against a congressional bill which would have imposed sanctions on Iraq following yet another attack against the Kurds, this time with gas and other chemical agents in 1988. The Bush administration blocked a congressional attempt to deny loan guarantees in protest against the now widespread practices of political killings, disappearances, and torture. Washington barely offered a response when an Iraqi plane, using a French-made Exocet missile, killed thirty-seven seamen aboard a U.S. Navy vessel. On October 27, 1989, Assistant Secretary of State John Kelly declared Iraq "an important state with great potential." Kelly went on to state that "we want to deepen and broaden our relationship" (quoted in Massing 1991:20). By 1990, however, Washington's relations with Baghdad had become more complicated, not because of concern over Iraq's military strength or Saddam's human rights record, but primarily because of the price of oil. Iraq needed higher prices to sustain its recovery from the war with Iran and to repay its debts. But the United States, supported by Kuwait and Saudi Arabia, wanted cheap oil. Negotiations among the oil-producing states failed to resolve Iraq's predicament, and mutual suspicions between Washington and Baghdad deepened (Kriesberg 1992).

It was in this context that the now-famous meeting between Saddam Hussein and April Glaspie, the U.S. Ambassador to Iraq, took place on July 25, 1990. After listening to Saddam's complaints about the pricing policy of his neighbors, Glaspie told the Iraqi leader, "We have no opinion on the Arab-Arab conflicts, like your border disagreement with Kuwait. I was in the American embassy in Kuwait during the late sixties. The instruction we had during this period was that we should express no opinion on this issue, and that the issue is not associated with America. [Secretary of State] James Baker has directed our official spokesmen to emphasize this instruction" (Glaspie 1991:130). Many have found these comments overly soft toward Saddam. They may have also signaled a U.S. policy of turning a blind eye towards a possible limited Iraqi military action against Kuwait. While many have found Glaspie responsible for failing to warn off Saddam, the ambassador herself does not deserve the blame for a policy conceived under two Republican presidents. The day before Glaspie's meeting with Saddam Hussein, State Department spokesperson Margaret Tutweiler, asked if the United States had any commitment to defend Kuwait militarily, responded, "We do not have any defense treaties with Kuwait, and there are no special defense or security commitments to Kuwait" (quoted in Bronner 1991:19). On July 31, Assistant Secretary of State for Near East and South Asian Affairs John Kelly was queried by Representative Lee Hamilton:

> *Hamilton:* Do we have a commitment to our friends in the Gulf in the event that they are engaged in oil or territorial disputes with their neighbors?
>
> *Kelly:* As I have said, Mr. Chairman, we have no defense treaty relationships with any of the countries. We have historically avoided taking a position on border disputes or on internal OPEC deliberations, but we have certainly, as have all administrations, resoundingly called for the peaceful settlement of disputes and differences in the area.

At that very moment, Iraqi troops were massing on the border, poised for their invasion of Kuwait. Hamilton asked another question:

> *Hamilton:* If Iraq, for example, charged across the border into Kuwait, for whatever reason, what would be our position with regard to the use of US forces?

Kelly: That, Mr Chairman, is a hypothetical or a contingency, the kind of which I can't get into. Suffice it to say we would be extremely concerned, but I cannot get into the realm of "what if" answers.

Hamilton: In that circumstance, it is correct to say, however, that we do not have a treaty commitment which would obligate us to engage U.S. forces?

Kelly: That is correct.

Three days later, Iraq invaded. The Bush administration never broke with Saddam. The mistake the Iraqi leader made was to think he had approval to take all of Kuwait.[11]

The Gulf War and the New World Order

From the standpoint of the Bush administration, the military devastation of Iraq strengthened each of the five elements of the old world order described above: preserving the need for enemies, the utility of military force projection, privileged access to resources, the cultural expectation of the inevitability of war, and the realist paradigm governing international relations. The remainder of this chapter outlines those elements of the Gulf War that served as harbingers of a new world order. They include, first, a more prolonged legitimation process, especially from the international community, which must take place before a major commitment of U.S. military force can be made; second, greater appreciation of the costs of war; and third, the increased influence of ethical codes and human rights norms in judging the behavior of governments. Taken together, these elements point toward the possibilities of a foreign policy based on common security rather than the preservation of military superiority.

11. In March, 1991, Glaspie testified before Congress, maintaining that she issued Saddam Hussein a stern warning during her meeting. According to cables obtained by the Senate Foreign Relations Committee and the *Washington Post*, however, the message delivered to Saddam was far weaker (*Boston Globe*, July 13, 1991). Some Arabs now think that Glaspie was setting a trap in which Iraq would be first encouraged to invade Kuwait and then crushed for doing so. If so, Saddam walked right into it. For his part, Tariq Aziz, then Iraq's Foreign Minister, does not think that the Glaspie interview was in itself that critical in the determination of Saddam's decisions (Viorst 1991b). For additional speculation on the possibility that Iraq was provoked see Viorst (1991c:63–64).

Legitimation Before Use of Military Force

Before committing the U.S. military to war, President Bush had to receive approval from important international and domestic bodies including the United Nations, Europe, Congress, and the Soviet Union. This process established a legacy that will constrain future unilateral U.S. military actions.

Toward the end of the Cold War, the United Nations finally made significant progress in enhancing its peacekeeping role (Urquhart 1991). In Namibia, Cambodia, Western Sahara, Afghanistan, the Iran-Iraq war, and Central America, the United Nations was able to be far more active in bringing warring factions together than it typically had been in addressing regional conflicts during the Cold War. In each case, the goal of a durable and just peace has yet to be achieved. But we have been able to glimpse the potential advantages of a stronger international authority capable of following a consistent code of peace. What was the impact of the United Nations during the Gulf crisis? Did the twelve resolutions passed by the Security Council enhance the international norms of the new world order and establish a legacy that will prevent Washington from committing military force unilaterally? Or did the United Nations merely provide a cloak for what was primarily an effort orchestrated by the Bush administration? Both sides of the case can be argued persuasively. The "orchestration" thesis is particularly powerful (and was summarized earlier in this chapter). Yet the role played by the United Nations during the Gulf crisis also contributed to its influence, which will be significantly greater than that exercised in the bilateral structure of the old world order. We have entered a period of great instability resulting from ethnic and religious conflict, the continued flow of arms, poverty and deep inequality, environmental crises, population pressure, and the migration of large numbers of people. The hope of ameliorating these significant strains can be realized only through collective actions organized by the United Nations. During the Gulf War and its immediate aftermath, the United Nations proposed new, more firm standards for controlling and taxing international arms trade. U.N. inspectors used intrusive inspection procedures in Iraq to investigate violations of international law regarding nuclear proliferation. These efforts were especially reassuring to the U.S. public. U.N. teams were also active in providing emergency health care and disaster relief in the immediate postwar period. Finally, the fact that the Bush administration worked so hard to obtain support for its actions from the Security Council is itself a strong indication of the new role for the international organization in the post–Cold War period. Securing United Nations agreement prior to the initiation of Operation Desert Storm may have been a prerequisite for support from the U.S. population. The maturation of an independent, active, and powerful United Nations will take time and additional support from a vast majority of the nations of the world. In the meantime, the U.S. public is willing to see the United Nations to play a much more active role, not only in approving the use of U.S. military force, but in enforcing international law and encouraging global development projects as well (see Chapter 3).[12]

Beyond the international community, President Bush also had to receive approval from the legislative branch before going to war. The congressional debate over the initiation of Operation Desert Storm stood in remarkable contrast to the discussion of the 1964 Gulf of Tonkin resolution that endorsed the Vietnam War. First, the 1991 congressional resolution mandated that the United States use "all appropriate diplomatic and other peaceful means to obtain compliance by Iraq . . . " before the initiation of armed hostilities. While everyone understood Congress to be giving the president the right to wage war, the call to exhaust all peaceful avenues was both a contrast with Vietnam and an affirmation of one of the central principles of just war doctrine (see below). Second, Congress registered significant dissent. Only two senators dissented from the Gulf of Tonkin resolution. The votes freeing President Bush's hand were in the Senate, 52 to 47, and in the House, 250 to 183. Third, the debate over the January 1991 resolution could not be characterized as the same rush to war that marked Vietnam era congressional decision making. Members of both houses were thoughtful and sometimes eloquent, especially when invoking the human cost of war. Some of the members who were Vietnam veterans referred to their own war experiences while speaking in opposition to the resolution, while others used biblical injunctions against war. What we are not fully able to judge is whether the debate, in combination with the costs of the war, left Congress less likely to approve of war policies in the future. What can be said with certainty is that the congressional mandate to review the decision of the president to declare war has been strengthened.

Approval from the foreign policy elite is another, albeit weaker layer of legitimation. While no significant opposition from this stra-

12. Many of the particular roles that could be played by the United Nations in the development of a new world order are explored by the World Federalist Association (1991).

tum could be detected once the Gulf War had actually started, the level of stated opposition to the premature initiation of armed conflict in the fall of 1990 was significant. Many in the foreign policy elite supported the continuation of economic sanctions. In contrast to the period leading up to the direct military commitments in Vietnam when the foreign policy elite spoke virtually with one voice, during the August–January period, op-ed pages, congressional testimony, and television debates all contained disagreement among the elite.[13] Of course, the willingness of experts to disagree with administration policy leading up to the start of the Gulf War must be contrasted with their silence in the general post-war euphoria. After January, their attitude could only be described as craven.

Public Appreciation of the Costs of War

Greater public appreciation of the costs of war is the second peace element or harbinger of the new world order. Policymakers considering armed conflict have become acutely sensitive to possible adverse public reaction, and their decisions are shaped by the desire to avoid provoking this incipient opposition. The costs and counterproductive aspects of the Gulf War are not fully crystallized in the public consciousness. Yet the objective nature of these costs, their spread, however uneven, in the collective memory, and the potential role of progressive political leadership in making these lessons more explicit can create a strong legacy affecting future U.S. military action, and possibly impart a "Gulf War syndrome" that will constrain future intervention. Awareness of the costs of war does not imply that officials are fully captured by public attitudes. Instead, they must make "forced choices" or otherwise accommodate themselves to public sensibilities. In this situation, the possibility exists that the public desire for peace may be circumvented. But the potentiality of developing alternative policies predicated explicitly on the awareness of the costs of war exists as well. A discussion of those costs, and how they affect the development of peace politics, follows.

---

13. Examples of the reasoning of the elite opposed to military force can be found in the testimony of former undersecretary of state George Ball, former assistant secretary of state Richard Murphy, and former deputy secretary of defense Paul Nitze (Federation of American Scientists 1991). Military officers, including former chairman of the Joint Chiefs of Staff Admiral William Crowe also testified in favor of economic sanctions. Other foreign policy elite dissenters included former secretary of state Cyrus Vance, former national security adviser Zbigniew Brzezinski, and former defense secretary James Schlesinger.

The human costs of the Gulf War were considerable. Casualties to the United States and its allies were comparatively light (389 Americans were killed and 357 wounded; other members of the coalition counted 77 dead and 830 wounded). Operation Desert Storm also caused considerable emotional impact on the families of those sent to the Gulf and a yet-to-be-determined monetary obligation to veterans of the operation. To the Iraqis, of course, the cost was far higher. While the exact number killed will never be determined, a conservative estimate is 60,000 military and 80,000 civilians deaths.[14] According to a French source, Iraq estimated its own dead at 110,000 to 150,000, including 35,000 to 45,000 civilians and 75,000 to 100,000 soldiers (*Boston Globe*, May 27, 1991).[15] A United Nations team that visited Iraq in early March 1991 issued a report describing the impact of U.S. bombing as "near apocalyptic," with some 72,000 people left homeless, food, water, and health care scarce, and the Iraqi infrastructure reduced to a "preindustrial age." A Harvard University research group estimated that 170,000 children would die from disease, lack of treatment, and epidemics caused by the destruction of the food and health care delivery systems, and the destruction of eighteen of Iraq's twenty power plants which are necessary to run sewage and water purification systems (*Boston Globe*, May 22, 1991). An international study team visiting several months later found Iraq's public services functioning at only 5 to 10 percent of capacity. The mortality rate for children under five was 380 percent greater than before the Gulf crisis (Neuffer 1991). Julia Devin, a member of the group, later testified before the House Select Committee on Hunger: "Those suffering the most are children, elderly, women, and the poor. Food is still not available and the water is highly contaminated. Children play in the raw sewage which is backed up in the streets. . . . Two world renowned child psychologists stated that the children in Iraq were 'the most traumatized children of war ever described.' . . . The Iraqi economy is in a state of collapse. Real earnings are less than 7 percent of what they were before the start of the Gulf crisis" (in Draper 1992b).

---

14. *Time* magazine (June 17, 1991), citing a report prepared by the Natural Resources Defense Council and based on estimates of the Defense Intelligence Agency obtained by a Freedom of Information Act request, gives the figure of 100,000 Iraqi soldiers killed and 300,000 wounded. *Time* also cites several reasons why this figure may be high.

15. In November 1991, Middle East Watch issued a report that, while critical of the bombing campaign, placed the number of civilians directly killed by the bombing at "only" 2,500 to 3,500 (*Boston Globe*, November 17, 1991). Viorst (1991b) also downplays the direct damage to civilian targets in Baghdad.

From the standpoint of developing peace politics, the significance of this appalling record is that it must remain hidden. In the public perception, this was a war in which the Pentagon had to avoid killing civilians and to limit the number of military deaths as well. Announcements of even military casualties had to be avoided for fear of invoking a horrified response. This was a war in which ordinary people could not die and even Iraqi soldiers could not die—at least not in great numbers. For example, the Pentagon actually *underestimated* the number of Iraqis killed at the first ground engagement at Khafji. No body count was offered because this might incite sentiment hostile to the administration within the United States. When asked about Iraqi casualties at a January 18 press conference in Riyadh, General Schwarzkopf responded, "I have absolutely no idea what the Iraqi casualties are. And I tell you, if I have anything to say about it, we're never going to get into the body-count business." The public acquiesced, perhaps all too willingly, in the refusal to consider the implications of the way the war was conducted. But administration respect for latent opposition reflects accurately the reluctance of the public to tolerate the costs of war when these are made explicit.

The Bush administration also encountered difficulties in "demonizing," or creating an enemy image of Iraqis beyond Saddam Hussein himself. Consider the slaughter of retreating Iraqi troops at Mutlaa ridge (the "highway of death" on the road to Basra) as an example. Pictures of charred and broken bodies were an exception to press and media coverage that sanitized the portrayal of war. It now appears that the U.S. military command ordered the destruction of Iraqi troops even though they were in the midst of a retreat from Kuwait City. (Baghdad Radio announced a withdrawal late Monday, February 25, while the bombing of the trapped troops and vehicles took place throughout the day on the twenty-sixth.) As General Merrill "Tony" McPeak, air force chief of staff, explained in a briefing: "When enemy armies are defeated, they retreat, often in disorder, and we have what is known in the business as the exploitation phase. It's during this phase that the true fruits of victory are achieved from combat. . . . It's a tough business. . . . It often causes us to do very brutal things—that's the nature of war" (quoted by Walker and Stambler 1991:22). Washington evidently felt that a straightforward explanation of the destruction of the Iraqi military was not adequate. A carefully coordinated series of follow-up briefings, both in Riyadh and at the White House, conveyed the impression that the troops destroyed at Mutlaa had been planning to link up with Iraq's Republican Guard, where they would have continued to pose a threat to the allies rather than withdrawing from Kuwait (Coll and Branigin 1991:12). Also of interest are reports of the conduct of the U.S. ground troops. Unlike some fighter pilots who circled overhead waiting for clearance from air controllers before conducting strafing missions in specific "killing grids," many ground troops were appalled by the slaughter and chose to fire warning shots and take prisoners rather than continue the killing. As British Foreign Secretary Douglas Hurd later noted: "Some people argue that the coalition should have carried the fight to Baghdad and demanded Saddam's head. In fact, once the Iraqi forces had effectively lost their capacity to defend themselves, many pilots were reluctant to continue the fight." Sir David Craif, marshall of the Royal Air Force, noted that if the allies had continued the war, "I think we would have been rightly held to account for what would have seemed more and more like butchery" (*Times of London* quoted by Miller 1991) . In the British assessment, U.N. resolutions authorizing only the liberation of Kuwait and a fear of becoming bogged down in Iraqi politics were listed as secondary arguments, after the moral code, against the option of continuing the military push into Baghdad.

The catastrophic environmental costs of Operation Desert Storm serve both as a legacy of war's devastation and as a benchmark against which future discussions of the consequences of armed conflict will be measured. The Gulf War saw massive oil spills, threats of leakage of radioactive fuel and possibly other weapons-grade material, and burning oil fields in Kuwait that spread black soot throughout the region. Three months after Iraqi troops began blowing up wells in Kuwait, more than five hundred fires were still burning with an estimated 4.5 million gallons of oil going up in smoke daily (Fagan 1991). Quenching the fires took a toll on personal health and the region's environment. Those fires may raise the amount of carbon dioxide in the atmosphere an additional 2 percent (Linden 1991). The accompanying smoke was composed of hundreds of toxic chemicals, many of which are known to cause cancer. Still unknown but probably significant health effects were felt as far away as the Indian state of Kashmir, sixteen hundred miles to the east, where black snow fell. Some experts predict that the amount of soil stirred up by the Gulf War could double the intensity and frequency of sandstorms and the heat from the oil fires might push the monsoon line farther south so that much-needed rain will fall over the Indian Ocean rather than land. Other environmental threats included the bombing of nuclear and chemical weapons facilities, and the targeting of at least two Iraqi nuclear reactors. The Bush administration has played down the environmental impact of the war, partly to avoid the conclusion that modern warfare will inevitably carry considerable damage in this critical area.[16]

Despite claims of victory, the political consequences of Operation Desert Storm were ultimately negative, even on the terms established by the Bush administration. While the goal of forcing Iraq out of Kuwait was achieved, the means used multiplied the destruction that had been initiated by the Iraqi military. The war left several important issues unresolved and created new difficulties for the United States and the rest of the region. Saddam Hussein is still in power. The goal of establishing effective constraints on Iraq's capacity to build weapons of mass destruction remains elusive. Iraq is no more democratic now than before the war. Shiites and Kurds were encouraged to overthrow Saddam and then left with minimal support. The United States was also forced to reintervene in Turkish Kurdistan to avoid the unforseen destabilization of an ally in the war. All of these developments run counter to U.S. interests and perpetuate a pattern of U.S. military involvements, exhibited most recently in Southeast Asia and Central America, that have led to destabilization and high human costs without achieving significant progress on the underlying issues of political democracy and economic inequality.[17]

Ironically, of the various postwar possibilities, the Bush administration actually preferred that the Baath party and Saddam Hussein stay in power. One possible outcome, the balkanization of Iraq into Shiite and Kurdish autonomous regions, was opposed by all countries facing similar internal cleavages along ethnic lines. In another, Shiites, who predominate in the south of Iraq and are well represented in the military, could conceivably have overthrown Saddam, at least with outside support. But Shiites are precisely the school of Islam that Washington has invested so much political capital, and forfeited so much morality, opposing in neighboring Iran. A third possibility, in

---

16. Many U.S. journalists portrayed Saddam's decision to open the pumping station at Kuwait's Sea Island terminal, and the resulting spillage of millions of gallons of oil into the Persian Gulf, as the first deliberate acts of war against the environment. In fact, these actions were preceded by the widespread use of herbicides against vegetation and forests by U.S. forces in Vietnam. Quite apart from deliberate actions, virtually all modern wars have also had an indirect but still significant impact on the environment.

17. Those wars have also affected the United States in important ways. To cite but one example: millions of refugees were produced during the Indochina and Central American regional conflicts; their migration has changed the demographic character of the United States (Barnet 1991).

which the United States would support a more democratic and representative government, could have been achieved, but only through a more active policy of political intervention in the name of human rights. Such a policy would also have required extensive economic support. The United States would be obliged to such a government to repair at least part of the estimated two hundred billion dollars of infrastructure damage from the war. With Saddam in power, no such obligation is created. From the standpoint of the Bush administration and the goal of preserving the old world order, the precedent that such actions would produce, and the political impetus to enact similar interventions against other repressive regimes currently favored by Washington, were important to avoid. Finally, a democratically elected government would not have been favored by the unrepresentative regimes of the other Gulf states, especially Kuwait and Saudi Arabia (Viorst 1991c). Thus, in the aftermath of a war fought in the name of democracy, no country wanted a democratic Iraq. In effect, Bush has tilted, once again, toward Saddam, an enemy who is at once weak and vulnerable to rhetorical flagellation in ways that are politically useful.

The quality of U.S. democracy also suffered as a result of Operation Desert Storm. The most striking example was the failure of the press and media to convey adequately the political and social background of the war as well as its human consequences (*Deadline* 1991; Fialka 1992; Hallin 1991; Nickerson and Neuffer 1991).[18] The significance of the inadequate coverage for the development of peace politics can be developed in two directions. On one hand, U.S. opinion did not, in general, express horror at the loss of Iraqi lives. If, in the words of Robert Jay Lifton, in the end it was not a war but an "annihilation project," the public either was not informed or approved of the Pentagon's decision. On the other hand, the fact that the government saw a need for extensive public relations demonstrates its sensitivity to the inclination of the public to withdraw support from policies that carried significant human cost, even if those costs were suffered pri-

18. One of the most dramatic examples of press compliance with the administration's point of view concerns the claim that the Iraqi military were poised to invade Saudi Arabia and that a U.S. military intervention was necessary to block this possibility. The *St. Petersburg Times* published a story (January 6, 1991) based on Soviet satellite photos, taken in mid-September, five weeks after the invasion of Kuwait, which failed to show troop concentrations or other evidence of a threat to Saudi Arabia. The *Times* felt that the story, while not conclusive, was suitable for national distribution. Yet neither the Associated Press, nor the Scripps-Howard news service, of which the *St. Petersburg Times* is a member, chose to distribute it.

marily by the Iraqis. While efforts to control information are not unusual in wartime, in the case of Operation Desert Storm the U.S. government committed huge resources in this area, thereby acknowledging the reservoir of peace sentiment that lay beneath the relatively shallow public support.

The administration went to unusual lengths to control the press. On August 14 Captain Ron Wildermuth, General Norman Schwarzkopf's chief aide for public affairs, dispensed "Annex Foxtrot," which outlined the public information policy for Operation Desert Shield. "News representatives," he wrote, "will be escorted at all times. Repeat, at all times" (DeParle 1991:1). Defense Secretary Cheney delegated many particular decisions to military officers who, distrustful of what they perceived to be the role of the press during the Vietnam War, imposed strict rules regarding pool coverage and censorship. President Bush watched virtually every televised briefing, while his political aides recommended that some public relations officers be removed after their performances. It was the White House that promoted Lieutenant General Thomas Kelly as star briefer, and arranged daily rehearsal sessions for him. Chief Pentagon spokesperson Pete Williams held a series of fall meetings with news executives, during which he conveyed the misleading impression that opportunities for independent reporting would follow the temporary assignment of journalists to closely monitored teams or pools. The Pentagon provided free transportation for reporters from smaller towns and put them in direct contact with "their" soldiers to ensure that the dominant theme would be human interest rather than in-depth analysis. Instead of the fears expressed by some of these subjects, the typical story focused on skills, prowess, and determination to "do the job" and get home. Human interest stories overwhelmed the occasional article pointing out significant inequities within the armed forces. In 1990, for example, according to figures from the General Accounting Office, blacks comprised 20.8 percent and Hispanics 4.6 percent of the armed forces. In 1971, the respective figures were 11.1 percent and 3.6 percent. In the Persian Gulf, blacks comprised 29.8 percent of the army, 21.3 percent of the navy, and 13.5 percent of the air force. Blacks are roughly 12 percent of the total population. While blacks contributed nearly twice their proportional share to the military, youth from the country's wealthiest communities volunteered at one-fifth the national rate (Tye 1991b).

Those watching late-night cable television could sometimes view soldiers wearing peace symbols, listening to 1960s antiwar music, and expressing confusion about exactly why they had been ordered into the Saudi sands. Family support groups prayed for their relatives in the Gulf. Often they prayed for the Iraqi people as well. But such incidents were never culled by the press and media and presented as incipient peace sentiments, perhaps because White House staffers were so effective in screening articles written by reporters who filed for credentials to cover the war and in denying requests for interviews from those who seemed to be independent or critical. Martha Teichner of CBS offered the following assessment of press coverage of the Gulf War: "You've got incompetence from the bottom up and you've got resistance from the top down and it met where we were, in the pool. It all came together, and it was disastrous" (in Draper 1992b).

Once the war started, the Pentagon took pains to avoid making statements of the number killed in bombing missions and to avoid using concrete language to describe the impact of the war. According to what has been described as a metaphorical system for justifying the war (Lakoff 1991), the allied air forces were not trying to kill Iraqi soldiers but were trying to "soften them up" for a future ground attack. Civilian casualties were "collateral damage." We "targeted elite troops" or "Saddam's Republican Guard," never ordinary conscripts. The dead were transported in "human remains pouches," not "body bags." The Danish paper *Politiken* compiled the following comparison of terms used by the press:

The Allies have:	The Iraqis have:
Army, navy and air force	A war machine
Guidelines for journalists	Censorship
Briefings to the press	Propaganda
The Allies:	**The Iraqis:**
Eliminate	Kill
Neutralize	Kill
Hold on	Bury themselves
Conduct precision bombing	Fire wildly at anything
The Allied soldiers are:	**The Iraqi soldiers are:**
Professional	Brainwashed
Cautious	Cowardly
Full of courage	Cannon fodder
Loyal	Blindly obeying
Brave	Fanatic
The Allied missiles:	**The Iraqi missiles:**
Do extensive damage	Cause civilian deaths

George Bush is:	Saddam Hussein is:
Resolute	Intractable
Balanced	Mad

Every effort was made to portray this as a war without human cost, even for armies. Not only were pains taken to avoid estimates of civilian casualties, but the Pentagon remained silent on the question of how many uniformed enemy soldiers were being killed as well.

In the words of John Berger:

> Four or five times a day the public received a TV lesson about how to become deaf to the voice of their memory, or their conscience or of their imagination; deaf to a voice which might cry out that these bombers, used so extensively in Vietnam, became, across the world, a symbol of the horrors of war; deaf to a voice which might shout that the "carpet" bombing of a city suburb (whatever the claimed target) is a step towards genocide; deaf to a voice which might repeat that the cluster bombs being dropped on the cities contained 24 grenades, each one exploding into 2,000 high-velocity needle fragments designed so as to cause the maximum number of untreatable wounds; deaf to a voice which might recall that Islamic culture has probably contributed as much to the human dream of justice and reason as has Christianity. (1991)

That the public remained largely deaf is true. But as pre- and postwar polls indicate, the public also has an alternative voice. In fact, the public possesses both the capacity to not hear and the capacity to speak in favor of a new world order.

Influence of Moral Considerations

The two peace elements discussed thus far—constraints on the unilateral use of U.S. military force imposed by the need for extended legitimation prior to use, and increased public awareness of the costs of war—make up two building blocks of the new world order. A third block is the increased salience of moral considerations in the decision to go to war. Each of these elements will make it more difficult for policymakers to commit U.S. troops in the future. The application of moral codes will also limit the ability of presidents, on their own, to order troops into battle.

The use of international norms to judge the behavior of nation-states has never been more accepted, even though a gap between actual policy and those norms remains (Jones 1991; Little 1991). In the period leading up to the January 1991 initiation of hostilities, much of the debate over the possible use of U.S. military force, by both supporters and opponents of the Bush administration, was structured by the use of just war categories.[19] In Massachusetts, the Council of Churches, the largest Protestant ecumenical organization in the state, even issued a videotape, based on just war criteria, to help local congregations sort out their responses to the war (Higgins 1991b). A broad spectrum of religious leaders, including the leaders of twenty-six American Protestant and Orthodox denominations, fifteen Roman Catholic bishops, and one hundred church officials from around the world, declared their opposition to the war on moral grounds (Higgins 1991a). Ambiguity is inevitable when both supporters and opponents of Operation Desert Storm can appeal to identical reference points and use similar vocabulary to support their position.[20] Yet the increased use of just war criteria serves as a growing restraint on the employment of unilateral military intervention by the United States.

Human rights norms also figured prominently in the debate over the war. Concern for human rights informed critical assessments of the Iraqi regime and led to the question of whether the United States was guilty of hypocrisy when it supported the Kuwaiti and Saudi governments in the name of democracy. Human rights norms were an importance force behind international support for the provision of safe havens or enclaves for Kurds in the northern part of Iraq after the war. Such action actually compromised the principle of noninterference in the internal affairs of another country (Article II, Section 7 of the U.N. charter). The Bush administration's efforts to assist the Kurds were not motivated by a desire to follow a human rights code. Washington was forced to reintervene with military force by the glare of the public spotlight, and by the argument that the United States bore some responsibility for the destabilization of the Kurdish homeland. Yet the reintroduction of troops may serve as a precedent for other humanitarian actions that conflict with strict interpretations of nonintervention principles. Meanwhile, after the war, the emir of Kuwait, Sheikh Jaber al-Ahmad al-Sabah, extended martial law well

19. Just war criteria are usually divided into two groupings: *jus ad bellum*, or the right to go to war; and *jus in bello*, or the actual conduct or prosecution of a war. Criteria in the first group include but are not limited to the following: The cause must be just; the authority waging war must be legitimate; the ultimate objective or intention must be to secure peace; and going to war must be a last resort. Criteria belonging to the second category include: The means used and the damage produced must not be excessive; discrimination between combatants and noncombatants must be maintained; provisions on international law must be respected; and the enemy must be able to sue for peace.

20. For an example see the exchange between Fotion (1991) and Lopez (1991).

past the point that outside observers considered necessary (Viorst 1991c), while the Saudi government, which had put some of its less impressive practices on hold for the duration of the war, quickly returned to a selective pattern of brutal punishments, often enforced by the religious police.

Another moral aspect of the Gulf War concerns President Bush's comparison of Saddam Hussein with Adolf Hitler. The use of the Hitler analogy locked the administration into a strategy of applying the "lesson" of Munich—we must avoid appeasement and we must respond to aggression. Comparing Saddam to Hitler sometimes invoked a quasi-racist reaction among the population. Use of the image of the German dictator prompted the demonization of the "other" in which the Iraqi leader was seen as "typically" Arab in his cruelty, strangeness, and irrationality. While evidence of anti-Iraqi and anti-Arab attitudes on the part of Americans could certainly be found, the people-to-people level of hostility was less than expected. The combination of both racism and understanding was demonstrated, for example, by an incident in which a Dairy Queen fast-food restaurant owned by an Arab-American in a small Michigan town was burned down by the deliberate act of an individual. Immediately afterward, the townspeople got together and rebuilt it.

President Bush supplemented the Hitler analogy with a reliance on moral arguments to justify his decision, because the public would approve of military force only when it was viewed as a moral act.[21] Bush initially maintained that a military commitment was necessary to protect the American way of life and to guarantee cheap oil. These arguments were rejected by the public. As several commentators observed, when the dollar cost of the military commitment to the Gulf is included, the cost of a barrel of Middle East oil, which moved between $20 and $40 during the crisis, was actually somewhere between $180 and $280 (Barnet 1991). Public preference for a change in the conduct of international relations forced Bush to cloak decisions made to preserve the old world order in the rhetoric of creating a new world order.

Conclusion

Well before Saddam Hussein invaded Kuwait, he represented a threat to world security. Now that Iraqi troops have been forcefully repulsed, Saddam and the brutal repression he represents are still a threat. It is

21. The significance of another morality play, focused on the obligation of the United States to respond to the "rape" of Kuwait, is provided by Jeffords (1991).

now clear that Iraq had both chemical weapons and missiles with sufficient range to threaten many of its Middle East neighbors. Baghdad was also well on its way to acquiring a nuclear bomb. No one can be pleased by these developments. Operation Desert Storm and subsequent U.N. supervision of Iraq has put a temporary cap on the threat of weapons of mass destruction. But we must also remember the policies that gave Saddam the diplomatic and material encouragement necessary to develop these weapons in the first place. Here, the abysmal records of the Reagan and Bush administrations in the Persian Gulf clearly demonstrate the weakness of realist axioms and over-reliance on military force as foreign policy guides in the effort to create a genuine new world order. The more distance we achieve from the 1991 Gulf War, the more apparent the costs in human, ethical, environmental, and financial terms. Subsequent disclosures have weakened Washington's credibility as the defender of democracy in the Middle East region. The debate over the efficacy of economic sanctions as the means to remove Saddam from Kuwait continues. But the more central issue is how to conduct a foreign policy that favors democracy over dictators. And here the old world order approach has little to offer.

Despite a concerted effort by the Bush administration to bolster the principles of the old world order, Operation Desert Storm contained important elements of an alternative structure for global politics. Recognition of the need for a more protracted legitimation process prior to the use of military force, recognition of the costs and counterproductive aspects of war, and a strengthening of a moral code to judge the behavior of policymakers are important legacies. The war generated modest political momentum toward a new world order, but this political will would be further enhanced by the emergence of a progressive movement.

According to the premises of the new world order, the Gulf War also produced important "negative lessons" for the United States. First, foreign policy must not rest solely on realpolitik for such practices may become self-defeating. In the case of Iraq, Washington, following realist principles, supported the domestic power and regional status of Saddam Hussein. When Saddam misread signals, the United States responded with threatened and then actual military force. The war achieved only the goal of getting Iraq out of Kuwait. Otherwise the record of the Gulf War is not impressive. Other goals are still remote, including strengthening democracy in the entire region, creating more secure economies for the people of the Middle East, and addressing the grievances of marginalized populations.

Second, arms trade with tyrants is dangerous. As a world leader, the United States must use other avenues of influence. We may end up facing, as in the Gulf War, military equipment provided by our own defense contractors. On a global scale, the exchange of arms for influence and of arms for profit perpetuate the instabilities of the old world order. Third, the United States cannot afford to ignore festering economic grievances like those surrounding the pricing and supply of crude oil, for these will lead to political and military instabilities. This is not to suggest that Washington should attempt to control the market for natural commodities; security and stability in a new world order must be built upon more fair terms of trade between North and South and on the expectations that living conditions will continue to improve and that the development process will not introduce profound disruptions into the global economy. To meet these goals, the United States must be an active participant. Finally, the United States must reduce its dependency on foreign oil. If we do not, we may once again undertake policies that end up costing the population the equivalent of seven or eight dollars a gallon. The domestic policies of a new world order simply must include conservation efforts and research and development to provide greater energy efficiency (Flavin 1991; Kranish 1991; Romm 1991).

These goals can be achieved in part through a comprehensive peace conference whose duration would be on the order of years. From the standpoint of a new world order, a successful conference would have to resolve the Palestinian question, secure the withdrawal of Syrian forces from Lebanon, provide for the security and protection of Israel, and establish a regional development bank, funded at least in part by the oil-rich Arab states. The arms trade must be controlled and stringent arms control measures adopted. True peace cannot be established in the region until the Baath regime is removed from power in Iraq, and greater strides toward democracy occur within Saudi Arabia and Kuwait. These goals can be accomplished, but only through a stronger commitment to conflict resolution and a prolonged peace-building process (Kriesberg 1992). Above all, the Arab people must perceive that they are the masters of their own destiny, and that they are welcome to participate as equals in the creation of new world order. The need to take into account the aspirations of Arab peoples is not recognized by most of the West, and yet it is critical for peace. In the meantime, the cultural misperceptions held by many Westerners about Arab cultures are received, experienced, and twisted back into equally strong Arab misperceptions about the strength of the "Zionist lobby" and conspiracies directed by the Central Intelligence Agency (Said 1991).

Among the harbingers of a new world order illuminated by the Gulf War are public attitudes toward armed conflict. One point must be stressed: Until just before the January 15 deadline, most of the public favored the continuation of sanctions. A different president could have expected just as much support for economic sanctions as President Bush received for war if such a policy had been fully explained and legitimated by the authority of the office. My focus on the public may seem strange when we consider that, after Operation Desert Storm, President Bush enjoyed the highest performance ratings in history. The public was clearly proud of the military, and its success seemed to cement the status of the United States as the most powerful country on earth and to restore a sense of national purpose. At the same time, this interpretation of public opinion is much too simple. A majority of the public was simultaneously swayed by the political, military, and cultural trappings of Operation Desert Storm *and* willing to support a policy of seeking other means to remove Saddam Hussein from Kuwait. No new desire to support military interventions can be detected. In this respect, the impact of the Gulf War for the "Vietnam syndrome" has been overstated. While the public was emotionally satisfied by the display of U.S. military strength, polls also demonstrate strong support for a foreign policy that seeks to strengthen democracy as a global process. Despite the operational success of the U.S. military, the public continues to support both a reduction in the defense budget and a far more active government role in achieving social priorities.

3

National Security and the New World Order: What the Public Thinks

WHAT DOES the American public think about national security and the possibilities of a new world order? Is the population open to definitions of national security that incorporate environmental, economic, and human rights perspectives as well as the need for a strong military? What does the public think about nuclear weapons? The use of military force? Foreign aid? And how have the end of the Cold War and the Gulf War affected these views? The answers are important, for progressive policies cannot be imposed upon the public. Little change will occur if, after all is said and done, U.S. citizens genuinely support efforts to achieve nuclear superiority, a foreign policy that relies on military strength, and a "we should go it alone" approach to the world's economic, political, environmental, and health problems. Fortunately, they do not.

I argue that the attitudes Americans hold toward nuclear weapons and national security have undergone significant change. The potential for mobilizing the public around the themes of common security and the creation of a new world order now exists. Important areas of ambivalence can be found, yet a presidential campaign can appeal to the implicit support for the alternative approach to national security that can be detected within existing attitudes. The public supports programs that would depart significantly from the goals pursued by Washington during the Cold War. During the 1980s, the public became better educated on nuclear weapons issues, with the majority now appreciating the impossibility of fighting a war with strategic weapons. Most also believe that the concept of military superiority with respect to nuclear weapons no longer carries any meaning. The public supports a policy of basic deterrence. More ambitious political and military roles for nuclear weapons are rejected. While the recent Persian Gulf War had overwhelming popular support and recent Republican presidents have been favored with high levels of public approval in their handling of foreign affairs and defense issues, the longstanding distrust of Soviet intentions that characterized the Cold War era has now dissipated and the threat offered by substitute enemies is not nearly as great. There is no equivalent centerpiece that can sustain military spending at the levels needed to counter the Soviet threat.

The public is far more willing than the political elite to support new departures in arms control, including the elimination of chemical and nuclear arms—as long as these are carried out in concert with other countries and are verifiable. More broadly, the public supports the foreign policy goals of forming a more cooperative international order, supporting democracy over dictatorship, developing global economic policies that are environmentally sound, and strengthening the role of the United Nations. The meaning the public attaches to these goals is different from that expressed by current political leadership. In particular, the primacy of military force is not nearly as critical for the public. Alongside the tentative support for a new world order lies renewed public support for social spending and for a more active role for the federal government in protecting the environment, strengthening public education, and providing for better health care.

Important qualifications must be attached to this summary of the potential support for political realignment. Left to itself, public opinion will *not* be a major force in creating a revitalized progressive agenda in U.S. politics. Public attitudes must be tapped by more active political forces such as social movements and a presidential campaign. Potential support for reform exists. So does support for the continuation of the policies that have been at the center of Cold War foreign and defense policy. An extended dialogue must take place between the public and the political forces that attempt to represent the incipient opposition. The adjustment process will be mutual: Public policies must reflect public sentiments, but a successful movement can also draw out the support that already exists for new social priorities. In the meantime, even in the absence of a new direction for national politics, public attitudes constitute an effective obstacle to efforts to raise the military budget, carry out strategic modernization, and reestablish the centrality of Cold War themes in foreign policy. Public opinion has set new limits on existing policies without dictating an explicit set of policy alternatives. Even those policymakers guided by the traditions of the old world order must adjust to this new political terrain.

The argument proceeds in several steps. First, I look more closely at the concept of public opinion and its relationship to national policy. Second, I explore the history of U.S. attitudes toward nuclear weapons. Significant changes in public attitudes took place during the 1980s and these can be built upon to support a focused effort to adopt basic deterrence. Third, I address counterarguments to my assessment that latent support for a progressive foreign policy agenda now exists among the public. Fourth, I examine public support for the Gulf War, which in itself poses a significant challenge to my argument. Finally, I consider demographic differences including gender, race, age, education, income, and party affiliation. I use a comparison with public attitudes in West Germany to discuss the relative lack of importance of such factors for formulating a new approach to national security in the United States. The implication is that policies premised on the transition to a new world order carry nearly universal appeal.

Public Opinion and Public Policy

As used in this chapter, "public opinion" comprises only the attitudes held by individuals as measured by professionally conducted polls. The impact of other important forms of public influence, including organized peace movements (which are treated in the next chapter) and interest groups, is not included. This concept of public opinion is a limited measure of the popular will. Yet the relationship between attitudes and public policy remains a critical element in assessing the quality of democracy.

Classic democratic theory asserts that government policy is generally responsive to the preferences of citizens. The evolution of opinion polling itself has been based on the assumption that better knowledge of what the public wanted could be communicated to policymakers who would in turn develop the specific policies that incorporated citizen viewpoints. The implication is that public opinion should be an important element of policy formation. Few theorists now regard the impact of public opinion in such an optimistic light.[1]

---

1. Page and Shapiro (1983, 1989) have described public opinion as the proximate cause

There are too many examples demonstrating that the political elite develop their own policy preferences, and little evidence of their inclination to monitor the public for continuous approval. The general response among students of political power has been to change the concept of democracy, which is now said to exist when elite policy decisions do not diverge substantially from the underlying *values* held by the public, or when a congruence or basic compatibility between public attitudes and government policies is maintained. The role of public opinion is only to provide a retrospective check on government excesses rather than a prospective guide that decisionmakers should follow.[2] Public opinion constrains but does not direct policymakers. As stated by Gabriel Almond: "The function of the public in a democratic policy-making process is to set certain policy criteria in the form of widely held values and expectations. The policies themselves, however, are the product of leadership groups who carry on the specific work of policy formulation and policy advocacy" (1950:5–6). From the standpoint of peace politics, this limited sense of democracy is completely unacceptable. A more active role for the public must be structured.

The problem, at least in part, is that the very process of conducting polls tends to reinforce this limited definition of democracy. Taken by itself, polling restricts our sense of public participation. Many think that polling successfully taps the natural reservoir of public sentiment. But answers and results can be more artifacts of questions than accurate measures of what the public thinks. Polls enhance the power of those who formulate questions, and they reduce participation to a docile—and controlled—form of expression. Ginsberg, for example, argues that polling first "alters both what is expressed and what is perceived as the opinion of the mass public by transforming public

of policy, with policy affected by opinion change more consistently than the public is influenced by the efforts of government officials. Bruce Russett (1972) also presents a case for a modest impact of public opinion on the level of military expenditures. But these authors condition their arguments. Page and Shapiro, for example, caution that in one-third of their cases, government decisions did not follow the populist message.

2. Cohen's (1973) study of State Department officials is typical. He found a low opinion of the public's views on foreign policy issues. Even where the public was well informed, government officials saw their role as trying to carry out what in their judgment was the best, rather than the most popular policy. The implication is that the elite determines policy largely without regard for public sentiments, and that public opinion has an impact only in special circumstances. Cohen found that "public opinion as a political force has bearing on foreign policy to the extent that foreign policy makers perceive in the environment outside their political orbit some encouragements or limitations that facilitate or modify preferred behavior" (p. 7). These conditions exist only rarely, and policymakers are "autonomous," or relatively free from societal constraints.

opinion from a voluntary to an externally subsidized matter. Second, polling modifies the manner in which opinion is publicly presented by transforming public opinion from a behavioral to an attitudinal phenomenon. Third, polling changes the origin of information about public beliefs by transforming public opinion from a property of groups to an attribute of individuals. Finally, polling partially removes individuals' control over the subject matter of their own public expressions of opinion by transforming public opinion from a spontaneous assertion to a constrained response" (1989:274). The critique of polling (and of the limited definition of democracy) focuses on the ways in which polls mold opinion and help structure passivity. Recent book titles are harsh: *The Captive Public* (Ginsberg 1986), *Inventing Reality* (Parenti 1986), *Manipulating Public Opinion* (Margolis and Mauser 1989), and *Manufacturing Consent* (Chomsky and Herman 1988). Public opinion is no longer assumed to be an independent force, and a different set of questions have emerged: To what degree can government leaders force the public to accept their preferences? By what mechanisms is this "manipulation" (or "massaging") of the public carried out? Can the press and media play any role other than servant, cognizant or not, to policymakers? Is the contemporary politician interested in the public's view in any capacity other than how it may affect their chances for reelection? Can the public perform even the modest role of setting policy parameters within which decisionmakers are free to act?

The interpretation of public opinion on national security issues developed below recognizes polling as a form of social control but respects the ways in which public opinion can also constrain decisionmakers. On one level, government officials can follow their own policy preferences, with public opinion either approving or disapproving but essentially ignored. On another, governments can be forced to acknowledge the public even as the general will is inadequately communicated through the medium of opinion polling. Control is not complete. Some elements of public attitudes oppose government policy. Other elements either genuinely match official government positions or merely appear to because of manipulation and the influence of media framing. The influence paths are two-way. Government management of opinion and public constraints upon decisionmakers exist simultaneously and the balance between the two is in constant flux.[3]

3. The conventional typology describing the relationship among public opinion, the po-

The tendency of the public to side with government officials on foreign policy has several layers. Conscious deception exists, but it is less important than the overall acceptance of the premises that support the role of military power in the old world order. The world view of the policy-making elite is accepted as "natural." The public recognizes the authority of political leaders because they seem to possess more information, because their offices make them appear persuasive, or simply because they are viewed as legitimate authorities on complex issues. The authority and legitimacy generally accorded the president on foreign affairs and defense issues is particularly powerful. The support a president can expect from the public following a national speech or almost any other dramatic action is illustrative. No visible conflict or deception occurs or is necessary. Domination and control are embedded in the "normal" operations of society. The press and media also comply with the political elite because they are ideologically loyal, because their professional canons make it impossible for them to contest what the government presents, or because any capable administration is able to control the stories that the press and media, in their normal functioning, will select and present as tomorrow's news (Chomsky and Herman 1988; Hallin 1986; Hertsgaard 1989). Contrary views voiced by leaders of social movements or by dissident intellectuals are either ignored or marginalized. The mass media is not propagandistic in a strident way; the process is more subtle. The ideological impact of the press and media is to set the agenda and to determine which views are legitimate and which are not. Control over the news is not absolute. Diversity can be found and critical coverage of the government is present. But the range of views is not comprehensive (Bosso 1989; Qualter 1989). The quality of democracy is limited by elite control of "factual" information, but is further limited by the context in which that information is presented and received. Public officials are also able to manipulate opinion in a more direct manner. Here the elite, sometimes acting through a compliant press and media, self-consciously produce "public opinion" that is consistent with their own interests. Officials lie outright or use other deceptions, such as staged political and military crises, to dupe

---

litical elite, and policy is as follows: (1) The public and the elite differ and the public is the source of policy; (2) the public and the elite differ but the elite can follow its own policy preferences; and (3) a congruence exists between the public and the elite which policy reflects. This third school is sometimes subdivided into a "legitimate" branch whereby the public genuinely approves of government policies, and a "counterfeit" branch that focuses on the control of information and other methods of securing a compliant public.

the public. Bias in favor of government policies is reinforced by both the existing political culture and deliberate acts of disinformation (Parenti 1989).

On the other hand, the control exercised through political culture, political elites, and the mass media is not absolute. Public opinion is not fully molded by ideology and conscious deception. Public attitudes, while continually influenced by the prevailing political culture and government and press distortion, can nonetheless be an effective constraint. The influence of public opinion varies. Policy responds to public preferences on some issues, while public attitudes have little impact on others. At times, government officials can control the public effectively. But periods also exist in which public opinion, usually in combination with organized social movements, has an independent impact on government. Decisionmakers recognize that they must somehow accommodate themselves to this pressure. When attitudes coalesce into clear-cut opposition, the political leadership views the public as "a problem" to which they must respond. The press and media focus on the fact that the public and current policy are out of step (which also implies that a simplistic view of the press as a literal servant to their government masters must be modified). Prevailing attitudes have become a constraint on government autonomy. All three actors—the public, the press and media, and the political leadership—recognize that programs representing existing policy cannot continue. Decisionmakers may not be forced to adopt what the public prefers, but they most certainly are pressured to alter their policy in a way that alleviates public pressure.

There are many examples. The Vietnam War illustrates the mutual determinacy of government policy and public attitudes. While public opinion did not force the United States out of Vietnam, it did help establish limits on the number of troops in Vietnam and the extent of bombing of the North. The Johnson and Nixon administrations were unable to take the military measures that offered real hope of effectively countering the revolutionary forces arrayed against the Saigon government (Joseph 1987; Small 1988). Another example is the mobilization of public attitudes in favor of a nuclear freeze and against the nuclear buildup of the first Reagan administration. Ronald Reagan was able to circumvent this pressure to some degree, electorally through an economic recovery that pushed nuclear issues lower in the voters' list of priorities, and politically by deflecting part of the opposition through the promise of an effective defensive shield. Yet public attitudes were a key factor in Washington's shift from efforts to achieve strategic superiority and toward resumption of nuclear arms control. Finally, public hostility toward the use of U.S. ground troops in Central America throughout the 1980s ruled out their possible use in an invasion of Nicaragua to overthrow the Sandinista government. Public opinion (as well as active lobbying by the anti-intervention movement) led to a congressional vote against further U.S. aid to the contras, the military force seeking the overthrow of the Sandinistas. Yet public reaction was not sufficiently strong to force the Reagan administration to end all forms of military and economic pressures against Nicaragua, or to end its support of the oligarchy in El Salvador. Washington could appeal to anticommunist currents that remained strong among the public. But public opposition to the direct use of U.S. ground troops remained strong as well. The possibility that an invasion would transform the public mood was sufficiently strong to block the preferred option of direct military force.

The following letter, written by Rep. Newt Gingrich (R–Ga.) to then national security adviser John Poindexter, captures this dual character of public opinion perfectly. Gingrich favored continued military pressure against Central America but worried that the public would block this policy (two-thirds of the public disagreed with the Reagan administration's program of military aid). Gingrich tells Poindexter (who was later indicted for deceiving Congress about efforts to circumvent the ban that was placed on military aid):

> Our goal with the public at large must be for the absence of disapproval, rather than for approval. . . . The American people are by nature not inclined to seek out conflict, and not inclined to meddle in other people's affairs. If we ask for their positive approval, we will never get it. We must simply ask for the benefit of the doubt. We must keep the risks small enough so that people will tolerate it. . . . There is a fundamental difference between gaining public approval for our efforts, which is very difficult, and avoiding public disapproval, which is much easier. (1986, in *In These Times*, October 18–24, 1989)

Public attitudes on national security issues are contradictory. Many Americans endorse a policy of basic deterrence, significant reductions in the defense budget, and a new, more cooperative relationship with the world of nations based on law, respect for human rights, and the strengthening of democracy. At the same time, most of the public continues to respect the need for military strength, remains moderate in its ideological self-image, is hostile to foreign aid, and can be swayed by the president in a crisis.

U.S. Attitudes Toward Nuclear Weapons Before the End of the Cold War

Compared with the recent explosion of polls, we know relatively little about public attitudes before the 1980s. The incidence of public opinion surveys seems to follow world events. Polling peaks correspond to the use of nuclear weapons against Japan (1945), the first Soviet atomic explosion (1949), the hydrogen bomb tests (1953), and heightened tensions over Cuba during the early 1960s (Kramer, Kalick, and Milburn 1983). One early pattern discerned was general approval of the use of atomic weapons on the cities of Hiroshima and Nagasaki at the end of World War II. In 1945, two-thirds of the population supported this action, probably in the belief that the bombs were necessary to end the war quickly and to save American lives. Support for the use of atomic weapons against Japan has remained constant with 64 percent approving in 1971, 63 percent approving in 1982, and 65 percent approving in 1988 (Kramer, Kalick, and Milburn 1983:12; *Americans Talk Security* [hereafter cited as *ATS*], vol. 12).

In the early 1960s, public opinion—fueled by fears of leukemia, bone cancer, and long-term genetic damage, and by evidence of strontium-90 found in wheat and milk—played a major role, together with the antinuclear movement, in securing the Partial Nuclear Test Ban Treaty that was ratified by the Senate in September 1963 (Devine 1978; Wittner 1984). Between 1963 and 1980, there was relatively little public discussion and exploration of what Americans thought about nuclear weapons (Boyer 1984). A 1969 Gallup poll asking subjects to list the "two or three most important problems facing the nation" found 63 percent listing Vietnam and only 2 percent mentioning the danger of nuclear war. Before the 1980s, the public was consistently appreciative of the dangers of nuclear war and supported arms control measures between the United States and the Soviet Union. At the same time, most of the public accepted the basic premises of the Cold War, supported a posture of strong military force, regarded Moscow with suspicion, and saw no realistic alternative to the reliance on nuclear weapons to deter Soviet aggression (Davis and Kline 1988; Russett 1989; Shapiro and Page 1988). Over the next decade, that set of attitudes began to change.[4]

4. Many students of public opinion argue that public attitudes display overall continuity (Graham 1989). Everett Carll Ladd, for example, maintains that "American opinion on nuclear

In the early 1980s, Americans were forced to think more about nuclear weapons and the policies that guided their potential use. In many respects, their views changed significantly. The first shift concerned public fear about the possible outbreak of nuclear war. Those reporting that they worried about the prospect of a nuclear war increased from 14 percent in 1958 to 22 percent in 1961, and to 28 percent in 1982 (Kramer, Kalick, and Milburn 1983:21). By 1984, 38 percent, including 50 percent of those under thirty, believed that a nuclear war was likely to occur within the next ten years (Yankelovich and Doble 1984). Toward the end of the decade, the fear of nuclear war declined. Between October 1987 and March 1988 the number expecting a war within the next 25 years fell from 44 to 33 percent (Yankelovich and Smoke 1988:10; *ATS*, vols. 1 and 4), and by 1988 a direct Soviet attack on the United States was now considered a likely possibility by only 15 percent of the population. Terrorist attacks and regional wars that could draw in the superpowers were considered more pressing dangers (*ATS*, vol. 4). At the same time, the public became more realistic about their chances of surviving a nuclear war. In 1961, 49 percent thought their changes of surviving were 50–50 or better, but only 37 percent were so optimistic in 1982, and only 21 percent in 1984. Yankelovich and Doble (1984) summarize the renewed appreciation of the dangers of nuclear war as follows: (*a*) by 96 percent to 3 percent, Americans asserted that "picking a fight with the Soviet Union is too dangerous in a nuclear world"; (*b*) by 89 percent to 9 percent, Americans subscribe to the view "that there can be no winner in an all-out nuclear war; both the United States and the Soviet Union would be completely destroyed"; and (*c*) by 83 percent

---

weapons and war has changed scarcely at all over nearly four decades" (1982:20). In the conservative version of this view, widespread support for a nuclear freeze in the 1980s had to be balanced against widespread public support for almost any arms control proposal that the public perceived as fair. (By 1982, a congressional resolution calling for a bilateral moratorium on the testing, production, and deployment of nuclear weapons became the focal point for public debate on nuclear weapons policy.) Ladd points out that almost as large a proportion of the public supported Reagan's original START proposal as supported the freeze. Supporters of the nuclear status quo pointed to the public's skepticism of Moscow's desire to abide by any arms control treaty. In 1983, eighty percent maintained that "the Soviet Union would try to cheat on any nuclear freeze agreement and get an advantage over the U.S." (ABC News/*Washington Post*, in *Public Opinion* 1988) In the orthodox view, the tension formed by support for a freeze on the one hand and suspicion of Moscow on the other conferred responsibility upon the executive branch to harmonize the imperative for arms control with the deep fear of communism. Support for existing policy was the result. Public opinion did not send an unambiguous message to end the arms race with the Soviet Union.

TABLE 3-1
Changing Views about the Arsenals of the United States and the USSR

United States and Soviet Nuclear Arsenals Compared	*1955* %	*1961* %	*1982* %	*1984* %	*1986* %	*Oct 1987* %
USSR superior	9	21	41	27	23	24
The two sides are about equal*	0	11	41	57	54	60
U.S. superior *	78	56	7	10	14	11
Not sure	13	12	10	6	6	6

Sources: 1955—Gallup; 1961—*Minneapolis Tribune*; 1982—*Los Angeles Times*; 1984—Public Agenda Foundation; 1986—Gallup; 1987—*Americans Talk Security*.

Note: Percentages may not total 100 because of rounding.

*Gallup uses approximately comparable wording.

to 14 percent, Americans say that while in past wars we knew that no matter what happened some life would continue, "we cannot be certain that life on earth will continue after a nuclear war." This sober view was an important change from the comparative optimism of previous years regarding the outcome of nuclear war.

Public attitudes also changed on the issue of which side had the advantage in the arms race. At the outset of the postwar period, Americans found the United States to have the advantage. Only 9 percent in a 1955 poll placed the Soviets ahead (see Table 3-1). In 1961, 21 percent found Moscow ahead. The late 1970s witnessed a dramatic change in public perceptions. By 1982, 41 percent thought that Moscow had a stronger nuclear arsenal and only 7 percent found the United States stronger (Kramer, Kalick, and Milburn 1983:7).[5] The most significant development over the rest of the 1980s was not the slight shift back toward an appreciation of the relative strength of the United States compared with the Soviet Union, but the increased awareness among the public that the very concept of nuclear superiority had lost its meaning. On one level, this development was reflected in the increasing proportion of the public finding both sides

5. In part, this shift accurately reflects a change in the actual numbers of weapons held by both sides and the creation of mutual assured destruction by the late 1960s. At the same time, the public perception of a Soviet advantage in the early 1980s was not supported by the assessments of most experts. In this case, public views reflected more the propaganda successes of the Committee on the Present Danger (Sanders 1982) and the Reagan administration than a rational calculation of the strategic balance.

roughly equal (60 percent in 1987). On another, polls found overwhelming support (84 percent) for the thesis that the United States no longer held nuclear superiority and that we could never hope to regain it. If we did have a larger arsenal, the Soviets would simply keep building until they matched us (Public Agenda 1984).

Americans also became more critical of U.S. nuclear policy in important areas and more willing to entertain alternatives to it. For example, under the doctrine of extended deterrence, Washington was supposed to counter a Warsaw Pact land invasion with nuclear weapons. In 1949, 50 percent of respondents felt that the use of the bomb in this situation was justified. By 1955, support had declined to 44 percent. By 1982, opinion shifted still further with only 28 percent favoring first use of nuclear weapons against a Soviet invasion (Kramer, Kalick, and Milburn 1983:14). The 1984 Public Agenda poll found 77 percent saying that it should be U.S. policy *not* to use nuclear weapons to respond to a conventional Soviet attack.[6] Almost as many (74 percent) said that the United States should never use small nuclear weapons in a battlefield situation. Remarkably, a full third said it should be American policy *never* to use nuclear weapons under *any* circumstances. Finally, in 1988, only 8 percent agreed that it would be appropriate for the United States to initiate the use of nuclear weapons if the Soviets invaded Western Europe and were winning without using nuclear weapons (*ATS*, vol. 6:134). Of nine scenarios examining the public's willingness to use nuclear weapons, only one, a full-scale attack against the United States, elicited strong public support for their use (see Table 3-2). One other possibility, an attack on U.S. troops with nuclear weapons, received a bare plurality. All of the other scenarios were rejected, most strongly the situation for which the nuclear arsenal was actually designed, namely to respond to a Soviet invasion of Western Europe. Even after being informed that a conventional defense of Europe was the more expensive option, the public still believed that nuclear weapons should not be used in the role dictated by the policy of extended deterrence (*ATS*, vol. 12). A majority now supported a declaration of no first use of nuclear

---

6. Several historical reviews indicate that the public never supported a policy of first use, even during the period of atomic monopoly over the Soviet Union (Graham 1989; Shapiro and Page 1988). In this particular instance the "stability" thesis concerning attitudinal change is correct. The "change" has been the deepening of opposition to official policy over the nuclear era.

TABLE 3-2
Willingness to Use Nuclear Weapons: 1988

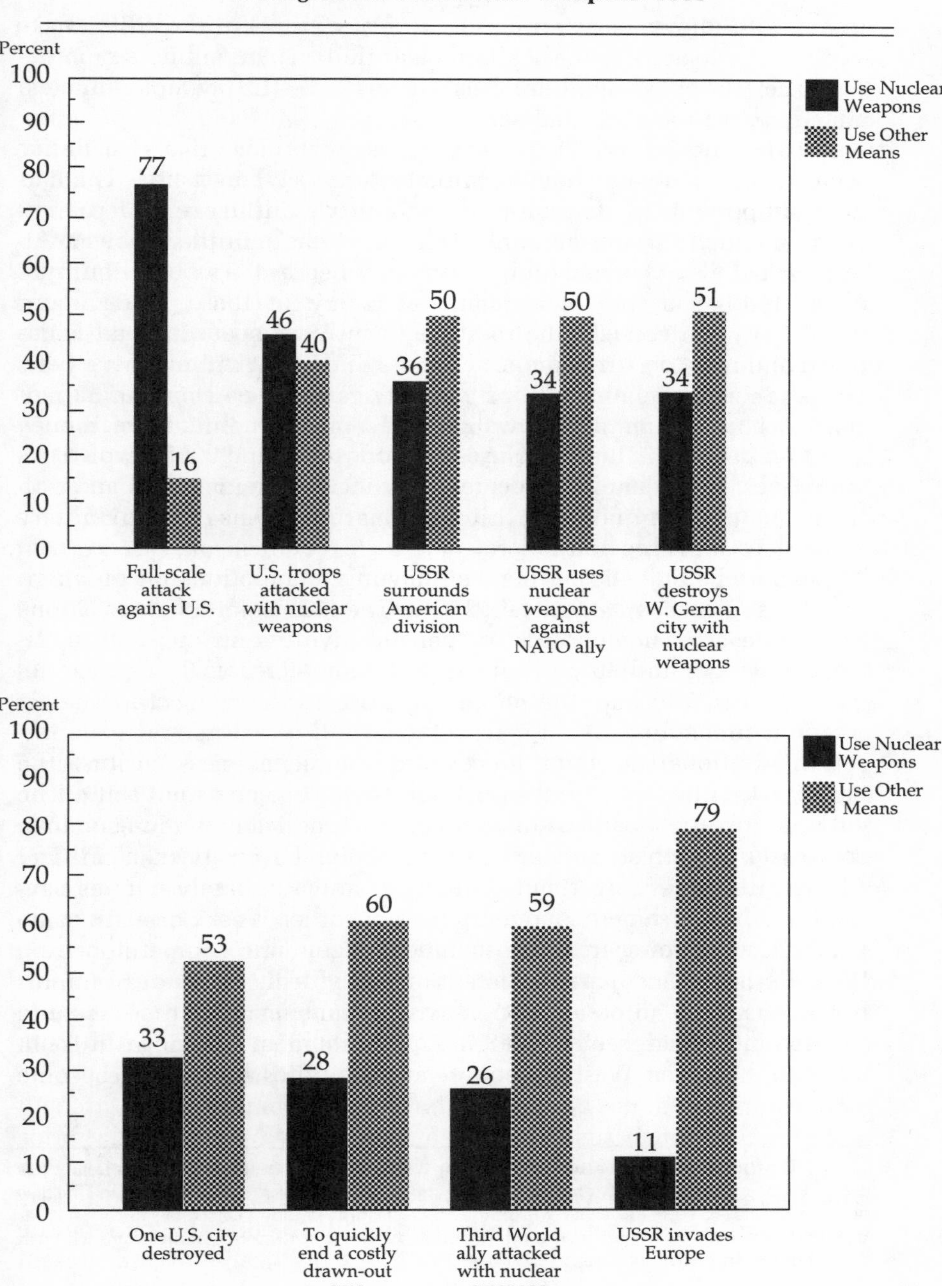

Source: ATS, vol. 9.

Note: "Don't Know" and "Refused to Answer" responses are excluded.

weapons.[7] Policymakers could not, for fear of invoking hostility, make explicit the logic of actual U.S. nuclear policy. The public supported only the use of weapons for basic deterrence—to prevent a nuclear attack against the U.S. homeland.

By the end of the 1980s, Americans were more likely to define security in economic than in military terms. When asked which is more important in determining a country's influence, 62 percent chose economic power and only 22 percent chose military power. Attitudes had also changed on the issue of whether the military buildup of the 1980s had been good for the economy. In 1983, polls showed that 53 percent thought the increase in military spending had had a positive impact on the economy. Forty-one percent did not. Five years later the respective proportions were reversed (39 percent and 53 percent). About 60 percent now believed that "the amount of money spent on defense is hurting our economic well-being" (*ATS*, vol. 3). A 1989 Gallup poll found 35 percent "strongly favoring," and an additional 39 percent "favoring," limitations on defense spending as a method of reducing the federal deficit. In contrast, only 11 percent "strongly favored" and 31 percent "favored" limitations on programs that assist blacks and other minorities. The Harris poll of August 1989 (see Table 3-3) showed only 10 percent favoring an increase in defense spending and 40 percent supporting a decrease. By a margin of more than two to one, the public supported cuts in specific nuclear weapons programs.

An additional aspect of the concern with economic security was a perceived increase in the threat posed by Europe and the Pacific Rim nations. By an almost two-to-one margin, Americans found economic competitors posing a greater threat to national security than military adversaries (Greenberg 1988). Americans now saw themselves as having roughly the same economic power as either West Germany or Japan. Those agreeing with the statement "economic competition from West Germany and Japan represent more of a threat to our nation's future than the threat of communist expansion ever did" roughly equaled those disagreeing (*ATS*, 6:73). While most Americans did not think that this competition would turn our allies into enemies, there

7. Roughly 80 percent of the public erroneously think that the United States already has a no first use policy (Russett and Starr 1985; chap. 10). Measured support for a no first use declaration varies with the exact wording of the question (although it consistently receives majority support). For historical examples of this variation see Kramer, Kalick, and Milburn 1983. For current examples see *ATS* 9:77–80.

TABLE 3-3
Defense Spending

"IN GENERAL, DO YOU FAVOR INCREASING OR DECREASING THE PRESENT DEFENSE BUDGET, OR KEEPING IT THE SAME AS IT IS NOW?"

	Increasing (%)	Decreasing (%)	Keep It as Now (%)	Not Sure (%)
August 1989	10	40	46	4
July 1988	14	31	53	2
July 1987	22	28	49	1
October 1986	23	25	49	3
October 1985	26	21	51	2
June 1983	22	33	42	3
October 1982	17	24	54	5
August 1981	58	16	22	4
February 1980	71	6	21	2
October 1979	58	9	30	3
November 1978	50	9	38	3
December 1976	25	27	38	10
March 1971	10	44	36	10

"DO YOU FAVOR CONGRESS MAINTAINING THE SAME SPENDING LEVELS ON [INSERT ITEM] OR DO YOU THINK THE AMOUNT SPENT ON [INSERT ITEM] SHOULD BE CUT?"

	Maintain Same Spending Levels (%)	Cut Spending Levels (%)	Not Sure (%)
The MX Missile	26	65	9
The Stealth B-2 Bomber	27	65	8
The Midgetman Missile	25	61	14
Strategic Defense Initiative or SDI (Star Wars)	33	61	6

Source: Harris Poll, October 1989.

was considerable disgruntlement on this score. A Baltimore respondent cited in the 1988 Public Agenda study exemplified this attitude: "We're going down the same path that the Roman Empire went down. We're playing 'Big Brother' all over the world but we're 'Big Brothering' ourselves right down the drain. I'm talking about the Japanese *owning* New York City. I'm talking about Germany who puts up absolutely nothing for its defense" (p. 68). Three-quarters of the population felt that the United States should make its allies pay more of the cost of their defense, even if that meant losing influence over them on economic issues.[8]

Finally, a large proportion of Americans wanted to see greater U.S.–Soviet cooperation on a range of issues including combating environmental pollution, controlling illicit drug trade and terrorism, expanding cultural exchanges, resolving conflicts in the Middle East and other trouble spots, and eliminating most nuclear weapons by the year 2000 (*ATS*, vol. 7). The most important documentation of this shift in American attitudes toward nuclear weapons and the U.S.–Soviet relationship was conducted by the Center for Foreign Policy Development at Brown University and the Public Agenda Foundation.[9] Participants in the study were asked to consider the following possible four Futures for U.S.–Soviet relations for the year 2010:

Future 1: U.S. Gains the Upper Hand

By 2010 the U.S. will achieve superiority over the USSR in political, military and other ways. Realizing that the Soviets, no matter what they pretend, aim to dominate the world. Americans will have risen to the challenge. By 2010 the U.S. will have deployed a panoply of advanced offensive and defensive weapons, potentially including defenses against missiles. The USSR will be perceived worldwide as technologically inferior, economically backward, and simply not on the same plane of power.

Future 2: Eliminate the Nuclear Threat; Compete Otherwise

By 2010 the U.S. and USSR, realizing that a nuclear war "cannot be won and must never be fought," have taken far-reaching steps to remove that danger. They will have drastically cut their nuclear arsenals, to the point that a world-destroying holocaust is impossible, and will have reached agreements preventing any dangerous escalation of a crisis. But they will

8. Then, as now, public attitudes held the potential for supporting a form of economic nationalism that could provide a substitute for the Cold War enemy.

9. The poll is particularly sophisticated in two important ways: First, unlike most surveys, opinions on particular issues were solicited in a context—that of the feasibility and risks of different possible economic and military futures in the year 2010; and second, opinions were solicited both before and after an opportunity to clarify issues and to discuss the strengths and weaknesses of the different futures in a "focus group." Each future combines long-term goals and short-term policies needed to reach them, and participants were asked to assess risks and costs as well as advantages of each. Discussions lasted three hours. The other major source of information on public attitudes is the multivolume compilation of polls published under the title *Americans Talk Security*.

consider it unrealistic to try to end the overall political conflict, and they still compete for influence in the Third World.

Future 3: Cooperative Problem Solving

By 2010 the U.S. and Soviet Union will have fundamentally changed their relationship, somewhat as the U.S. and China did in the 1970s. This will have been achieved by working together on problems that faced both sides and did not have their origin in either side. Examples include terrorism, nuclear proliferation, AIDS, and environmental problems. Success in greatly reducing mutual mistrust has enabled the two sides to work successfully on removing the nuclear threat.

Future 4: Defend Only North America

By 2010 Americans will have realized that the U.S. does not need to be deeply involved in political and military affairs all around the world. U.S. alliances (except in Canada and Mexico) will have been phased out, and U.S. forces brought home. The U.S. maintains a strong defense of North America, potentially including defenses against missiles. Otherwise America is concentrating on resolving problems at home. Relations with the USSR are simply not a priority.

Future 3, favoring cooperative problem solving, received the greatest support and was ranked first by 46 percent. Future 2 received 28 percent support, and Future 1, 24 percent. Only 21 percent either strongly or somewhat opposed Future 3, while 38 percent opposed Future 2 and 41 percent opposed Future 1. The quasi-isolationist position, Future 4, received only minimal support. Those participating in the discussions agreed that the Soviet military threat had become less critical than terrorism, economic competition from other countries, nuclear proliferation, and long-term environmental hazards. A majority also opposed aiding anticommunist efforts in the Third World if that meant "sometimes supporting dictators and others who do not believe in democracy."[10]

10. The Futures study also found the public leery of the Soviet Union in several respects. While Future Two, which provides for arms control but continued competition in other areas, received less support, many sided with particular arguments in favor of that position, such as the expectation of Soviet military expansion and Soviet support for groups opposed to the United States in the Third World, and the possibility of the need for a significant conventional build up to compensate for deep nuclear reductions. These concerns are now moot.

TABLE 3-4
Support for Four Futures: 1988

	Post-Test Rank Order		
	First Choice (%)	*Second Choice (%)*	*First or Second Choice (%)*
Future 1: The U.S. gains the upper hand	24	15	39
Future 2: Eliminate the nuclear threat; compete otherwise	28	46	74
Future 3: Cooperative problem solving	46	30	76
Future 4: Defend North America only	4	8	12

	Strongly Favor	*Somewhat Favor*	*Strongly Oppose*	*Somewhat Oppose*
	%	%	%	%
Future 1	26	23	17	24
Future 2	21	34	21	13
Future 3	39	31	13	8
Future 4	14	15	23	42

Source: *Public Agenda Foundation* 1988.

At the very end of the decade, U.S. opinion on security issues seemed to be supportive of changed government priorities and a renewed commitment to social spending. Eastern Europe was undergoing political and economic transformation and the Soviet Union had initiated the process of perestroika. These changes in the world security environment made more possible a thorough reexamination of the direction of U.S. domestic policy. According to a major poll conducted for the World Policy Institute, the public, by a majority of 81 percent to 17 percent, favored "new and sweeping programs involving increased domestic spending, a smaller restructured military, and more taxes on high-income individuals" (Greenberg and Lake 1989). The same poll found a clear majority, 52 to 43 percent, supporting a more active role for government in solving problems. Almost 80 percent favored the creation of a "national economic plan that helps direct private sector investment to strengthen America's economic posi-

TABLE 3-5
Defense vs. Social Programs: 1989

"If you had to choose, would you prefer to see sharp cuts in (read each item) or in defense spending?"

	Cut Other (%)	*Cut Defense (%)*	*Cut Neither or Both (%)*	*Not Sure (%)*
Social Security				
1989	6	89	3	2
1985	x	x	x	x
1984	14	76	5	5
Medical benefits				
1989	7	87	3	3
1985	18	73	7	2
Veteran's health benefits				
1989	7	86	4	3
1985	19	71	6	4
Medicaid benefits				
1989	10	84	3	3
1985	18	74	6	2
Federal aid to education				
1989	11	83	3	3
1985	23	69	4	4
Federal aid to the homeless				
1989 (new)	12	81	3	4
Federal health and nutrition programs				
1989	13	81	3	3
1985	25	67	5	3

Source: Harris Poll, October 1989.

Note: x = not asked.

tion in the world."[11] In a similar vein, three of every four voters wanted the United States to take the lead in combating global warming

11. The Greenberg-Lake survey (1989) established several important themes. Almost two out of three voters said that "our federal budget priorities are wrong: that we are spending too much on the military and shortchanging our economic, social, and environmental needs." More than 90 percent of the sample wanted substantial increases in education funding to create a more literate and productive work force. Environmental problems, including the cleanup of nuclear and toxic waste dumps, global warming and the greenhouse effect were considered more serious security threats than Soviet aggression or Third World dictators. Many of the same themes, especially public support for a large peace dividend that could be applied to social problems, can be found in the publication *Americans Talk Security* (vol. 13).

(Union of Concerned Scientists 1989). An October 1989 Harris poll documented the public's support of a range of social problems over defense spending (see Table 3-5).[12] These changes in public opinion over the postwar period were all the more remarkable for they occurred despite the failure of an established political authority to articulate and legitimate the principal themes. Yet a majority of the public was especially open to the possibilities of significant policy departures. These views did not reflect unthinking public volatility. They were the consequence of a decade of important debate within the United States and a result of the beginnings of a new international situation.

In August 1990, however, Iraq invaded Kuwait. The United States responded with military deployment, and the possibilities of progressive change that were represented by public attitudes were quickly submerged beneath the awe of military might and media hyperbole. Despite initial opposition to the early use of military force, the public was swayed by the urgency of supporting their troops and their president. That process presents a strong challenge to the argument that there is incipient support for new peace policies predicated upon common security and the creation of a new world order. But before examining the impact of the Gulf War, we need to take a closer look at public attitudes as they existed at the end of the 1980s, particularly my thesis that embryonic support for political realignment existed in the population.

Counterarguments

I will consider two kinds of counterarguments to my contention that incipient support now exists for progressive politics and the creation of a new world order. The first considers empirical findings that point in a different direction. Public opinion is more ambiguous than has been shown thus far. Second, in many ways the overall character of U.S. political life weighs against the chances of an issue-oriented, oppositional program. The next section addresses the contradictions in public opinion. The broader problem of political culture and its relationship to progressive politics is introduced in this chapter and addressed more completely in the final chapter, which assesses the prospects for political change.

12. At the same time, President George Bush, who opposed significant changes in social and government priorities, continued to enjoy 70 percent approval ratings (*ATS* 13:10).

In the late 1980s, a moderate interpretation of public attitudes toward nuclear weapons could be expressed in the following paradox: "The public wants an immediate, verifiable freeze on testing, production, and deployment of nuclear weapons; wants the complete elimination of all nuclear arms in the world; thinks nuclear arms reductions too important to be held up by any objections over other things the Soviets are doing; and thinks the weapons create more problems than they solve, and do not, in fact, even prevent us from going to war." On the other hand, the majority of the public "also thinks it was necessary to drop the atom bomb on Japan; also believes U.S. leaders' declaration that the purpose of the weapons is to deter war; agrees that they have been the major component in preventing a major war; and believes that they will likely do the same for the immediate future" (Stucky n.d.).[13]

By the end of the Cold War, the first half of the paradox was already stronger than the second and was in the process of becoming stronger still. Yet it must be acknowledged that public attitudes on security issues were not fully aligned with a progressive foreign policy agenda. At the end of the 1980s, public attitudes were rapidly changing. Yet U.S. citizens continued to want a strong military. They did not want to spend as much on it, and certainly did not want to continue the arms race. But there was renewed confidence in the military as an institution (61 percent expressed such confidence in 1987, up from 50 percent in 1981—and higher than the level of confidence expressed in any other institution in U.S. society save the church) (Gallup 1987). By a two-to-one margin, the public thought that the Reagan military build up was necessary and that more accommodating Soviet behavior was a response to the increased strength of the United States (*ATS*, vol. 6).[14] Most Americans wanted to move toward a cooperative relationship with the Soviet Union, but at a cautious pace.[15]

Many Americans continued to harbor deep distrust of Soviet intentions. Two-thirds of the public endorsed the view that the "Soviet

---

13. Rielly (1992) also presents poll results in a manner that supports this paradox.

14. Equally important, a vast majority of the public felt that there was no need for a further buildup (*ATS*, vol. 3). Much of the public (unlike the press and the government) also thought that the peace movement in Europe and the United States was a major reason for the INF Treaty (*ATS*, vol. 2).

15. Despite these caveats, it is significant that by the wide margin of 59 percent to 16 percent the public would have preferred to support efforts to help the Soviet Union carry out democratic restructuring and economic reform rather than to try and undermine that society.

Union used detente as an opportunity to build up their armed forces while lulling us into a false sense of security" (Public Agenda 1984). The Four Futures study cited above found the public roughly divided in their reaction to the statement that "The Soviet Union is like Hitler's Germany—an evil empire trying to rule the world," although attitudes on this particular issue were changing. In 1984, the public agreed with the statement by a 56 percent to 36 percent margin (Public Agenda 1984). An October 1987 study found this claim rejected by 58 percent to 38 percent (*ATS*, vol. 1). A similar pattern could be detected in attitudes toward Soviet aims. The relatively harsh judgment that existed during the end of the 1970s and the first years of the Reagan administration changed by the end of the decade. In the early 1980s, approximately one-third of the public agreed with the statement, "Russia seeks global domination and will risk a major war to achieve that domination if it can't be achieved by other means." By 1988, the view that the Soviet Union would risk a major war to achieve global domination fell to last among the four options considered (Roper 1988). Most of the drop occurred between 1981 and 1986, before Gorbachev's policies could exercise their ameliorating influence.

Verification of arms control treaties was another issue where Americans continued to be cautious, although here too opinion moderated. In 1982, only 17 percent of the public thought the Soviet Union could be trusted to keep its part in nuclear arms control agreements, while 66 percent thought they could not be trusted. Expectations of trustworthiness rose only slightly, to 24 percent in November 1985 and again to 35 percent in January 1988 (*Public Opinion* 1988). Later polls found the public divided more or less evenly. The verification issue went deeper than could be captured by polling data. According to Yankelovich and Smoke (1988), the public desired "a low-risk, working relationship that improves only if and when the good faith of the other side is clearly demonstrated." Verification seemed to be a code for the development of mutual perceptions that each side fully respects the other's security. Here, the provisions in the INF Treaty that provided for on-site inspection were especially important.

In fact, the process in which Americans increasingly felt that the people of the former Soviet Union were becoming more like ourselves was already well developed. Soviets became popular in all of the principal expressions of popular culture (even as the Soviet identity was dissolving in the Soviet Union itself). U.S. and Soviet cops teamed up in the movies to smash a dope ring. U.S. and Soviet athletes were on the same side in tag-team wrestling. A perestroika boutique opened up in Bloomingdale's, and a Soviet actress appeared in *Playboy*. Rock critics celebrated Soviet heavy metal groups as being more faithful to the spirit of rebellion than U.S. bands. Travel increased. So did the perception that the Soviets wanted the same things we do: clothes, good schools for their kids, a sense of freedom, a place to go for vacation. We began to identify with them, and no one wants to go to war with people who are like oneself.

Another source of public ambivalence was the Strategic Defense Initiative.[16] After the program was announced in March 1983, a majority supported SDI (*ATS*, vol. 16; Bard 1987). The Four Futures study, for example, found 56 percent to 39 percent support for the statement, "We should build SDI even if that means giving up the chance to negotiate deep cuts in nuclear arms" (Public Agenda 1988). This support for SDI weighed against a possible shift toward programs predicated on common security. More recently, opposition to SDI has deepened among the public.[17] Yet there continues to linger the hope that the United States can acquire security through technological means.

An additional factor to consider in weighing the impact of opinion on policymakers is the seeming lack of knowledge, and the presence of misinformation among the public. In one telling example, 81 percent (mistakenly) agreed with the statement that it "is current policy to use nuclear weapons against the Soviets if and only if they attack the United States first with nuclear weapons" (Public Agenda 1984). In fact, U.S. policy is based on the possible first use of nuclear

16. SDI represented different things to different people. To the Soviets it was a new step in the arms race, the costs of which might produce still more problems for their economy. To many in the peace movement, SDI was another attempt to achieve strategic superiority. To the nation's scientists and engineers, SDI established research and development priorities. To the President and the Republican Party, SDI became a rather successful effort to undercut the strength of the movement for a nuclear freeze and to regain the moral high ground through its accompanying rhetoric of peace and security. For many Americans imbued with a traditional faith in scientific and technical solutions, SDI carried the promise of providing effective defense for the population against the threat of nuclear annihilation.

17. Support for SDI has always been shallow when detailed follow-up questions are asked. For example, only a minority favored the program when economic costs were mentioned. A *Los Angeles Times* poll found 59 percent agreeing that $26 billion for five years was too much to spend on SDI given the nation's budget situation (November 1985). Support also dropped when SDI was presented as a program for missile and not population defense. Finally, support also fell when SDI was presented in the context of a possible cooperative working relationship with the Soviet Union. The Four Futures study found 59 percent agreeing with and 36 percent opposed to the statement, "We should work with the Soviets, even if it means not building or sharing SDI" (Public Agenda foundation 1988).

weapons to protect both the homeland and our allies. Apparent contradiction is another pattern. For example, 71 percent of the public either strongly approved or somewhat approved of the statement, "We should build up our conventional forces such as tanks, ships, planes, and soldiers to make up for cuts in our nuclear weapons." On the other hand, 70 percent either strongly or somewhat approved of the statement, "Instead of increasing our conventional forces such as tanks, ships, planes and soldiers, we should negotiate with the Soviets to reduce their conventional forces" (*ATS*, vol. 11). With some reflection, it is possible to understand how someone could respond positively to both statements. But the face value contradiction enables policymakers to argue that they cannot responsibly follow what the public wants because the public itself does not know what it wants.

These cautious elements in the public mood at the end of the 1980s can be balanced by evidence of public support for several bold proposals. Resolution of the pressing safety and environmental problems surrounding U.S. nuclear weapons production plants is one example. The cost of remedying these problems is more than $150 billion, and 61 percent of the public supported holding off rebuilding the plants to see if we could get an agreement for deep reductions in nuclear weapons. Only 33 percent said that Washington should rebuild the plants as quickly as possible in order to negotiate from a position of strength (*ATS*, vol. 12). While the public preferred bilateral measures to reduce the threat of nuclear war, one poll found a majority (61 percent) favoring the idea of declaring a *unilateral* six-month moratorium on the development of nuclear weapons (Hart Research Associates 1984). Two-thirds of the public said they would be willing to pay higher taxes for the more expensive conventional forces that might be necessary to replace nuclear weapons (Public Agenda 1984).[18] By 1984, expanding trade with the Soviets and using other cooperative gestures to make them feel more secure was supported by 55 percent of the public (Public Agenda 1984:36).

The Cold War was premised on an external enemy who posed a continual threat to the United States. By the end of the 1980s, we had lost our enemy. The potential consequences for domestic politics were enormous. But the defenders of the old world order were fortunate. They found a new enemy and were able to fight a war against it.

18. This question assumes that a trade-off between nuclear and conventional forces was necessary, but that may not have been the case.

The Gulf War and the New World Order

Public attitudes toward the Gulf War also illustrate the complexity of polls, public opinion, and policy, as well as the hazards of assuming that the public supports progressive change and the adoption of a new world order in any unequivocal sense. As argued in the previous chapter, Operation Desert Storm was conducted by the Bush administration to secure the old world order and traditional definitions of security. And the public, despite its seeming desire for changes in Washington's relations with the rest of the world, supported that war enthusiastically. This paradox can be developed in more depth.

The first issue concerns the dramatic shifts in public opinion regarding the use of military force in the Gulf. U.S. troops were deployed in August 1990. Until the end of the year, poll after poll, by at least a two-to-one margin, showed opposition to the initiation of military force and support for the extension of economic sanctions. In September 1990, only 17 percent of the public felt that the United States should go to war with Iraq, and 61 percent wanted to wait to give sanctions more time (with most willing to give sanctions a year or more to work) (*ATS*, vol. 14). Yet the public overwhelmingly supported Operation Desert Storm and gave President George Bush record-breaking approval ratings. Despite strong indications that the public would have supported more protracted diplomacy and other nonviolent measures to remove Iraq from Kuwait, a direct, swift, and seemingly successful military operation with little direct human cost to Americans was able to decisively reverse the public's disinclination to support a war. The public even recast its former rejection of the military option as a means to remove Saddam Hussein from Kuwait. In March 1991, approximately two-thirds of the public said that they had favored the military option before the war. Only 24 percent said that they had wanted to give sanctions a longer time to work (*ATS*, vol. 15).[19] The dramatic reversal of opinion at the start of the war is also documented in postwar polls, which reflect strongly held percep-

19. This reversal is also documented by Applebome (1991) and may reflect a historical pattern in which the public has been consistently less supportive of hypothetical future military commitments and more approving of past use of military force. The public approves of the way the U.S. military was used in the Cuban missile crisis, the bombing of Libya, the Korean War, the invasion of Grenada, and the peacekeeping mission in Lebanon. Dissatisfaction in the case of Vietnam is the exception (*ATS*, vol. 9).

tions that the war was a "great victory" for the United States, that the war increased U.S. influence in the world, and that sanctions would not have brought a better result (*ATS*, vol. 15). Despite these results, I believe that the public would have supported with equal favor a policy of economic sanctions and negotiation to remove Saddam Hussein from Kuwait *provided such a policy was forcefully presented by a president as being consistent with United States security and with prevailing values in the U.S. that are hostile to dictators and to the arbitrary use of force.*

Second, broad political and cultural influences may overwhelm what would otherwise be a person's judgments about a particular policy. During the Gulf War the public displayed a strong desire to support our troops in the field, respect the authority commanded by a president during a crisis, and remain loyal to the flag while the country was at war. People were impressed by the diffuse, but still powerful sense that the country was finally doing something right, and celebrated a newfound social cohesion.[20] These powerful feelings were less reflective of attitudes toward the war than of the political culture as whole. Yet they carried significant impact. Another cultural element affecting the public's policy judgment of the Gulf War was fascination with the high-tech wizardry allegedly displayed by the newer weapons (many of which promised to reduce the human cost of war). Patriotism also played a role, particularly in that the public identified President Bush and Republicans with that term. Until patriotism is attached to the themes of a progressive foreign policy, change will be limited.

Third, public enthusiasm for the Gulf War has moderated somewhat since March 1991. A vast majority of the public (80 percent) remains convinced that Washington was right in sending troops to the Persian Gulf. Only a third thinks that giving sanctions a chance to

---

20. In July 1990, 60 percent of those polled told ABC News that the United States was headed down the wrong track (Farrell 1991). By October, that figure increased to 79 percent. Within 48 hours after the air war began there was a 30-point shift (*ATS*, vol. 15). By the middle of February, that proportion had changed a remarkable 40 points with only 39 percent now feeling pessimistic about the country.

After the war came a reversal. By April 1991, 51 percent thought that we were back on the wrong track (*Washington Post*, April 12, 1991:A4). By July that figure had risen back to 60 percent (thus completing a return to the level of the previous year) (Farrell 1991). Note that these results are greatly affected by perceptions of the economy and cannot be used as an indication of how people feel about the war, except to support the hypothesis that Operation Desert Storm was popular because it enabled the public to at least temporarily forget domestic problems (Tye 1991a).

work would have produced a better outcome. Yet doubts remain. In July 1991, a majority of 62 percent believed the war was a "great victory" (a 22-point decline from March when 84 percent saw the war in that light) (*ATS*, vol. 16:19). A moderate majority (57 percent) agree that a "better result could have been obtained if we had been more vigorous in enforcing sanctions and had strengthened diplomatic initiatives" (*ATS*, vol. 17).[21] The majority also say that they are upset either "all the time" or "a lot" by the fact that Saddam Hussein remains in power, by environmental damage to the Persian Gulf, and by the suppression of the Kurdish rebellion (see Table 3-6) (*ATS*, vol. 16). After a brief period of support for greater military spending, the public has reverted to a preference for reductions.

Fourth, the values displayed by the public at the end of the Cold War were not significantly changed by Operation Desert Storm. Despite the intentions of the Bush administration, the circumstances surrounding the war have actually reinforced several new world order themes including the necessity of securing international approval prior to Washington's use of military force, an appreciation of the costs of war, and the use of ethical codes and moral judgments rather than self-interest to justify going to war. Despite support for Operation Desert Storm and the handling of the crisis by President George Bush, postwar opinion polls also illustrate public approval of these and other important elements of the new world order.

Americans want to increase the role of the United Nations in the world. In 1989, roughly two-thirds of the population held a favored view of the U.N. and believed that continued U.S. participation was important. Post–Gulf War surveys show that the United Nations rather than the United States is the preferred leader in opposing aggression. Three-quarters of the public have a favorable view of the organization, with the same proportion expressing "warm" feelings when asked where they place themselves on a thermometer scale. Even more (86 percent) feel that the United Nations "should play a much bigger peacekeeping and diplomatic role than it did before the Gulf War" (*ATS*, vol. 15). A majority of the public even feel that where necessary, U.N. resolutions should have the force of law and

---

21. The issue of economic sanctions provides an interesting example of how wording can affect public opinion results. A majority of the public supports sanctions and diplomacy when the question refers, as above, to "vigor" and "strength." Approval for a milder formulation of a policy of sanctions drops 22 points (a "better result could have been obtained if we had had more patience with sanctions and diplomatic initiatives") (*ATS* 17:16).

TABLE 3-6
U.S. Attitudes on the Aftermath of the Gulf War: 1991

"Does this upset you almost all the time, a lot, sometimes, or almost never?"

	All the Time	*A Lot*	*Sometimes*	*Almost Never*	*Don't Know*
"Saddam Hussein is still in power in Iraq."	44	35	14	6	0
"The oil released in the Persian Gulf has done more damage to the environment than the Exxon *Valdez* spill in Alaska."	31	38	22	8	1
"Saddam Hussein was able to crush the rebellion of the Kurds and other minorities when the U.S. Army is trying to protect and feed the hundreds of thousands of refugees."	22	30	34	13	1
"Kuwait is governed now, as before, by a ruling family that is opposed to genuine democracy."	15	23	38	23	1
"Things in the Middle East are pretty much unchanged, with dictators and sheikdoms still in power and the Arab-Israeli conflict still going on."	17	30	37	16	0
"It is estimated that one hundred thousand Iraqi troops and many more civilians were killed, and Iraq is threatened by epidemics, malnutrition and related diseases."	16	30	32	21	0
"Terrorist states, like Iran and Syria, may emerge even stronger from the war."	17	29	33	20	1
"The flow of oil from Kuwait has stopped, and may be reduced for many years because of damage done during the war."	12	23	39	27	1

TABLE 3-6 (*Cont.*)

"DOES THIS UPSET YOU ALMOST ALL THE TIME, A LOT, SOMETIMES, OR ALMOST NEVER?"

	All the Time	*A Lot*	*Sometimes*	*Almost Never*	*Don't Know*
"The United States uses as much Middle East oil as before the war, and may be just as vulnerable to the actions of unstable Arab states."	18	31	36	14	1
"Some people say the President has been spending so much time on the Middle East and foreign affairs that he's neglecting to address domestic problems here in America."	23	24	33	20	1

Source: ATS, vol. 16.

Note: Percentages may not total 100 because of rounding.

precedence over U.S. law and the laws of other nations (*ATS*, vol. 16). More specifically, 75 percent support a proposal for the United Nations to monitor and tax international arms sales with the money to be used for humanitarian purposes; 59 percent say U.N. resolutions should "rule over the actions and laws of individual countries, including the United States"; and 75 percent approve of the job being done by the United Nations (*ATS*, 16:2).

The public is also willing to support a broad range of coordinated global actions against security threats posed by atomic, biological and chemical weapons, global environmental problems, and dictators who represent a threat to democracy. Coordinated international action against world environmental problems ranks the highest of all tested new world order concepts (greater than 90 percent). By comparison, only one-quarter of the public thinks the United States should take the lead military role in securing international stability (*ATS*, vol. 16). By roughly a three to two margin, the public even supports the elimination of nuclear and chemical arms by balanced, verifiable agreements rather than continuing deterrence through nuclear weapons. The meaning of the new world order assigned by Republican administrations—a leading military role for the United States and the use of

TABLE 3-7
Possible Courses of Action in the "New World Order": 1991

	Agree (%)	*Disagree* (%)
U.S. gets others to act on environmental problems	93	6
Stop use of chemical and nuclear weapons with force	92	6
Expand role for United Nations	88	11
Stop invasion of one country by another with force	84	12
United Nations monitor and tax international arms sales	83	14
U.S. promote democracy in Eastern Europe and Middle East	78	19
U.S. force Europe and Asia to open markets	76	21
Rely on economy and diplomacy to handle threats	70	26
U.S. uses aid and weapons to balance power	62	33
U.S. takes leading military role/shares costs with other nations	57	38
U.S. takes leading military role	46	51

Source: Americans Talk Security, vol. 15.

Note: "Don't Know" and "Refused to Answer" excluded.

"aid, weapons, and alliances to maintain a balance of power between hostile countries in various parts of the world"—receives the *least* support of the options presented to the public (see Table 3-7) (*ATS* 15:17). Overwhelming support was given three projects consistent with the development of a new world order: "a bank that would finance environmental cleanup around the world and joint ventures with poorer countries to transfer environmentally sound technologies . . . an international organization like the Red Cross to take the lead in cleaning up environmental disasters, such as Chernobyl, the Exxon *Valdez* oil spill or the Persian Gulf oil spill and fires"; and a "bank to invest in all countries, to develop the use of more efficient energy systems in agriculture, industry, housing and transportation" (*ATS* 16:C-13).[22]

22. A poll taken just before the initiation of the Gulf War found 50 percent of the population believing that U.S. troops were sent there to protect oil supplies, and three out of four favoring a dramatic redirection of the nation's energy policy away from that pursued by the White House (Dumanoski 1991).

The public is particularly concerned about the threats posed by dictators and shows a remarkable willingness to take strong actions against them. Dictator-sponsored terrorism, possession of chemical, biological and nuclear weapons, and violations of human rights are considered "extremely serious" and "very serious" threats by more than 90 percent of the population (*ATS*, vol. 15). Significantly, Saddam Hussein embodied each of these themes. Public hostility toward him is probably grounded more in moral outrage and identification with new world order values than in acceptance of the traditional role of world policeman played by the United States during the Cold War.

Although it supports many proposals consistent with a new world order, the public does not reject a role for the U.S. military, especially when it is a last resort, when international approval has been obtained, and when the costs are shared with other nations. If a dictator violates international norms, a near consensus of the population says the United Nations and United States must put an end to that behavior, using force.[23] A majority of citizens even support unilateral military measures if the United Nations does not take action. At the same time, more than 50 percent of the public thinks that one thousand deaths would be "too many" on the other side if we are fighting a dictator and two-thirds think that ten thousand would be too many. During Operation Desert Storm, coalition forces killed, by conservative estimates, tens of thousands of Iraqi soldiers and over one hundred thousand civilians. And the public's instincts are not always democratic. A mid-February Gallup poll taken in the midst of the war found 63 percent of U.S. citizens agreeing it was "a bad thing" to protest while the country was at war (34 percent thought it was "a good thing"). Almost one-third would have supported a law banning antiwar demonstrations during wartime.

---

23. According to Alan Kay, president of the Americans Talk Security Foundation, from "80 to 90 percent of Americans support the United States and the United Nations taking clear action to stop dictators engaged in any of the following behaviors: sponsoring terrorism around the world; acquiring chemical, biological, and nuclear weapons; violating human rights including torturing and murdering many of its own citizens; sponsoring international drug trafficking; having gotten aid and support from the U.S. in the past, then turning against us and supporting our enemies; and engaging in a major arms build-up beyond what's needed for defending his own country. [A near consensus of] 77 percent favor using 'military intervention and combat if necessary' to stop such rogue behaviors" (*ATS* 17:20). In Kay's view, the public supports a more vigorous effort to create a new world order and does not shy away from the use of military force, particularly against dictators, provided the United Nations approves of such actions. Approval of the United States' acting on its own to counter these threats drops to a bare majority.

Economic concerns form a crosscurrent to support for new world order values. Americans are increasingly concerned about international economic competition, and see our principal competitors as more of a threat than any military adversary. No longer does the public see the United States as the world's dominant economic power. Burden sharing is a volatile political issue. Americans want our allies to pay their share of the costs of defense and expensive military interventions such as Operation Desert Storm. Most Americans now believe that military spending is hurting the economy.[24] There is tremendous concern about foreign investment in the United States, and the possibility that such fears will be used promote hostility toward all forms of international cooperation should not be overlooked. A "get tough" trade policy does not have strong public support. More would prefer to reduce the trade deficit by focusing on "improving the efficiency and productivity of U.S. industries" rather than "forcing other countries to adopt fairer trade practices" (*ATS*, vol. 4). But Americans are experiencing profound economic insecurity, and while a peace dividend and the development of a peace economy (see Chapter 5) may provide some answers, the connection between declining economic conditions and progressive politics is by no means automatic. The Gulf War has not had an impact on public attitudes toward military spending. Surveys taken in March 1988 and March 1991 show virtually the same proportion of the population (three-quarters) favoring economic programs to create jobs and economic growth. In March 1991, when asked which one of three areas of government spending should be cut, 56 percent said military spending and national security, 15 percent said social and domestic programs, and 22 percent said economic programs to create jobs and economic growth. This distribution is within three points of that obtained three years earlier (*ATS*, vol. 15). For the first time since World War II, the American people do not see either a nation or an ideology as the primary threat to national security. If this perception takes root, its economic impact on the military and the priorities of defense spending will be enormous.

At the same time, the public continues to rank foreign aid as a low

---

24. In 1988, 69 percent thought that the Reagan military buildup had been necessary, and a plurality thought that it had been good for the economy (*ATS*, vol. 1).

priority among a list of government programs. Yet international development assistance is a key element of the revitalization of the world's economy—especially if future development is to proceed with a stronger commitment to preservation of the environment. In 1988, only 12 percent of the population favored an increase in foreign aid —more than three times as many wanted to decrease the level of funding, even though respondents were informed that the funding level of $13 billion represented only 1 percent of federal budget (*ATS*, vol. 8).[25]

Conclusion

What, then, is the overall significance of current public opinion in the United States regarding war, security, nuclear weapons, and the possible adoption of a new world order? Contradictions and ambiguities remain, but the policy parameters supported by the public have moved away from the tenets of the Cold War. At a minimum, the public is now open to considering new approaches to national security. U.S. citizens continue to feel that they need a strong military. They do not support radical cuts in nuclear or conventional strength if they are unilateral. But the public is remarkably open to an entirely different set of policies that would secure international cooperation. One of these policies is basic deterrence (see Chapter 6). Once the logic of nuclear weapons policy is made explicit, the majority of the population does not support the more ambitious political and military roles called for by extended deterrence. It is important to note that much of this change in public opinion came during the first half of the 1980s, before the wave of reforms now sweeping the former Soviet Union and Eastern Europe. By the end of the decade, in a near consensus, the population supported an expanded agenda of cooperation with Moscow. The single most popular argument for or against any of the Four

25. Yet, by a margin of better than two to one, the public favors economic over military aid as the type that will best advance U.S. interests. The public also feels that humanitarian aid should be increased (*ATS*, vol. 16). Only 7 percent thought that military aid should be increased. During the dramatic events of the fall of 1989 and spring of 1990, less than one-half of the public thought that helping Eastern European countries "become more democratic and avoid economic collapse" was a very important goal for the nation. Aid for Eastern Europe ranked 16th out of 17 possible goals (*ATS*, vol. 13).

Futures considered by the Public Agenda/Center for Foreign Policy Development study was the need for superpower cooperation in combating common problems including AIDS, terrorism, environmental pollution, and nuclear weapons proliferation. That these significant changes in public attitudes emerged without being strongly articulated by a national leader is remarkable. Since the 1989 transformation of Eastern Europe the public has identified even more strongly with a new world order that is very different from the version pursued by recent presidents. The values favored by the public include concern for physical safety and economic prosperity, a desire to defend and even to extend democracy, faith that pragmatic solutions to global problems can be found, and the belief that the United States should remain a "strong" country in the international arena (Lindeman 1989). These values can be fulfilled more completely by the programs associated with common security, than with the continuation of the policies of the old world order.[26]

Does public opinion, by itself, constitute a significant political force for change? To what degree will policy be influenced by the incipient support that now exists for programs based on common security? By itself, public opinion is not strong enough to force meaningful change.[27] At the same time, current attitudes are an obstacle to the readoption of the most severe measures of the Cold War. Despite the Gulf War and the support of the public for it, no blanket endorsement for the unilateral use of military force now exists. The public wants neither increases in military spending nor a new program of strategic modernization. On the cultural plane, the images sustaining the Soviet threat have disappeared.

But enough areas of ambiguity in opinion remain that politicians who oppose the adoption of progressive politics have plenty of room

---

26. It should be noted that the term "common security" has virtually no meaning for the public. Many individuals support the policies that are implied by common security, but the overall connotation of this alternative approach to the national interest has not been communicated effectively.

27. Risse-Kappen (1990) argues that public opinion "can directly affect top decision-makers' choices by (a) influencing specific policy decisions; (b) defining a range of choices which decision-makers have without losing public support; or (c) providing a certain 'climate of opinion' setting rather broad and unspecified limits to policy-makers' actions. Public opinion may also affect the coalition-building processes among the elites which in turn determine policies." I would argue that public opinion can have this effect, but only in combination with other social forces.

for maneuver. Public opinion is not yet mobilized around clear policy alternatives. Politicians and decisionmakers view public attitudes as a potential cost of improper political management rather than a directive to which they must immediately respond. They are reinforced in this view by responses reflecting misinformation among the American public, and by inconsistencies between responses indicating an openness toward new policies and those demonstrating the need for caution, skepticism, and continued suspicion of "the other." Public opinion is less a clear-cut pressure that is forcing out orthodox policies than a permeable barrier that policymakers must circumvent in order to perpetuate existing foreign policy priorities.

In addition to the qualifications that arise from a detailed review of opinion polls, other obstacles to a progressive agenda on security, which derive from the fundamental character of U.S. politics, need to be weighed. In particular, we need to look more closely at the argument that these shifts in public *opinion* can be used by social movements and presidential candidates to bring about significant changes in U.S. political *culture*. A shift in attitudes as measured by polls may not signify public willingness to support truly substantive change. The issues here are complex, and each is the subject of a significant literature. My strategy is to outline only the principal issues here and then to return in the concluding chapter to the overall implications of a fundamental realignment of U.S. politics.

One tendency of U.S. political culture is that programmatic liberalism accompanies ideological conservatism. The shifts in attitudes than can be recorded issue by issue have not been accompanied by a switch from the Republican to the Democratic party or by any other indicator of support for a new and broad political agenda. This may be partly explained by the reluctance of the Democratic party or any of its presidential candidates to develop and articulate alternative approaches to security.

The claim that the public may be open to new politics may be countered by other arguments as well. Miller (1989) has argued that recent polling data supporting a revitalized commitment to social spending represents, not a shift toward liberalism, but a need on the part of the public to redress the conservative policies of the 1980s. Attitudes have not changed in any long-term sense—the public is merely trying to move back toward the center. Recent change is more a phase in an ongoing cycle than a secular shift. Moreover, public opinion is still "politically soft." It is still possible for political leaders to follow status quo policies, develop most weapons systems, and use U.S. troops overseas. It may be possible to find substitute "enemies" to replace the Soviet Union, such as international terrorism or even economic competition from Europe and Japan. Even most Democrats seem to accept the need to restructure U.S. military forces in a way that still permits rapid deployment to the Third World. The emergence and acceptance of these competing "others" weighs against the formation and acceptance of a foreign policy predicated on international cooperation.

Americans are also reluctant to support changes that are perceived to adversely affect the economy. In the absence of clear, specific proposals and an accompanying explanation of how a new foreign policy will be in the national interest, the public will probably follow the more cautious attitude that "we have more to lose than we have to gain by changing." Some may perceive a new global U.S. leadership role as too expensive—just another way of raising the taxes of the middle class. The need to develop precise policy proposals to fill out the vision of progressive politics remains. Another problem is that of communicating a more complex approach to national security through a mass media that seems to require the collapse of a political perspective into ten-second sound bites. Finally, much of the political culture continues to focus more on personality than on substantive issues. Presidents Reagan and Bush have been popular despite the fact that a large majority have opposed many of their specific policies. Each of these considerations is important in assessing the current potential for progressive politics in the United States.

The three principal factors affecting the future development of public opinion on national security are global events, the reemergence of a peace movement within a broader coalition of social activism, and the potential emergence of a presidential candidate who could respect the ambiguity that now exists in public attitudes and simultaneously articulate the vision of a new world order. As emphasized in this chapter, the last decade has seen a significant shift in the patterns of these ambiguities, but the fact remains that contradictions continue to exist. Consequently, the influence of public opinion as a force in its own right is greatly circumscribed. Public opinion can play a larger role if a president initiates a dialogue over the meaning of security. A candidate could appeal to the public using end of the Cold War themes and stressing the need for greater international cooperation without becoming politically vulnerable. In fact, a president would *have* to mobilize the incipient support for significant change that now exists in order to overcome the opposition that will emerge in response to any attempt at domestic realignment. In short, public attitudes reflect both continued passivity—a product of inner contradiction and manipulation—*and* the potential to support progressive change. The situation is fluid.

Postscript: Comparison of the United States and (Former) West Germany

In many ways, public opinion in former West Germany on peace and security issues paralleled that in the United States. Each country rejected its government's reliance on nuclear first use. Over the first half of the 1980s, both populations became more critical of Washington's nuclear policies and of defense spending in general.[28] There are, however, three important differences. First, German opinion after 1987 increasingly favored the complete denuclearization of Europe, while U.S. opinion did not reject all roles for nuclear weapons. Second, the German public earlier rejected the Cold War images of the Soviet threat. Third, German opinion is rooted more firmly in the system of political parties and varies more significantly with other social variables such as income, age, and education. In the United States, the relative detachment of attitudes from a particular sociological base signifies that a presidential candidate attempting to build a progressive coalition can use common security as a political unifier. No specialized appeal to a particular segment of the population is necessary.

Many of the military and political aspects of the Cold War revolved around the possibility of a Soviet conventional invasion of Europe. The recent and dizzying rate of change affecting such basic premises should not prevent us from appreciating the significant

28. This comparison focuses on public opinion only. The peace movements that emerged in both countries are assessed in the next chapter.

changes in opinion that transpired over the 1980s in West Germany. In the first half of the decade, the previously dominant image of a world divided into a good superpower (the United States) versus a bad superpower (the Soviet Union) was replaced by a more complex view that increasingly held both superpowers responsible for the arms race (Rochon 1988). Majorities in both countries were opposed to NATO's policy of threatened first use of nuclear weapons. In 1986, in West Germany, about 40 percent of the population believed that nuclear weapons should not be used under any circumstances, and another 40 percent believed they should be used only if the USSR used atomic weapons first. Less than 20 percent advocated their use, even in the face of overwhelming conventional force (Eichenberg 1988). In the United States, only 8 percent believed Washington should respond with nuclear weapons in such circumstances (88 percent believed other means should be explored) (*ATS* 6:134).

German and American perceptions regarding the military balance between the United States and Soviet Union were also similar. In each country, those finding the United States superior in military strength increased slightly, those finding the United States not as strong as the Soviet Union declined, while those perceiving rough parity increased significantly.[29] Increased opposition to defense spending also developed in parallel—although the opposition of the German public was more pronounced. Before the fall of the Berlin Wall, almost 40 percent of the population favored decreased defense spending while only 7 percent supported an increase (Eichenberg 1988; Rochon 1988). (Table 3-3, presented earlier in this chapter, documents the declining support for defense spending in the United States.)[30]

---

29. For U.S. opinions see Table 3-1; for the FRG those finding the Soviets ahead dropped from 44 percent in 1981 to 20 percent in 1985, while those finding rough parity increased from 24 percent in 1981 to 47 percent in 1985. For both countries, most of the change took place between 1983 and 1985, before Gorbachev came to power (Eichenberg 1988).

30. Despite these changes, the West German public remained identified with the West. Annoyance with U.S. policy existed during the 1980s, but apprehension that the Atlantic Alliance would crumble was not justified. Even at the height of opposition to INF deployment, for example, the German public did not reject NATO. At least two-thirds of the population rejected Pershing II and GLCM, the two new intermediate-range land-based missiles. Yet a 1983 poll found members of the Social Democrats, Christian Democrats, and Free Democrats continuing to support NATO by 86 percent, 96 percent, and 95 percent respectively. Support for a policy of withdrawal from NATO did increase over the early 1980s, but only to slightly over 10 percent. Even 56 percent of the Green Party found the military alliance necessary (Domke, Eichenberg and Kelleher 1987:385).

TABLE 3-8
West German Attitudes Toward the Superpowers: 1982

	The United States/Soviet Union act to promote			
	U.S. = Peace USSR = War (%)	*U.S. = Peace USSR = Peace* (%)	*U.S. = War USSR = War* (%)	*U.S. = War USSR = Peace* (%)
All respondents	41.1	12.3	41.4	5.3
The Greens	5.4	1.2	86.9	6.4
Social Democrats	28.3	18.2	44.4	9.1
Free Democrats	39.8	17.0	27.7	15.5
Christian Democrats	57.7	12.6	26.6	3.1

Source: Eurobarometer 17, April 1982.

Note: Respondents were asked, "On balance, do you think that the (United States'/Soviet Union's) policies and actions during the past year have done more to promote peace or more to increase the risk of war?"

The principal difference between U.S. and German opinions lies not in the overall pattern of increased rejection of Cold War premises but in the social roots that sustain that pattern. In particular, German opinion is more closely tied to party affiliation. Table 3-8, which examines attitudes toward the two superpowers by political party in 1982, shows that 41 percent of the entire German public judged the United States to be acting to promote peace and the USSR to be acting to promote war. Another 41 percent found both superpowers acting to promote war. Only 12 percent found both countries acting to promote peace. Those finding the U.S. more warlike than the Soviet Union numbered 5 percent. Significant deviation from the overall pattern appears when respondents are separated by political party. Almost 58 percent of the Christian Democrats found the United States acting to promote peace and the Soviet Union war, compared with 28 percent of the Social Democrats (SPD), and 5 percent of the Greens. Conversely, only 27 percent of the Christian Democrats (CDU/CSU) blamed both superpowers for war-promoting behaviors, compared with 44 percent of the SPD and almost 87 percent of the Greens. Interestingly, the party most closely associated with active opposition to the further deployment of nuclear weapons, the Greens, tended to blame both superpowers instead of only the United States. The centrist Free Democrats were three times as likely as the Greens to find the United States acting to promote war and the Soviet Union acting to promote peace. Party affiliation also is very important in explaining variation in opposition to defense spending (in 1983, Green opposition was roughly 90 percent, Social Democrats 60 percent, Free Democrats 46 percent, and CDU/CSU 34 percent).[31]

In contrast, the impact of party affiliation in the United States is relatively weak. Differences between Republicans and Democrats can be found on specific questions such a support for SDI or preferred level of defense spending, but the gap is less than the differences between political parties in West Germany. Table 3-9, examining the impact of various variables on the overall choice of one of four possible Futures for the year 2010, does indicate a variation between political parties, but only by 10 percentage points for Futures 2 and 3. Only one-quarter of *both* parties support Future 1. Future 3 received the highest level of support from *both* parties. And independents, or possible swing voters, are more likely than either Republicans or Democrats to support Future 3.

A "generation gap" in which younger people are held to be more dovish is frequently thought to have an effect on attitudes toward war and peace issues. Save for a limited period during the Vietnam War, there is surprisingly little support for the impact of age, either historically on attitudes toward pacifism, or more recently on attitudes toward the nuclear arms race. No significant generation gap on attitudes exists regarding the use of nuclear weapons over Hiroshima and Nagasaki (Kramer, Kalick, and Milburn 1983), nor does age seem to be associated with support for the any of the Four Futures of the Public Agenda study.

Another characteristic of public attitudes toward the arms race is the so-called gender gap, in which women are held to have more dovish opinions than their male counterparts. Over the 1980s, by a consistent margin of ten to fifteen percentage points, women were more fearful of the possible outbreak of nuclear war, less trusting of a leader who appeared bellicose, and more opposed to the development of most weapons systems. A 1982 poll, for example, found 59 percent of the men but only 45 percent of the women "trusting of Ronald Reagan to make the right kind of decisions about the control of nuclear weapons" (CBS/*New York Times*). Many polls document the existence

---

31. While party voting retains the strongest correlation with opinion, modest support for the relationship of age, educational level, and adherence to post-materialist values to opinions concerning defense issues can also be detected (Mueller and Risse-Kappen 1987).

TABLE 3-9
Impact of Gender, Age, Education, Party, Religion, Income, and Ideology on Choice of Future

Futures Ranked First in Preference	Future 1 Fully Competitive	*Future 2 Arms Control Compete Elsewhere*	*Future 3 Cooperative Problem Solving*	*Future 4 Isolationist*
Gender				
Male	21	28	47	4
Female	23	26	47	4
Age				
18–29	19	24	53	4
30–39	22	29	45	4
40–49	21	24	51	3
50–64	28	29	39	4
65 and over	21	30	44	5
Education				
Less than high school	34	25	36	4
High school graduate	26	21	47	6
Some college	21	30	46	3
College graduate/more	17	30	51	2
Party Affiliation				
Democrat	26	23	47	4
Independent	13	22	59	6
Republican	25	33	38	4
Religion				
Protestant	22	31	44	3
Catholic	25	30	41	5
Jewish	18	17	63	2
Family Income				
Less than $5,000	27	24	46	3
$15,000–24,999	23	24	48	6
$25,000–34,999	22	25	50	4
$35,000–49,999	22	28	48	2
$50,000–74,999	20	30	47	4
$75,000 and over	11	46	38	5
Ideological Identification				
Liberal	19	19	61	2
Moderate liberal	14	29	53	4
Moderate	19	32	47	3
Moderate conservative	23	29	45	3
Conservative	39	31	25	5

Source: Public Agenda Foundation/Center for Foreign Policy Development. Mark Lindeman was kind enough to provide statistical assistance.

of a gender gap affecting opposition to the development of the Strategic Defense Initiative (Gallup, March 1985; Public Agenda 1988). Women are now, more than men, cautious about military spending and the possibilities of a new military role in the Persian Gulf. On all questions examining future military activities there is a 10 to 15 point gap between men and women (*ATS* 15:15). For the Gulf War the gender gap was wider than any other recent military action with some prewar polls reaching more than 25 points (see Table 3-10) (Harris 1990; Pertman 1991; Tye 1990).

Republican party strategists have feared that the gender gap on war and peace issues extends far deeper, perhaps even to the point of underpinning a more permanent form of opposition among women to their political party. On the other hand, the gender gap seems to appear on only some dimensions of public opinion. Questions that tap fears of an unchecked arms race or military conflict are likely to produce a significant difference between men and women. Issues that are formulated along explicit policy lines do not. For example, Table 3-9 does not indicate an appreciable difference in choice of Future by gender.[32]

Opposition to the Gulf War was also stronger among African Americans than among whites. An ABC News/*Washington Post* poll in early February found support for the war among 84 percent of whites, but only 48 percent of blacks (*Boston Globe*, February 16, 1991) (see Table 3-11). Postwar polls showed 64 percent of African Americans disagreeing with the initial use of force, or roughly double the percentage for the population as a whole.

With reference to the other variables and their possible influence on choice of Future, religion does not seem to have an impact, except that Jews are more likely to support Future 3. The impact of income is erratic, with only the highest bracket least likely to accept Future 1 and most likely to support Future 2. Educational level has a modest effect, with those with an advanced degree more likely to support Future 3. Even among those without a high school diploma, however, no strong support for Future 1 can be detected. Only ideological orientation along a left-to-right political spectrum seems to have a strong impact. In the final analysis, religion, income, age, gender, education, and even party identification play comparatively weak roles in ex-

32. Measuring the gender gap and explaining its origins has spawned an important literature (Brandes 1992; Brock-Utne 1985; Lamare 1989; and Carol Mueller 1988).

TABLE 3-10
The Gender Gap in Attitudes Toward Recent U.S. Military Interventions

Polls show a wider gap between women's disapproval of military action, and men's approval, in the Persian Gulf than in any other recent U.S. military intervention.

Yes | No | Undecided/No response

VIETNAM: Was it a mistake sending troops?

Year	Group	Yes	No
1969	MALES	52%	41%
	FEMALES	52%	37%
1971	MALES	60%	32%
	FEMALES	62%	23%
1973	MALES	61%	31%
	FEMALES	59%	28%

GRENADA: Do you approve of President Reagan's handling?

Year	Group	Yes	No
1983	MALES	66%	28%
	FEMALES	54%	35%

PANAMA: Do you approve of President Bush's handling?

Year	Group	Yes	No
Jan. 1990	MALES	70%	21%
	FEMALES	61%	22%

PERSIAN GULF: Do you approve of President Bush's handling?

Year	Group	Yes	No
Nov. 1990	MALES	70%	26%
	FEMALES	52%	41%

PERSIAN GULF: Was it a mistake sending troops?

Year	Group	Yes	No
Nov. 1990	MALES	21%	76%
	FEMALES	34%	60%

Source: Gallup Poll, in Tye 1990.

TABLE 3-11
Differences by Race in Attitudes Toward the Gulf War: 1991

"Do you or are you"*

	White (%)	Black (%)
Willing to see your own children fight Iraq?	58	31
Believe blacks would bear an unfair burden in Mideast fighting?	24	58
Approve of Bush's handling of the crisis?	61	35
"Very confident" U.S. military can achieve its objective?	56	40
Believe forcing Iraq out of Kuwait is a "very good" reason to have the troops in the Gulf?	51	34
Support an attack if Iraq has not withdrawn from Kuwait by Jan. 15?	59	38

"Do you approve or disapprove of the way George Bush is handling Iraq's invasion of Kuwait?"**

	White (%)	Black (%)
Approve	60	30
Disapprove	32	60
Don't know	8	10
*"Do you think the United States did the right thing in sending troops to Saudi Arabia, or should we have stayed out?"***		
Right thing	65	36
Stayed out	27	55
Don't know	8	9
*"The troubles between Iraq, Kuwait, and Saudi Arabia are just a conflict between different groups of Arabs that the U.S. should stay out of. Do you agree or disagree?"***		
Agree	34	53
Disagree	60	36
Don't know	6	11

Sources: Gordon S. Black Corp. for *U.S.A. Today*, December 29–30, 1990; CBS News/*New York Times* Poll, Dec. 9–11, 1990.

*N = 1,008 adults nationwide.

**N = 1,044 adults.

plaining differences among U.S. citizens.[33] A comprehensive review (Milburn, Watanabe, and Kramer 1986) also found little difference among social groups in their support for a nuclear freeze. Save for a tendency for the general public to be more dovish on nuclear weapons issues than the elite in the United States, the appeal for common security is as universal as one is likely to find in the U.S. political system (Eichenberg 1988; Russett 1990; Wittkopf 1990). No potentially divisive appeal to one segment of the population is necessary. It is not a "special interest" issue.

33. Demographic differences do not entirely disappear on security issues. On some issues, for example, the perception that "The Soviet Union Is Like Hitler's Germany—An Evil Empire Trying to Rule the World," age, education, income, ideology, and gender did have an impact (Public Agenda Foundation 1988).

4

Peace Movements Make a Difference

PEACE MOVEMENTS are expressions of hope. People give their time, money, talent, and energy against what appear to be overwhelming odds. Indeed, in the United States, a nation whose culture does not encourage political activism, it sometimes appears that a pessimistic appraisal of the chances for success is the only reasonable one. By almost any measure, the resources of a peace movement are far less than the political, economic, and symbolic assets possessed by the national government. And yet a vision of peace remains. Governments cloak themselves in national glory, national duty, and the national interest. Citizens are sometimes swayed by these appeals. But many are also moved by the images of children sacrificed for no apparent gain, economic destruction for no possible good, and the perpetuation of international violence as a totally illegitimate method to solve problems. Opposition develops, protest deepens, and the motivation to make more safe their lives and the lives of others intensifies. In the process, peace movements succeed in making inroads against the particular policies and strategies chosen by government officials. They hold up the promise, even if imperfect and fleeting, of achieving a more true and secure peace than that achieved by the threat of military force.

The prevailing interpretation of peace movements, however, discounts their impact. The resources commanded by governments are immense and the pressures against which any social movement must struggle to sustain itself over time are significant. In foreign affairs, a president who enjoys an even modest level of popular approval can define an issue to his own liking. Within limits, a president also can manipulate circumstances to his advantage, even to the point of manufacturing convenient crises. The executive branch commands the powerful image of the flag, legitimates itself through expertise and the military hierarchy, and does not expect significant opposition to be generated by the press and media. The political leverage of social movements are usually weaker.

One does not have to look farther than the 1980s anti–nuclear weapons movement to find support for this point of view. Even though it mobilized millions of citizens against U.S. policy, the movement failed in its efforts to institute a bilateral freeze between the superpowers. A nuclear freeze resolution was passed by the House of Representatives, but its provisions were nonbinding. The administration, the press, and even many in the movement itself saw the measure as a hollow victory. Not one significant weapons system that the movement opposed—not the MX, SDI, the Trident II missile, or the Midgetman—was blocked. Movement-supported measures such as a halt to nuclear testing or a ban against antisatellite weapons were not passed by Congress. Despite strenuous efforts, the anti–nuclear weapons movement did not significantly affect the outcome of more than a few national or local political races. By the middle of the decade, large-scale mobilization efforts were exhausted and membership in most organizations began to decline. The movement became fragmented, torn by internal disagreements that hurt its overall effectiveness.

The argument in this chapter proceeds in three steps: First, in an account that contrasts with prevailing orthodoxy and is consistent with the vision of peace and its importance for citizen activism, I demonstrate the impact of the 1980s movement against nuclear weapons in some detail. The movement made a significant though rarely acknowledged contribution to the end of the Cold War, and it is important to rescue that fact. Second, I examine efforts to oppose the Gulf War and their implications for redefining national security. Finally, I compare the U.S. and West German peace movements, especially in terms of the role played by political parties in each country. The twentieth century has seen important cycles of opposition to war: resistance to conscription in World War I, to massive deployment of troops in Korea and Vietnam, to testing of nuclear warheads and the development of nuclear weapons systems, and to military intervention in Central America and the Persian Gulf. But my purpose is more than to document the influence of particular peace movements at particular moments in time. Linked to each example of opposition to war is a broader current of peace sentiment that transcends particular victories and defeats. These peace movements have been a critical source of ideas and political will. They have raised issues and expanded political agendas. The ideas represented by peace movements were not adopted in their entirety, and the process of translating their social impact into concrete decisions and government policy was complex. But an important motivation for change emanated from the movements themselves. Only rarely did political elites change their policy orientation without pressure from below. The recurrence of social mobilization has created a legacy of positive peace, which any effective movement to redefine national security must draw upon. A close examination of the peace movement will provide valuable clues to how a broad coalition of social movements focused on political realignment might be revived over the 1990s.

Definition and Characterization of the U.S. Peace Movement

Peace movements are examples of social movements or "sustained interactions in which mobilized people, acting in the name of a defined interest, make repeated broad demands on powerful others via means which go beyond the current prescriptions of authorities" (Tilly 1978: 313). More specifically, peace movements are *efforts to transform government strategies that (a) present ideas and policy options that go beyond the boundaries of elite policy discourse; (b) convey a sense of urgency in their opposition to prevailing policy; (c) employ influence strategies that focus on existing political institutions, such as lobbying and coalition building, with activities that permit direct popular participation in protest, such as demonstrations and civil disobedience; and (d) attempt to speak for and mobilize a broader, unorganized constituency than the formal members of the organizations that make up the movement itself.* A significant component of modern peace movements has been the attempt to build a *culture of peace*, not only by advancing a critique of policy, but also in opposing more generally the use of war, militarism, and the threat of organized violence to settle international disputes. Following Gamson (1990), we can specify further components of peace movements: *social movement organizations*, or the specific groups that carry this challenge to the political system; *targets of influence*, or the individuals, groups, policies, and social institutions that the challengers seek to alter; *constituencies*, or the population to whom the social movement organization appeals in advancing its quest; and *benefits*, or the newly acquired advantages that are to be distributed to the social movement organization, to the constituency, or to both. Finally, it is important to remember that social movements are agents of change. They do not write, implement, or administer policy and their impact is not to be judged by these criteria.

It has been estimated that some three thousand independent antinuclear groups existed over the course of the 1980s (Conetta 1988). The movement contained different organizational, tactical and cultural faces, many of which drew upon important twentieth century precedents (Chatfield 1973; Cooper 1991; DeBenedetti 1973, 1980; Katz 1986; Taylor and Young 1987; Wittner 1984). The movement was at once "radical and moderate, structured and amorphous, organized and chaotic, religious and secular, routinized and spontaneous, simple and complex" (Benford 1988:238). To make sense out of this diversity, we must characterize the organizational strategies and activities that were employed by the antinuclear movement.

Peace movement organizations pursued different objectives in their quest to achieve a nuclear freeze. Several organizations devoted themselves to blocking specific weapons systems such as the MX missile, the B-1 bomber, and the Strategic Defense Initiative. Others took as their first priority the resumption of the arms control process, which appeared stalled by the failure to ratify SALT II and by the overall attitude of the first Reagan administration. The imperative to resume arms control was also part of the massive effort to persuade Congress to pass a resolution that would freeze the testing, production, and deployment of nuclear weapons. The majority of the individuals in the peace movement had a nuclear freeze as their goal. Other peace movement organizations were committed to the more ambitious goal of total nuclear disarmament. For them, measures such as a nuclear freeze or a comprehensive test ban would be only the first step toward that goal. Finally, still other organizations viewed the effort to cap the nuclear arms race as important in itself, but also as an opportunity to advance a broader range of issues including opposition to military intervention in Central America, attaining ecological stability and global development, securing reproductive rights, and achieving greater social justice within the United States itself.

The relative commitment to local versus national organizing activities constitutes the second set of differences among peace movement organizations. In the early 1980s, the freeze movement succeeded in having many local governments pass resolutions against the further testing, production and deployment of nuclear weapons. In some areas, nuclear-free zones were declared as well. Many activists maintained that local, grass-roots activity was necessary not only build a political base but also to avoid the process of co-optation and dilution that can accompany efforts to influence national political leaders through legitimate channels. Other movement organizations mounted a national effort to have the House of Representatives pass the freeze resolution (Meyer 1990; Solo 1988; Waller 1987). Attached to this national focus were efforts to secure financial and organizational resources for those political candidates who supported the arms control process. The Council for a Livable World, National Freeze Voter, and state level Freeze PACs serve as examples.

A third highly varied dimension of the peace movement was organizational structure. The mobilization against the arms race included centralized and hierarchical organizations such as SANE (the Committee for a Sane Nuclear Policy) and the Federation of American Scientists. Other organizations such as local freeze groups, Women's Pentagon Action, and coalitions established for a particular purpose such as organizing a demonstration were more decentralized with an informal leadership structure and no formal membership (Hall 1984:478).

Peace movement organizations also differed over tactics. Tactics are important because it is the "face" of the movement that the public, through press and media accounts, sees most clearly. Virtually every organization in the peace movement supported the organization of national and local demonstrations as peaceful and necessary expressions of protest. But significant disagreement also existed, particularly over the role of civil disobedience, and over the contention that lobbying, electoral activity, and other efforts to affect the political process directly only sapped the movement of its energy and creativity. Some peace movement organizations sought change only through means that were considered legitimate, such as lobbying Congress, public education, and electoral activity. Others, such as Greenpeace, Plowshares, the War Resister's League, and numerous ad hoc groups, favored more direct forms of protest including civil disobedience, tax refusal, blockading nuclear weapons production facilities, and even breaking into plants or submarine pens, either to destroy warheads with hammers or to pour blood over weapons to register symbolically their opposition.

It is possible to combine these four areas of divergence in order to compare the more moderate "coalition movements," having relatively moderate political goals, orthodox organizational structures, and legitimate tactics that demand comparatively little commitment from their members, with the more radical "prophetic minorities," having decentralized structures and tending toward more militant tactics that demand much greater levels of personal commitment. The size of the first set of groups fluctuated dramatically with the ebb and flow of the peace movement. The second set of organizations contained a smaller, but more stable number of adherents (Everts 1989).

Other tendencies within the peace movement were important. Some organizations sought to establish and then deepen a feeling of global identity that would extend across international borders the sense of "us" that animates all social movements. Foremost among these efforts was "citizen diplomacy"—the proliferation of initiatives undertaken by individuals and various movement organizations with the purpose of building a more constructive relationship between the United States and the Soviet Union. These initiatives were aimed less at achieving immediate policy change than at the creation of mutual understanding and popular forms of cooperation between the peoples of both nations. More than four hundred organizations engaged in citizen diplomacy with the USSR, with a 200 percent increase between 1983 and 1986 (Schauffler 1988). An extensive range of organizations established contacts with their counterparts in the Soviet Union. Mountaineering and fishing clubs, athletes and entertainers, sister cities, and even lawyers organized exchange visits.

The peace movement also contained professional groups, which used the expertise of their respective occupations in peacemaking efforts (Meyer 1990; Zald 1987). The model for this activity, the Physicians for Social Responsibility (PSR) was actually formed in 1961 during an earlier wave of social activism. After its revival it served as the prototype for dozens of other professional groups including Educators for Social Responsibility, Artists Against Nuclear War, Architects Against Nuclear War, Social Scientists Against Nuclear War, and the Lawyers Alliance for Nuclear Arms Control.

The Church's role in the peace movement of the 1980s was strong, especially in comparison with organized religion's relatively low profile during the movement against the war in Vietnam. While the Catholic church played the leading role in using the traditions of pacifism and just war to challenge the doctrine of nuclear deterrence, many Protestant denominations and Jews also developed moral arguments against the continuation of the arms race, became centers of organizing activity, and encouraged their constituencies to act as their ethics dictated. One exception to this trend was the rise of fundamentalist Christian sects, which generally supported the military buildup of the Reagan administration.

Feminist organizations comprised still another dimension of the movement. Women's peace groups ranged from relatively well-established organizations, such as Peace Links and the Women's League for Peace and Freedom, to more radical groups that favored tactics of direct action and decentralized organizational structures, and sought to build an alternative culture linking opposition to militarism with efforts to transform the culture of patriarchy. Examples include the Seneca Falls Peace Encampment and Women's Action for Nuclear Disarmament.

Support for efforts against the arms race within higher education, represented by United Campuses to Prevent Nuclear War (UCAM), and in secondary schools, represented by Student/Teacher Organizations to Prevent Nuclear War (STOP), was another dimension of peace movement activity. Two of the groups active in educational efforts, Educators for Social Responsibility and Ground Zero, straddled the boundaries of the peace movement. On the one hand, they were formally neutral, refusing to take a position in their educational activities. On the other hand, it is probably fair to say that most participants in these two organizations believed that furthering the education of the American public would also deepen opposition to Washington's policies. Other education projects were carried out by the Federation of American Scientists and the Union of Concerned Scientists. Some felt that the freeze movement should have spent more time in self- and public education before moving into the political arena (Molander and Molander 1990).

A final focus was on the economic impact of military spending. Groups such as Jobs with Peace made the case that defense spending has a negative impact on the rest of the economy, prepared alternative budgets containing much-reduced expenditures for defense, and promoted the concept of economic conversion. In some cases, these groups attempted to establish alliances with those trade unions that would have been most affected by a significant reduction in the military budget.

This summary of different tendencies in the peace movement was intended to give a sense of its breadth and diversity. I turn now to the question of its effectiveness.

Peace Movement Effectiveness

The assessment of the peace movement that follows flows from the major thesis of this book: The renewal of progressive politics in the United States can evolve only through the development of a coherent perspective on common security, a remobilized peace movement, and a presidential campaign. A presidential campaign and revitalized peace movement can develop the embryonic support for common security that already exists among the American public, but only by recognizing the positive legacy of earlier peace movements.

Peace movements can have an impact in many ways. The goal of advancing specific demands and thus affecting government policy decisions is important for movements. But we will miss many avenues of influence if we focus only on immediate forms of impact. Because influence channels are varied and indirect, participants in peace movements themselves do not always appreciate the impact of their efforts. Unambiguous victories occur only rarely. Even where mobilization is successful, the short- and medium-term result is not a clear-cut victory for either the peace movement or the government. During these periods, influence becomes more fluid as decisions reflect contradictory impulses. As Nigel Young has argued: "With peace movements, as with other social movements, the results of public activity are always ambiguous. Like other great social change or social protest campaigns, they have both latent and manifest consequences. They may actually prolong the wars they aim to stop. They may alienate public opinion. Their relative success or failure always depends on other independent or external factors, not just the degree or level of activity achieved" (1986:210). Yet peace movements are reticent about claiming victory in the midst of ambiguous forms of progress. Peace movement leaders often have a difficult job of informing their constituencies and the public of movement influence, especially when the evidence of success is difficult to disentangle from events that seem to preserve existing policy orientations. Where new advantages for the movement have been created, many see only co-optation. Sometimes peace movements give up just as their impact is becoming significant. Another problem is that overt forms of mobilization such as large-scale demonstrations may wane while the influence of the movement is carried by other social agencies. Government officials may be deterred from decisions out of fear of rekindling a movement whose most visible manifestations are in decline. To capture all this we need to measure both the direct impact of social movements on policy, and the more oblique patterns of influence that are mediated by third parties and refracted through altered social contexts. To appreciate better the impact of peace movements, we must peer behind the contradictory voting pattern of a congressman, and examine closely the businessman who complains about the improper management of the economy, the editor who finally agrees to run the reporter's more critical story, and the quickening pace of arms control negotiations. In short, to understand fully the varied forms of influence stemming from the mobilization of the public, we have to become social detectives. What follows is an assessment of the 1980s peace movement according to each of nine criteria of movement effectiveness.[1]

1. The classic measure of movement success is forcing an actual change in policy goals. Government officials either accommodate the demands of the peace movement or accept the challenging group as a legitimate constituency, at which point the movement becomes a factor in the policy-making process, as policy change is acknowledged to be the goal.

Shortly after assuming office, the Reagan administration adopted what it called a "countervailing strategy" for nuclear weapons (Jervis 1984). Despite the new name, the countervailing strategy was only an extension of the long-standing policy of developing counterforce that would put the Soviet retaliatory forces and military command centers at risk and give Washington at least the potential of winning a nuclear war. The movement for a nuclear freeze began to mobilize against the more explicit public statements that reaffirmed this policy, and against renewed efforts to make this policy more credible by building up nuclear capability. At the same time, the movement was divided between those who saw the nuclear freeze proposal as a commitment to arms control and those who saw the proposal as a first step in the transformation of domestic politics and the international system. The tension between the two positions was usually articulated in the form of the question whether the campaign to freeze nuclear weapons should be a single-issue movement. Responding in the forum of the inaugural issue of *Nuclear Times*, a periodical devoted to coverage of the peace movement, Jeremy Stone, director of the Federation of American Scientists articulated the first tendency:

> The freeze is immensely popular, precisely because, being unlinked to other issues it is free to appeal to a very broad spectrum. If linking the

1. For a similar application of these nine criteria of effectiveness to the movement against the war in Vietnam, see Joseph 1992.

> freeze to other issues means appealing only to selected audiences, then, obviously, this would be counterproductive. In my opinion, the freeze is more popular than any other related issue to which it might be linked. It is the freeze that has the coattails, and they should be used sparingly. (October 1982:6)

David Cortright, director of SANE, outlined the alternative:

> We must not view nuclear issues in a vacuum, ignoring vital political and economic issues. The arms race is most directly connected to U.S. foreign and military policy. The assumption and objectives underlying American's role in the world determine these priorities. Thus there is a direct connection between opposition to military intervention and the prevention of nuclear war. The decision to increase U.S. nuclear and military spending is as much a matter of economic and social priorities as foreign policy. The diversion of funds from domestic programs to weaponry has already set off a time bomb of sorts in many low-income and working-class communities. All of us talk about the need for outreach to women, minorities, and labor. We cannot expect the involvement of these people, however, unless we show interest in their concerns for economic survival and social justice. (October 1982:6)

After nearly ten years of effort, neither viewpoint led to the achievement of a genuine change in policy. The first, or "lowest common denominator" orientation, came to dominate because it was thought that unification around a minimal position would attract more broadly based support. Several assumptions were built into this position: First, that an arms control movement would be more attractive than a peace movement. Second, that the simplicity of the freeze proposal was itself an important asset to retain. And third, that it was possible to stop the arms race without stopping the Cold War. Though the originators of the "Call to Halt the Arms Race" did not expect early success for the measure, especially by working through Congress, the passage of a resolution eventually consumed much of the energy and resources of the movement. The language of the resolution was gradually weakened, the resolution itself was nonbinding, and many Representatives voted both for the freeze *and* for the very nuclear weapons systems that the freeze was supposed to block. Despite its success in mobilizing millions of people in a protest against the arms race, the peace movement itself imposed no explicit change in policy. The failure to develop an explicit policy alternative led to fatal flaws. The dominance of the arms control imperative within the movement meant that attention became focused on technical debates, such as whether a freeze could be verified. It also meant that many of the characteristics that gave the peace movement its initial strength—such as its break with the very language of the Cold War—were lost. Similarly, no strategy for how to relate simultaneously to official Soviet bloc peace groups and to independent peace groups in the Soviet Union and Eastern Europe emerged.[2]

> 2. Peace movements may block the specific programs and strategies that are necessary for government officials to implement a policy. Overall goals do not change, but the measures necessary to carry out policy are denied. The result is a contradictory situation that contains both the impact of the oppositional movement and the continued efforts of authorities to pursue traditional policy objectives through a different strategy. Peace movements may create an impasse without creating an explicit change in overall policy.

The peace movement achieved only modest success in blocking the specific weapons programs of the Reagan administration. One of the most important campaigns was against the MX missile, two hundred of which were to be deployed in an invulnerable basing mode. In the end, due to public opposition, especially in the areas where the MX was to be deployed, only fifty missiles were built (MacDougall 1991b). These were deployed in existing (and theoretically vulnerable) Minuteman III silos.[3] The ability of the movement to block new missile silos and the other basing modes proposed by the Pentagon forced President Reagan to establish the Scowcroft Commission in an effort to find a solution. The commission's eventual recommendations undermined a principal contention of the Reagan administration, namely, that U.S. land-based missiles were subject to a "window of

---

2. The difficulty of transforming the mobilization of large numbers of demonstrators into immediate influence on policy is noted by Rochon (1988:109) with reference to the movement against the deployment of intermediate range missiles in Europe: "The Netherlands had the largest of the peace demonstrations, with 550,000 or 4 percent of the population in the streets of the Hague in October 1983. It also had the largest actions of any sort, a petition campaign that gathered signatures from over three million people, better than a quarter of the adult population. Even with these enormous numbers, the Dutch government was not forced to do the peace movement's bidding."

3. While the failure to block totally the MX should be marked up as at least a partial failure, the strategic arithmetic of the remaining fifty missiles, while arcane, is nonetheless significant. The MX carries ten warheads with a CEP (circular error probable) of a tenth of a mile. Two hundred missiles represents two thousand warheads or enough counterforce to put virtually the entire arsenal of land-based Soviet missiles at risk. The reduction of the MX warhead total to five hundred (fifty missiles with ten warheads per missile) meant that the program could no longer fulfill the first-strike mission that the planners originally intended for it.

vulnerability" (Drew 1985). Elsewhere, the extent to which the peace movement was able to muster sufficient political strength to block other weapons systems was disappointing—although not entirely so. Funding for the Strategic Defense Initiative continued, although—at least in part due to the organized efforts of the peace movement—at levels that were totally inadequate for any serious development program. Under pressure from the peace movement, Congress came close to passing a measure that would have banned antisatellite weapons (MacDougall 1991a). Momentum developed for a comprehensive test ban and a congressional cutoff of funds. On the other hand, opposition to INF missile deployment was slow in developing and unsuccessful in the short run.

3. Peace movements also try to educate or otherwise influence the attitudes held by the general public.

The impact of the organized peace movement on the public attitudes is difficult to determine. Ambitious claims have been made on behalf of the movement. Supporters argue that the movement "educated" the public and succeeded in placing war and peace issues closer to the center of public concerns. Movement activities are held to have increased the amount of information available to the public and demonstrated by example the importance of making a commitment to oppose the arms race. In turn, this commitment may have prompted even those individuals who did not join the movement to reconsider and even to alter their position on nuclear issues. These claims are impossible to address fully, but a beginning can be made by offering a distinction between public attitudes at the level that can be measured by concrete poll results, and public attitudes at the level of more deeply rooted values and concerns. At the first level, an argument can be made that the peace movement had a modest but significant impact. A close review of the poll results cited in the previous chapter shows a shift of roughly fifteen percentage points toward the positions generally favored by the peace movement between 1981 and 1984, the period of its peak activity. During that time the public became more aware of the dangers of nuclear war and more willing to part company with specific aspects of the Reagan administration's policies. It is important to note that these developments occurred before Mikhail Gorbachev became leader of the Soviet Union and thus cannot be ascribed to more flexible policies from Moscow. On the other hand, the movement did not succeed in keeping war and peace issues at the center of public concerns. By the 1984 national election, nuclear weapons had receded in importance relative to economic issues, a development that aided the reelection efforts of Ronald Reagan.[4]

It is even more difficult to assess the impact of the movement on what might be called the subliminal level of public attitudes. What influence did the activity of millions of people have on the long-term willingness of Americans to consider the possibilities of peace policies that go beyond nuclear deterrence? Has, for example, the shift in public opinion toward the incipient policies of common security that were detailed in the previous chapter been eased by previous spadework carried out by the peace movement? Is it possible to chart a sequence in which the prospect of a world without nuclear weapons was presented to Americans by peace movement activities, kept in abeyance because of continued fear of the Soviet Union, and is being considered again as more acceptable now that dramatic changes are taking place? Did the peace movement legitimate the concept of nuclear disarmament for a slightly later date? As for the answers to such questions, one can only speculate.[5]

---

4. A similar pattern occurred in Western Europe. In every country, peace movements failed to displace economic issues from the top of the agenda. Yet movement activity did create more public interest in the subject which, in turn, had the effect of moving discussion of nuclear policy to more open forums including parliaments, political parties, and the press (Rochon 1988).

5. The Netherlands presents an example of the possible impact of the peace movement on the underlying structure of political debate. The population arguably has considered the nuclear issue more thoroughly than any other. Philip Everts (1989) notes that Dutch opinion reveals "a remarkable continuity of opinion on general issues such as the need for armed forces, the need for military balance, membership in NATO, the relationship of nuclear weapons to war prevention, and preferred levels of defense spending. In 1975, for example, long before the new peace movement appeared, a large majority of Dutch citizens favored removing nuclear weapons from their country, and this did not change.

"The same is true of more specific questions such as whether cruise missiles should be deployed. The distribution of public attitudes on this issue, which deeply divided the country between 1979 and 1986, merely fluctuated a little in those years but showed no change that would indicate a trend. On the average, some 40 percent opposed the missiles, 15 percent supported the missiles, and 40 percent wavered.

"Not surprisingly, those figures echo another consistent distribution of attitudes in the Netherlands: some 35–40 percent of citizens oppose present military policies, considering themselves nuclear pacifists; some 25 percent support established NATO doctrine on nuclear deterrence; and the rest waver or do not care. These basic attitudes are strongly related to the general political left-right dimension, and one's position on this dimension, like personality traits, changes little, if at all.

"Although the peace movement had little influence on individual attitudes in the Netherlands, it caused people to act on their opinions, and caused these opinions to be seen as important. This, in turn, influenced policy to a certain extent because conditions were right in the political structure. Opposition to cruise missiles was not more widespread in the

4. Peace movement effectiveness is also measured by its impact on third parties including (*a*) Congress and local governments, (*b*) expert opinion, (*c*) religious groups, (*d*) the press and media, and (*e*) other social movements.

In its first few years, the burgeoning freeze movement focused its attention on local political activities. By the end of 1983, 23 state legislatures, 370 city councils, 71 county councils, and 446 town meetings had passed resolutions endorsing a nuclear freeze. In addition, the freeze was supported by 10 national labor unions, 140 Catholic bishops, many prominent individuals, the United Nations General Assembly and 150 national and international organizations (McCrea and Markle 1989:15). The effort invested in this activity was important for the organizational development of the movement and left a legacy supportive of broader policy change.

The peace movement also had a significant impact on Congress and local governments. Under pressure from the movement, sentiment for arms control resurfaced in Congress. On a modest scale, individual members became better informed about nuclear issues. Due to direct lobbying and the perceived shift in public sentiment in favor of peace, important aspects of the movement's critique of the nuclear arms race gained additional support within Congress (MacDougall 1990). These tenets included recognition of the impossibility of winning a nuclear war and of the need to develop measures that would ensure nuclear stability, the desire to open non-belligerent channels of communication with the Soviet Union, and increasing skepticism toward Pentagon budgetary requests. However, the movement did not change the prevailing pattern in which most congressmen support defense projects in their respective districts regardless of the overall rationale for those projects and their impact on strategy (Adams 1981; Smith 1989).

The peace movement also had a significant impact on professional strategists and the arms control community. Mayer Zald notes that "experts play a role in defining facts and issues for many [modern] movements" and that such movements "become battles over expert definitions, and the ability of parties to command expertise becomes

Netherlands than elsewhere, but it was relatively more successful, probably due to the openness of Dutch society, where it is relatively easy to put issues on the political agenda and keep them there. And although foreign policy making remains an elitist activity, some members and spokesmen of the peace movement are now recognized members of the informal Dutch foreign policy elite. A broader range of views has become acceptable, and this may be the most important and lasting effect of the peace movement" (p. 29).

an important part of the power equation" (1987:323). Yet, at its inception, the peace movement did not enjoy significant levels of support from even the more liberal professionals who devoted their careers to strategic issues. Consultations between the movement and experts prior to Randall Forsberg's issuing of the "Call to Halt the Arms Race" involved only two or three experts besides Forsberg herself. The ideas behind the call emanated from peace movement organizations rather than the strategic community. The prevailing sentiment, even among sympathetic experts, was that the freeze conveyed a good message but was an inadequate arms control proposal because it could not be verified. In the early 1980s, even those strategists who rejected the Reagan administration's policies supported a managerialist approach that stressed the inevitability of nuclear weapons in a nation's defense and in world politics. By 1987, well before the full extent of the political changes in Soviet Union and Eastern Europe were known, a significant change had taken place among strategists. It became more common to advocate basic deterrence, accept the tenet that nuclear weapons could play no military role other than inflicting spasmodic punishment, and argue for a much lower profile for nuclear weapons within overall U.S. foreign policy. Four experts in particular, McGeorge Bundy, Robert McNamara, George Kennan, and Gerald Smith (1982), were critical to this shift. Each had played a central role in key aspects of nuclear weapons policy. Their defection from prevailing orthodoxy, or their willingness to make their defection public, was only part of a broader process culminating in the virtual rejection by civilian analysts of the military utility of nuclear weapons. Over the course of the decade, and especially after the most dramatic forms of citizen mobilization began to wane, movement leaders were increasingly able to legitimize their positions by citing expert opinions.

The peace movement also had an impact among strategic hawks, although here the channels of influence are difficult to trace. Several notable defenders of counterforce, including members of the Reagan administration such as Fred Ikle, no longer feel that such formerly important centerpieces of strategic modernization as solving land-based vulnerability; improving war-fighting command, control, and communications; hardening against electromagnetic pulse; and developing SDI, are very important. Even before the dramatic changes in Eastern Europe in 1989, there had been a significant decline in the urgency to define military options for nuclear weapons that lie between all-out retaliation and surrender. It is probably impossible to pinpoint the precise role of the peace movement in the decade-long erosion of support for modernizing nuclear weapons that occurred among strategists, but that there was a role for the movement seems equally impossible to deny.

The peace movement also had a profound impact on the religious community (as religious groups had on the movement). The concept of a nuclear freeze was endorsed by the National Conference of Catholic Bishops, the American Baptists, the Lutheran Church of America, the Episcopalian House of Bishops, the United Presbyterian Church, the Reformed Church, American Hebrew Congregations, the United Methodists, the United Church of Christ, and the Unitarians (McCrea and Markle 1989:111). Among these, the most important was the controversial and well-publicized pastoral letter of the National Conference of Catholic Bishops titled "The Challenge of Peace: God's Promise and Our Response" (National Conference of Catholic Bishops 1983). The bishops used traditional just war doctrine as a basis for their opposition to nuclear strategy. Further, they appealed to Catholics to work actively against the arms race ("We are called to move from discussion to witness and action," (p.26). A few bishops went on to invoke the tradition of Jesus and the kingdom of God in their advocacy of unilateral steps toward nuclear disarmament and support for civil disobedience actions. While unanimity did not exist within the Church and it is not difficult to find a theologically grounded defense of nuclear weapons, much of the Church has moved against nuclear orthodoxy over the past decade.

The initial impact of the peace movement on the national press and media was significant in itself, and also aided the further growth of the movement. By 1984, however, national coverage of the peace movement had changed and was no longer positive. For approximately one year, the national peace movement and efforts to pass freeze resolutions in local city councils formed one of the major stories for both the press and the media. The symbolic frame used to characterize the freeze was one of moral justice and sympathy: local citizens (rather than crazy kids) were practicing the very democratic traditions (rather than violent revolutionary acts) that had been formed in the midst of the American revolution (local town meetings are perfectly legitimate). Peace movement activists were depicted as concerned, committed, and energetic. Their actions were for the common good. It was respectable to take steps against the further escalation of the nuclear arms race. The presentation of the peace movement as being as American as apple pie probably helped swell the ranks of the movement. The same image also helped counter conservative attempts to red-bait the movement (Donner 1982; Isaac and Issac 1982; Radosh 1983). Both the *New York Times* and the *Wall Street Journal* editorialized against efforts to smear the movement by alleging that it was controlled by the Soviet Union.

By the 1984 presidential campaign, however, the press and media were no longer interested in the peace movement. Town meetings no longer warranted coverage. The peace movement was no longer intriguing, save for the growing fragmentation among its leaders as they sought to regain momentum.[6] The peace movement, perhaps because many core activists saw themselves as opposed to mainstream cultural institutions, did not develop an effective strategy, or indeed any form of strategy with respect to the media. Instead of thinking out how its message could be presented effectively through an "alien" environment, the movement chose only to keep its message "simple" (as observed above, the simplicity of the freeze was seen by many in the movement as an asset that should be retained at almost any cost). As editors rediscovered the importance of arms control, they turned to experts who did not take the freeze as a serious proposal. The peace movement could not break out of the conceptual straitjacket of being perceived as no more than an "event" with dramatic appeal, a vast outpouring of popular and emotional sentiment against the danger of nuclear war, and a symbolic statement with only diffuse policy impact.

The story of the relationship of the 1980s peace movement to other social movements is one of lost opportunity. The failure to build longstanding connections flowed from the tension between the very ambitious goal of ending the nuclear arms race and the desire to utilize a relatively modest strategy with near universal appeal. By 1982, the operating assumption of the peace movement was that Congress, prompted by pressure from a single-issue constituency, would have the political will as well as the power to halt the testing, deployment, and production of nuclear weapons. As a result, ties with other social movements, especially those for racial equality and economic justice, were developed only at the most rudimentary level. Many of those involved originally with the antiwar movement became committed, after 1984, to working against U.S. intervention in Central America. Eventually, these activists had a significant impact on congressional

6. The Vietnam movement "solved" the dilemma of declining press coverage by adopting ever more militant and bizarre tactics that retained media attention while simultaneously undermining its own effectiveness (Gitlin 1980).

votes that restricted, at least temporarily, military aid to El Salvador and support to the contras. The connection between the two issues was never established organizationally, although many individual members of both movements thought that they could and should be tied together.

This brings us to the finding, often cited by students of social movements, that single-issue movements are more successful than their multi-issue counterparts in bringing new advantages to their constituents and in gaining recognition from established authorities (Gamson 1990). At issue here is the composition of "new advantages" for the peace movement. If the standard was only renewed attention to an arms control process, then the strategy of basing the movement on common denominator politics was probably correct. Economic, ecological, ethnic, and gender issues, with their attendant social movements, represented extra baggage that probably was not necessary to prompt Congress and pressure the administration. However, if new advantages meant an end to the nuclear arms race and significant reductions in the military budget, a strategy that included a working relationship with a broader constituency was required. The peace movement could have demonstrated how a nuclear freeze would contribute to the material benefit of the constituents of other movements. A reduced military budget would aid environmental, feminist, labor, and ethnic activists. Support from these movements was also necessary if the goal was to make a genuine break with Cold War orthodoxy. The political intricacies of such a coalition would have been considerable. Some of the issues involved in working from a broad definition of peace, establishing a working coalition, and placing progressive politics on the political agenda are treated in the final chapter.

5. Peace movement effectiveness is also measured by the ability to maintain an oppositional organizational culture. Movements need to make individuals feel that their actions are contributing, even if in the long run, to a better life. Peace movements need to create and sustain feelings of affiliation, social connection, belonging, and participation (Parkin 1968). Participation helps produce a vision that sustains local actions on the one hand, and feelings of membership in a global community on the other. Effectiveness means creating a sense of collective identity, social consciousness, and a commitment to work for peace. The form of this expression varies from bearing "moral witness" in the case of the Quakers to experiencing "empowerment" or other forms of personal growth in movements influenced by feminist perspectives. The challenge is to develop

> tactics that permit this expressive function of political participation to coexist alongside and even to enhance the more instrumental function of influencing policy change.

Most participants in the peace movement did not see themselves as radicals. At the same time, the freeze proposal was perceived by most of its supporters as a departure from the conventional arms control process. In this respect the freeze was different, and it was understood by most Americans as being different. The freeze was radical in the sense that it would have placed a limit on an institutionalized process that furthered the interests of powerful groups in both the United States and the Soviet Union. Yet the strategy adopted by the movement did not reflect the depth of the challenge that the freeze resolution represented. The assessment that follows of the limitations of the movement's inner life should not be viewed as an argument that lobbying efforts or electoral activity should have been jettisoned in favor of more radical tactics such as civil disobedience. To do so would have been equally suicidal. But the movement had to nurture the understanding that already existed among supporters of the freeze, namely, that it was a measure that broke fundamentally with prevailing orthodoxy. The core activists of the movement had to transform this understanding into a coherent attack on the arms race and its connections with military intervention, foreign policy, and economic interests. Lobbying and electoral efforts would have continued. So too would have acts of civil disobedience by a small part of the movement (Epstein 1991; Rogne and Harper 1990). But the most important development would have been the transformed meaning of each of these activities for the participants, the movement's constituency, and the target group of government officials—a meaning reflected in the gradual creation of a shared vision of a redefined national security and of concrete programs predicated on the realization of that vision.

The stress on local, decentralized, and participatory organizational structures that characterized the initial stages of the peace movement was simultaneously a source of attraction and a constraint on its ability to develop a coherent strategy. During the three-year peak of the peace movement, many forms of activity were offered and many individuals found ways to participate that expressed their own commitment to peace. By creating diverse ways to act for peace, the movement was a success. At the same time, this eclectic form of organizing came at expense of a coherent strategy. Because of the initial stress on local organizing activity and getting the political and civic leadership of communities on record as supporting a freeze, the central structure for the national freeze organization became a "clearinghouse" (located in St. Louis) rather than the directing committee (located in Washington, D.C.). The strategy paper of the 1983 Nuclear Weapons Freeze Campaign argued that "This (local organizing) is the work that most local Freeze Campaigns have thus far done best and, again, it is the foundation, the bedrock, of all future efforts" (Nuclear Weapons Freeze Campaign quoted in Solo 1988:130). I do not mean to imply that this emphasis was misdirected. As already noted, the impact of local activity was considerable. As many have recognized, it is essential for peace groups to establish a local presence beyond writing letters to Congress or mobilizing transportation to take people to large national demonstrations. The limitations lay in the failure to integrate this local activity into a national strategy and to link the passage of freeze resolutions by local authorities with efforts to build up conscious opposition to the Cold War. In its own way, decentralization and the identification of democratic process with the personal involvement of many individuals in every decision that had to be made replicated the tendencies toward fragmentation in the political culture that the peace movement sought to transform. The movement remained suspicious of leaders and buried the reports of task forces set up with the purpose of developing an overall strategy. Movement resistance to visible leaders did not, in reality, create a more democratic structure. The tendency to deny or minimize the function of leaders meant that the leadership style that did emerge was informal, personalistic and characterized by multiple and confusing lines of communication. In 1983, two consultants from Collaborative Change Associates concluded:

> A central conflict within the organization is the unacknowledged struggle for power and status. The Freeze as a movement has gained national recognition and power. There is confusion right now about how best to make use of that power. There are those within the organization who have strong opinions about how the organization should move—and want a personal role in shaping the organization. As a first step, this conflict needs to be surfaced in a constructive manner. The power brokering will go on and is probably healthy, but must be managed well in order to keep it from destroying the whole endeavor. (Solo 1988:144)

It would have been far better to have accountable leaders who were elected on the basis of their skills and political positions and who could then provide for more coherent direction. Instead, the movement tended to blur the issue of leadership in a fruitless identification of internal democracy with decentralization and constraints on formal leadership.

Lacking a strategy and sense of the true significance of a nuclear freeze, the peace movement flipped from its previous focus on local activity to concentrate on an effort to persuade Congress to pass the freeze resolution and to influence selected elections for national office. The May 4, 1983, House of Representatives vote in favor of a freeze was interpreted by some as a success for the movement, and by others as a hollow victory. Because the movement did not develop an overall strategy, it could not see the resolution as both a victory *and* a measure that by itself remained incomplete. That the movement was able to muster the influence to put Congress on record in opposition to the Reagan administration was certainly significant. But to assume that a positive vote on a resolution, even one with stronger language, would be an end to the arms race was an act in self-delusion. The movement claimed victory. The press claimed the congressional vote was a essentially meaningless. Neither had a sense of the vote within a broader context. Social movements need to be able to claim victories under such circumstances, when some progress has been made but the achievement of ultimate goals remains in the future.

The results of the peace movement's electoral strategy were disappointing, even while the funds that were raised to support sympathetic candidates were, by movement standards, impressive. But neither that money nor peace movement volunteers had a significant impact on either the outcome of the 1984 presidential election or more than a handful of congressional elections. The reaction to this failure was typical of American social movements—escalate the militancy of tactics. In 1969, for example, after the perceived failure of large demonstrations to bring peace in Vietnam, and the 1968 election choice between Hubert Humphrey and Richard Nixon, each of whom was identified with the war, the peace movement vented its frustrations with more militant tactics that were largely self-destructive. In the 1980s, a significant core of activists turned their attention to building resistance through a program of "direct action." The working definition of being "really" against the arms race was to offer oneself up for arrest. Civil disobedience has a legitimate role in peace movements, and many people feel strongly the need to live a life that is morally correct. But the collapse of a significant component of the movement's political activity into the tactics of direct action greatly restricted the movement's capacity to develop the culture and organizational resources that would have permitted the development of a coherent strategy of opposition.

Nor did the movement manage to develop a political psychology of mobilization more sophisticated than the attempt to scare people by projecting the consequences of nuclear war.[7] A discussion of the limitations of a recruitment strategy based upon fear emerged within part of the movement, but not until long after its membership peak had passed. Closely related to the inability to develop a coherent strategy was a similar difficulty in articulating both a vision and a practical program that contained hope and promise.[8]

Many in the movement also overestimated the strength of their public support and the ease with which sympathetic opinion could be turned into policy. The result was inflated expectations. For example, virtually everyone in the movement, citing numerous public opinion polls, felt that 75 to 80 percent of the public supported the freeze resolution. However, the 60 percent level of support recorded during the 1982 elections (when nearly one-third of the population had an opportunity to vote on freeze referenda) represents a truer figure. The gap between the results at the electoral booth and those of opinion polls can be explained by the sentiment of a segment of the public in favor of almost any form of arms control (Reagan's START proposal received almost as much support as the freeze). The act of voting requires at least somewhat more careful consideration of the merits of a proposal than being canvassed by a pollster. The lower levels of support found when people actually were asked to vote for the freeze, while still significant, fell somewhat short of the mandate that most in the peace movement thought they had from the public.

Many in the movement who thought that it would be possible to halt the arms race by working through Congress felt betrayed when the resolution that was eventually passed contained relatively weak language, and when many congressmen voted for both the resolution and for major weapons systems. In fact, the nonbinding version of the freeze resolution that passed the House of Representatives was probably all that could have been secured given the composition of the House at that time. One hundred eighty-six members voted for the

7. For an example of the negative reaction to this fear message see Coles 1985b.

8. Ironically, social psychologists have developed an appreciation of the role of hope—the expectation that significant change will occur—in sustaining social movements (Ennis 1987).

freeze resolution and against the MX. Their number could be considered as the maximum who voted for the freeze with the same intention as those in the peace movement, namely to end the nuclear arms race with the Soviet Union. An additional one hundred members voted both for the freeze and for the MX. In this respect, the freeze could claim a victory of sorts. Lobbying efforts were able to convey public sentiment in such a way that a significant proportion of the House voted for the resolution despite their inclination to support nuclear orthodoxy. Thus the May 1983 vote, while not a total victory, was nonetheless a realistic assessment of what was possible at that moment. The expectation that Congress would stop the arms race that year was unrealistic. What the organizational culture of the movement could not do was develop a strategy outlining what was immediately possible and what could be achieved over five years and more, and present those expectations to its constituency and to the press and media in a way that illuminated both near- and long-term progress toward the goal of ending the arms race.

In the final analysis, the movement did succeed in creating short-term opportunities for members of its constituency to express their desire for peace. Enabling people to participate directly is both a success in itself and a critical element in the development of a still stronger movement. Yet, in other ways, the internal culture of the movement and its organizational practices lacked the elements necessary to develop more influence. Failing to develop a coherent and appropriate strategy, the movement only rarely demonstrated the requisite patience or a sense of a longer time frame. The dilemma has been well stated by Pam Solo in the form of a question: "Can we inspire a social movement capable of generating sustained public support for a new vision of U.S. global responsibilities, with a specific political program and policy objectives to which we can hold decision makers accountable?" (1988:25). In my opinion, while the peace movement can in the future develop a more coherent strategy and provide important and necessary resources in the struggle for peace, limitations imposed by the very nature of social movements imply that a presidential campaign is an additional requirement for developing progressive policies and a vision of common security.

6. Peace movements can contribute to the formation of internal cleavages within the political elite. In general, policymakers do not regard peace movements and their leaders as legitimate. However, the influence of these movements may raise the costs of certain policies, in turn prompting

> those more sensitive to the constraints of popular pressures to distance themselves, either privately or publicly, from prevailing orthodoxy. The official dissenters command status and are respected by the press, the media, and specialized journals of opinion. Unlike those of movement leaders, these views "count." Elite opposition receives special attention and may even encourage a new round of popular dissent. The emergence of elite opposition reflects more deep-seated popular pressure.

The peace movement had one minor and one major impact on the deliberations of the Reagan administration. The minor impact involved the issue of INF deployment and its relationship to widespread political protest in Europe. Paul Nitze, who was conducting negotiations for the Reagan administration, felt that peace movement opposition constituted a political threat to NATO and the alliance structure, and that the United States had to back off from its commitment to deploy both Pershing IIs and GLCMs (Talbott 1984). Nitze advocated a compromise, known as the "walk in the woods" proposal because its was presented during an informal stroll with a Soviet negotiator, that would have permitted an equal number of GLCMs (ground-launched cruise missiles) and SS-20 warheads but no Pershing IIs. Nitze was opposed in his efforts by most of the Reagan administration and especially by Defense Department official Richard Perle. Perle felt that Washington should not bend to the European peace movement in any way, and that the Western European governments would be able to withstand political pressure and support deployment. Perle won the battle in the short run. No concessions were offered formally to Moscow, and deployment proceeded. Nitze and others, including Arms Control and Disarmament Agency Director Eugene Rostow, who also favored concessions to renew the arms control process and to undercut the strength of the European movements, either resigned or were marginalized within the administration. (The overall impact of the peace movement on the INF Treaty is more complex and is treated below.)

The major impact of the peace movement was on Ronald Reagan himself. The president's views on national security included both a deeply felt hostility toward the Soviet Union (the "evil empire" image) as well as a more idealist impulse that envisioned a world without nuclear weapons. Under Reagan, neither impulse enjoyed sophisticated elaboration, yet each was felt strongly by the President, and each was embodied in specific decisions and proposals. An indirect accomplishment of the peace movement was to alter the relative weight of these two images so that by the end of his term, Reagan was acting more on the idealist vision than on that of the Soviet Union as an evil empire. On one level, the motivation for this shift was political advantage. Given the strong expression of sentiment for peace that emanated from the movement, Republicans stood to do better electorally if Reagan moved away from an intractable stance against arms control. Favorable portrayal of the freeze movement in the media affected the White House and resulted in more moderate rhetoric. A similar element of political calculation can be seen in the program to develop the Strategic Defense Initiative and its promise of a world freed from the threat of nuclear missiles. But self-interest does not fully explain Reagan's shift. The peace movement forced Reagan to adopt arms control rhetoric, and to start a summit process that led to the leaders of the two superpowers' contemplating dramatic cuts in the nuclear arsenal. Thereafter, a new standard had been set for arms treaties. The political will for negotiations flowed from a political climate established by the peace movement, and from the interplay between political self-interest and Reagan's own vision of a world without nuclear weapons. Later, political vulnerabilities and low popularity ratings, especially during the "contragate" scandal (Cortright 1991), forced Reagan to act even more strongly on the more idealist subset of his own beliefs. In short, the peace movement forced Reagan to say yes to the more peaceful part of his own political and psychological composition. The INF Treaty was the result.

> 7. Another criterion for effectiveness is a more accommodating stance on the part of governmental authorities toward the challenging group. Gamson (1990:32) defines four possibilities: (*a*) "consultation" in which the views of members of selected peace movement organizations are actively solicited; (*b*) "negotiations" in which a government agency enters into discussions on a continual basis with a peace movement organization; (*c*) "formal recognition" in which the government recognizes the challenging group as a legitimate representative of a constituency; and (*d*) "inclusion" in which some members of the challenging group become members of the government organizational structure.

Peace movement recognition differs for the executive and legislative branches. From the executive branch, none of the four types of recognition was achieved. Nor could it be said that recognition from the executive branch was a significant goal of the peace movement. Relations between Congress and the peace movement are more complex. Initially, the movement placed priority on building up its local strength. The goal was to create an active bloc in each congressional district and only then to move on to the national level. The strategy of seeking immediate legitimacy from national authorities was viewed as a trap. But because the movement grew more rapidly than expected, adjustments were made in the original timetable. Senators Kennedy and Hatfield, as well as several liberal congressmen, were interested in the freeze as an important issue in itself, and as a factor that could enhance their own national prominence. In turn, the movement had to consider its working relations with Capitol Hill sooner than originally anticipated. In formal terms, extensive "consultation" and even "negotiation" occurred between movement leaders and members of Congress who sponsored the freeze resolution (Solo 1988; Waller 1987). Several staff members acted as liaisons between congressmen and leaders of the freeze movement.

Quite apart from efforts to develop and pass a freeze resolution, many moderate and even some radical peace movement organizations had good working relations with a significant portion of Congress. Since the movement did not set itself the goal of formal inclusion in the government policy-making process, the relationship with Congress was about as much as could be expected. At issue are the consequences of this "success" for the movement. On the positive side, the endorsement of leading congressmen brought more visibility to the movement and probably helped its recruitment efforts. The existence of a working relationship also made it more difficult for mainstream Democrats to dismiss the peace movement as dominated by "crazies" (as was common during the anti-Vietnam movement). These members were more likely to consider the merits of the freeze proposal than they would have been had the movement remained distanced from Washington. On the other hand, the early entry into national politics and the process of negotiating the passage of the freeze resolution commanded an increased proportion of movement resources, diluted the longer vision, and ensnared movement leaders in the technical details of verification. The movement was also forced to be defensive about keeping the freeze bilateral and cautious on the issue of whether the language of the resolution should be binding. All of this resulted in the sacrifice of both local political activity and the capacity of the movement to develop a strategy that went beyond the passage of the freeze resolution itself.

8. Peace movements can have an indirect effect on policy by transforming surrounding social conditions which may in turn influence the process of policy formulation. The impact of peace movements on targets of influ-

> ence operates not directly but through mediating elements. The benefits that trickle down to the constituency of the peace movement are not the same as originally conceived, but can still be significant. No theory can predict the precise ways that the original protest emanating from the movement will reverberate throughout other institutions. Methodologically, it becomes extremely difficult to isolate and measure the precise impact of the movement. Instead, peace movements and government policy coexist within a changing social context in which influence is mutual. The challenge is to detect the impact of peace movements behind the intermediate social filters.

As with the movement against the Vietnam War, the 1980s peace movement had several indirect effects on the overall context in which policy was formulated. The first of these is the reemergence of an antinuclear culture. A previous wave of antinuclear activism at the end of the 1950s was accompanied by critical films, such as *Dr. Strangelove*, and novels, such as Nevil Shute's *On the Beach*. Similarly, ABC's *The Day After*, its artistic merits aside, was shown to a large audience in November 1983 and touched a powerful nerve. Several popular films, each drawing on the public fear of nuclear war, followed. Jonathan Schell's 1982 book *The Fate of the Earth* became a best-seller and found a central place in teaching about the dangers of nuclear war. Significant elements of popular culture now reflected greater awareness of the danger of nuclear war and of the necessity of counting oneself in opposition to that possibility. Indifference and resignation were still present. But an additional impact of the peace movement was to raise expectations of what future arms control treaties would provide in terms of securing a more stable peace. The vision of a world without nuclear weapons has been brought closer. It is also likely, although it is impossible either to demonstrate or to disprove the point, that the movement has contributed to a stronger sense of collective identity and has thus, modestly, countered some of the excess individualism of the dominant culture.

Another indirect impact of the peace movement was on the university academy (Nusbaumer 1990). Shortly after the movement identified the threat of nuclear war as an urgent social problem, individual scholars responded with a new wave of important research. We now have more detailed historical studies of the development of strategic doctrine and nuclear weapons. Physicians have detailed the impact of nuclear weapons and the impossibility of mounting an effective medical response. The debate among strategic professionals intensified. Within the social sciences, chapters on militarism were included in social problems texts. Scientists began to explore new areas such as the possible impact of nuclear detonations on the global climate ("nuclear winter") and the possible psychological impact of the threat of nuclear war ("nuclearism"). Feminist approaches to war and peace issues were developed. Also within the academy, new joint projects involving Soviet and American scholars produced an academic version of global consciousness that worked against the Cold War order and Cold War scholarship. Finally, many peace studies programs emerged, as did new courses on peace and disarmament at the nation's colleges and universities. In general, these trends revealed renewed appreciation of the importance of war and peace issues as the central problem of our age.

9. The last criterion for measuring peace movement effectiveness is the degree to which conditions for a long-term change in policy have been established. In this case, the targets of influence are deeply ingrained institutional practices and ideological assumptions regarding the nature of national security. Examples of partial success might include, at the levels of both public and intellectual discourse, a deeper understanding of the roots of war and the emergence of coherent alternatives to prevailing concepts of security and defense. Policy formation over relatively long periods may also be affected by latent public opposition, or the potential for renewed mobilization against government decisions. Even where the visible strength of a social movement has receded, decision makers can be deterred from the commitment of military force by the anticipation of a new period of opposition. In this manner, social movements may affect policy formation even where the most visible manifestations of influence—large-scale demonstrations, fund-raising, petition drives, lobbying efforts, and membership in social movement organizations—are in apparent decline.

The classic example of the latent power of a peace movement is the "Vietnam syndrome," or the reaction to the defeat of the U.S. government that culminated in the April 1975 seizure of power by revolutionary forces throughout the southern part of Vietnam.[9] Both popular and elite disgust over Washington's failure—despite thirty years of effort, hundreds of billions of dollars, and the loss of close to sixty thousand Americans (let alone two million Vietnamese)—led to the inability of the executive branch to send U.S. ground troops into sustained combat when they might suffer more than minimal casualties.

---

9. Although I retain the term "Vietnam syndrome," I find something irksome about the implication that the unwillingness of Americans to support the blanket commitment of troops to overseas combat is some sort of "sickness" from which we will someday recover.

The constraints against U.S. military force under the Vietnam syndrome were not absolute. After the end of the war, naval and air power were exercised on several occasions. The Vietnam syndrome did not rule out small, short-term commitments of ground troops such as the invasions of Grenada and Panama. Nonetheless, public opposition to a major ground war did exclude the possibility of the direct use of U.S. military force to overthrow the government of Nicaragua. Until the Gulf War, the Vietnam syndrome was a significant restriction on the use of military force that had been imposed by the movement against the Vietnam War.

We will return to the Vietnam syndrome and examine the impact of the recent Gulf War on it, but first the long-term effects of the 1980s movement must be assessed. The antinuclear movement, while less successful in blocking specific weapons programs such as the MX missile or SDI, had a significant impact upon the parameters of the policy discussion, and opened up the possibility of meaningful reform. On the principal intellectual issues of strategic policy—such as the possibility of controlling and winning a nuclear war, the dangers associated with threatened first use, and damage that one does to one's own security by putting the other side's retaliatory forces at risk—the positions advanced by the peace movement acquired greater influence within the strategic community and among policymakers. A critique of U.S. nuclear policy had been formulated before the 1980s. But the influence of these criticisms spread considerably further in the context of the mobilization provided by the movement. Indeed, by the end of the decade, a credible defense of extended deterrence was difficult to find. Even former advocates of nuclear war–fighting capability distanced themselves from their previous positions. The intellectual credibility of counterforce and nuclear war fighting had weakened, and the concept that nuclear weapons carried political and military utility, while still present, had clearly become a minority position. Significant and balanced cuts in nuclear weapons has become the criteria for future arms control measures. Stronger, more informed support for arms control existed within Congress, and the continuation of major nuclear weapons systems took place more through inertia than strategic rationale.

Even before the transformation of the Eastern bloc, the peace movement had contributed significantly to a changed political environment that promoted new ideas of how a nation's security might best be achieved. It is now possible to conceive of a world where nuclear weapons do not play a significant political and military role.

There can be no doubt that the revolutionary changes now under way in the former Soviet Union and Eastern Europe have hastened this process. But the shift in the nuclear debate was already well underway by the time Gorbachev and Reagan initiated their series of summit meetings. The fundamental questions are now how to prevent the proliferation of nuclear weapons, and how to best carry out reductions. The political and military utility of nuclear weapons no longer occupies the center stage that it enjoyed earlier in the decade. This evolution stands as evidence of the impact of a movement on the language and practices of the Cold War.

A new component of the political culture of the United States has emerged and can be characterized by the term "nuclear Vietnam syndrome," or the inability of political and military leaders representing the old world order to launch a concerted effort to gain strategic superiority. The possibilities for funding another round of weaponry that would sustain counterforce and war-fighting strategies is extremely limited and will remain so. As with the Vietnam syndrome, important caveats remain. Nuclear weapons exist, and as long as they do, a danger of their use is still present. Additionally, the nuclear Vietnam syndrome is not an explicit alternative but more of a "proto-policy" representing latent opposition that will congeal against any effort to follow an ambitious modernization program. Washington can manipulate cuts in nuclear weapons without explicitly adopting the alternative policy of basic deterrence, which would make Americans more secure while saving a considerable amount of money (see Chapter 6). Nonetheless, the "syndrome" remains an effective obstacle to any attempt to resurrect Cold War policies.

What can be said in summary concerning the impact of the 1980s peace movement? Advocates of the "peace through military strength" security model identify the Reagan military buildup as the key influence on Soviet moderation in foreign policy and even on the motivation to begin domestic reform. In their view, U.S. fortitude, backed by strategic and conventional weapons modernization, promoted the transformation of the Eastern bloc and the eventual end of the Cold War (Krauthammer 1989; Weinberger 1990). This argument does not recognize the impact of the peace movement, both in the United States and in Europe, in bringing about the end of the Cold War. Many of changes in the Reagan administration occurred *before* the 1985 ascendancy of Gorbachev to political power. After 1983, official rhetoric on the possibility of winning a nuclear war was modified. In 1984, President Reagan announced his intention to resume arms control negotiations with the Soviet Union. And by 1985, defense spending had peaked in real dollars (Marullo and Meyer 1991). Each change reflected the influence of the 1980s peace movement, and each change had a positive impact on superpower relations. Moscow returned to the bargaining table *after* Ronald Reagan softened his rhetoric, not as a result of the nuclear weapons buildup. Furthermore, transnational alliances were built between those favoring a stronger peace policy in the West and those favoring a stronger commitment to human rights in the East. By establishing extensive contacts with East European reformers, Western peace activists drew attention to the problems of dissidents, provided a measure of protection for them, and furthered the process of democratization that was central to the end of the Cold War. Finally, several prominent foreign policy and defense advisors to Gorbachev have credited Western peace institutes as the source of ideas that inspired the concrete proposals that reflected "new thinking" in international relations. Western peace institutes were particularly influential in prompting Soviet "alternative" or "non-offensive" defense proposals, contributed to the growing Soviet disinclination to "bean counting" in determining the strategic weapons balance, and may have encouraged bold initiatives such as the unilateral moratorium on nuclear testing. Thus, the 1980s anti-nuclear movement constrained the Reagan military buildup and forced that administration back to the acceptance of arms control. The movement created a political environment in which the West chose to cooperate with rather than to exploit Soviet efforts at domestic reform. And the peace movement has brought new ideas on security and defense policy to the edge of the political mainstream. We turn now to a brief discussion of grassroots mobilization against the Gulf War.

The "Vietnam Syndrome" and the Movement Against the Gulf War

In the fall of 1990, movement activists mobilized against the prospect of U.S. military intervention in the Persian Gulf within a social context characterized by the Vietnam syndrome. An unanticipated consequence was the emergence of a strong nationalist sentiment with regard to casualties. A central theme of the prewar debate in Congress, in the press, and within the movement itself was the anticipated extent and public reaction to U.S. military casualties. This debate produced an opportunity for the Bush administration to fight the war in a way that preserved U.S. lives at the expense of Iraqis. The prolonged bombing before the final ground onslaught led to tremendous casualties (see Chapter 2). To some degree, the peace movement, while aware of the consequences, had trapped itself by focusing on the prospect of U.S. deaths. When the military cost turned out to be relatively low, the voice of movement opposition was considerably weakened. Two problems for peace movements are raised by this situation: first, how to project a globally based sense of morality while remaining effective within a particular domestic context; and second, how to avoid the unanticipated consequences of movement activity.

Together with the fear of the loss of human (American) life, other significant aspects of peace sentiment were present. Polls demonstrating public preferences to extend economic sanctions were summarized in the previous chapter. A core of experienced peace activists existed. Those from the Vietnam era were determined to avoid their earlier cultural and tactical mistakes and to appeal more effectively to the majority of the population. The movement was also more diverse than either the Vietnam or antinuclear movement.

At the same time, recent peace movements had not succeeded in creating more durable and powerful symbols of peace within popular culture that the movement against the Gulf War could draw upon. Such modifications in popular culture would have enabled Americans to see in other parts of the world a search for democracy and improved living conditions that expressed many of the very values that we already hold dear. The prevailing view of human nature is focused largely on our capacity to do evil. We could just as easily recognize our capacity to befriend others, to show compassion, and to recognize the common humanity in people who seem to be different from ourselves. Another peace element that the movement against the Gulf War might possibly have drawn on was people's confidence in conflict resolution mechanisms as opposed to models of security based on the concept of peace through strength. But faith in diplomacy and negotiation do not resonate as strongly as the belief in the efficacy of military force. Previous peace movements did not establish an appreciation of the connection between global peace and domestic renewal. Nor did much of the public feel dishonored by a national policy that killed more than one hundred thousand Iraqi women and children. As a result, the movement drew largely from the fear of what war might mean for individual Americans, rather than on the strength of more positive images of peace residing in the popular culture.

Thus, the possibilities in the period immediately prior to the Gulf

War were contradictory. On one side, the public was not enthusiastic about the prospect of war. In addition to the human toll, the prospective dollar cost seemed high when measured against pressing domestic priorities. Most citizens were not swayed by the appeals of the Bush administration predicated on self-interest. The public was not willing to go to war over the price and availability of oil. Only the moral argument, that Saddam Hussein represented such overwhelming evil that it became an obligation to oppose him, was convincing. Progressive political leadership could have appealed to these inclinations, and strengthened and legitimated them with expert opinion. *In fact, a careful explanation from a president of a policy of economic sanctions and diplomacy would have received as much support from the American people as did the initiation of Operation Desert Storm.* And yet the Gulf War had overwhelming support. Without political leadership, the fragmentary peace elements that existed within the populace were overwhelmed by nationalism and by presidential appeals to support the office. The media failed to offer any significant alternative presentation of the situation in the Gulf to supplement that offered by the administration. "Spectator militarism" also played a major role in muting those aspects of popular culture opposed to the initiation of war. The public—awed by the presentation of military technology, by the establishment of "us" versus "them" categories, by arguments that commitments, once made, should be seen through to the end, by the dazzle of power, by the vicarious pleasure of winning, and by the reassurance that the country was finally doing something effectively—demonstrated a capacity to turn a blind eye to the human consequences of war.

Until the initiation of war in January 1991, public sentiments regarding the prospect of war in the Gulf were roughly in balance. Among the population were strong advocates of a policy favoring economic sanctions, as well as those who felt strongly about the need to go to war to stop Saddam Hussein. Others were more ambivalent and expressed aspects of each side of the culture of peace and war. After the initiation of hostilities, however, the peace elements were virtually destroyed. The war produced a political and cultural warp in which the capacity of the organized movement to reach out beyond itself was reduced to virtual insignificance. Two congressional votes on President Bush's policy signified the rapid evaporation of peace sentiment. The first, taken just before the war, was a virtual dead heat. The second, taken a few days after the start of the bombing, provided virtually unanimous support for the war. Large demonstrations were organized in Washington, D.C., and on the west coast, but discussions with movement activists about this period contain a recurring theme: the number of individuals involved in organized activities before January, including demonstrations, teach-ins, petition drives, and letter-writing campaigns, dropped off precipitously after the war began. By the end of January, the majority of those who had been actively opposed to the war, let alone the public at large, were themselves silenced. For many, participation in the peace movement was reduced to bearing witness, to a moral act without any hope of immediate political impact.

In light of the self-consciously moderate stance of most of the movement, the treatment it now received from the country and established authorities was remarkable. Media coverage distorted the movement, either by ignoring it or by focusing upon people with unconventional dress engaged in unconventional behavior (such as burning a flag or blocking traffic in a major thoroughfare). A final media option was to provide "balance" by giving equal coverage to large antiwar and small pro-administration demonstrations. The majority of the public, awed by the fact that we were actually at war, became hostile to the movement. The moral certitude that sprang from opposition to evil was now applied against the movement itself.

Since the war, however, peace elements have gradually returned to the political surface. Public opinion polls have documented new doubts about the war. Negative legacies of war have been created: environmental destruction, control of the press, destruction of the civilian infrastructure, and postwar instability. How we remember the war is becoming more contested. From the standpoint of the history of peace movements in the twentieth century, the current "disappearance" of organized activity is unlikely to be permanent. Support for Operation Desert Storm materialized under special circumstances, and it is unlikely that the result will be undiscriminating public support for future military intervention. This brings us to the question of the future of the peace movement and its connection to progressive politics.

Movement Opportunities and a Vision of Peace

Students of social movements use the term "political opportunity structure" to describe the possibilities or social space for movements to grow (Tarrow 1989). As these opportunities change, the mobilized strength of peace movements may ebb and flow, even as the message of the movement remains essentially the same. Some opportunity structures are relatively stable and can be identified only through comparisons with other countries. The political institutions and culture of the United States, for example, make it relatively easy for citizens to participate in community activity and to gain access to local elected officials. Our system also contains a large amount of information that is available to the public, and permits a relatively broad range of political views to be expressed. The possibilities for public mobilization are always present. On the other hand, the same institutions and political culture effectively limit the chances of having a significant impact on national policy. Neither access nor freedom of expression guarantees influence. The result is a rather murky combination of opportunity and dispersion of the public will.

A second, more variable, opportunity structure for social movements is the emergence of a gap between administration policy and public opinion. Differences between policy and opinion become especially acute when no established organization or individual seems to be representing the public's point of view. The disjuncture can be further increased by visible actions taken by an administration. Political leaders can draw attention to issues in ways that encourage social mobilization. For example, in the early 1980s, the political opportunity for a peace movement was heightened, first, by the gap between the administration's nuclear war–fighting policy and public preferences for arms control; second, by the administration's rhetorical flourishes concerning the possibilities for fighting and winning a nuclear war; and third, by concrete choices, such as to renew efforts to provide a civil defense and to modernize the strategic arsenal. Other established political authorities, such as the Democratic party, were slow to take up the opposition to the Reagan Administration. The field was left open to the peace movement, which benefited from yet another opportunity structure: a network of organizers left by opposition to the Vietnam war and by the environmental movement of the 1970s.

Other opportunity structures affecting the growth of movements include publicity from media coverage, and the legitimation of movement positions by experts or scientists who convey them in a respected voice. The policy debate may deepen and the movement may broaden still further if the political elite splits under the pressure of public protest. The government's response, which can range from repression through partial co-optation to total acceptance, also affects the pace of movement development. In the case of the 1980s anti–

nuclear weapons movement, each factor favored early growth. By 1984, however, the political opportunities for continued growth were more restricted. The Reagan administration changed its rhetoric by dropping all references to the first and early use of atomic bombs, and moderated its previous critique of arms control. President Reagan also used the Strategic Defense Initiative to reassure at least some of the public that it might be possible to obtain protection from destruction by nuclear weapons. For the media, the movement became less interesting. Stories had been filed on New England town meetings, people chained to fences surrounding military bases, and grandmothers trekking to Washington, D.C., to participate in demonstrations. Now the media needed a new story, and the new moderation of the administration itself became that story. As far as the media was concerned, the movement was lost. The movement presence that the media had effectively established for the public earlier in the decade was now gone. For its part, the movement had to demonstrate its continued impact even as the most visible signs of successful mobilization were declining. This task proved to be daunting, in part because movement leaders seemed unaware that the conditions that had fostered the movement's growth had changed. While development of the strategic arsenal continued, the public's perception of an administration dedicated to building whatever weapons it possibly could had now been modified. The peace movement itself did not find much of a change in the policies of the Reagan administration, and tried to say as much. But the gap between the policies favored by public opinion and what the public thought were the new policies of the administration had been significantly reduced (Meyer 1990, 1991b).

What are the implications of this analysis of political opportunity structure for the future of the peace movement? Several of the elements that sustained the previous cycle of mobilization are unlikely to reappear. The end of the Cold War, with its emphasis on establishing a response to the Soviet threat, has changed the political terrain, both for Washington and for the peace movement. Administration rhetoric will probably be moderate. Nuclear arms control will seem to be proceeding, the number of nuclear weapons will decline, and the military budget will start to shrink. In other words, the factors that sustained recent U.S. peace movement mobilization—against a particular war, against a particular weapons system, against ominous administration rhetoric—will probably not return with the same strength. On one level, these developments are significant in themselves. They serve as an important legacy of peace movements and should be appreciated as such. But the near term will probably not offer the mobilization possibilities offered by a Vietnam or Gulf War, a new nuclear missile, or even a bellicose posture from a president. Given the startling changes underway in the former Soviet Union and Eastern Europe it is unlikely that a 1990s peace movement will be offered the "advantage" of opposing the old world order inclination to respond to a threat with visible military means. The question is stark: what role can a peace movement play during a period of relative peace?

The spread of peace, in the sense of the steady reduction of both the threat from the former Soviet Union and military tension between NATO and the Warsaw Pact, will be secured more by changing national images than by the activities of peace movements. Europe is now undergoing a convergence and within a decade the terms "East" and "West" will appear outmoded. Continuing to prepare for a massive land invasion, a task that consumes half of our military budget, seems foolish. Unfortunately, without a change in leadership, Washington will remain relatively passive with respect to the possibilities offered by the outbreak of peace. Defense spending will decline only marginally. Thus far, there is little indication that a program of global cooperation and domestic revitalization will originate from either Republicans or the more established Democrats.

Those acting in the name of peace must take up a broader agenda. A peace movement is still necessary to raise issues that are not generated by the political mainstream, cultivate the political will necessary to develop new national priorities, and build ties with other movements that seek progressive change. Despite its decline in numbers and visibility, in many respects the organizational structure of the peace movement remains intact. But its message must become more positive. Previously, the peace movement represented a groundswell of indignant opinion. The movement conveyed urgency from its large base to the press and media and to established politicians. It spoke for the public, which was greatly concerned about the threat of nuclear war. But the movement commodities of urgency, concern, and fear are no longer available. We are in the midst of a change to what might be called an "entrepreneurial" movement in which leaders and a relatively small core of activists speak for a constituency that is more distant. Issues and alternative policies are represented, but without the same intensity. This does not mean that the movement has no voice. Nor has its capacity to remobilize the public at some point in the future been lost. But the precipitating incidents that do occur must be used to give peace a positive connotation in the context of a redefinition of security. Opposition to particular aspects of the war system must be linked to a stronger economy, environmental protection, and, ultimately, to strengthening a culture that embodies a commitment to nonviolent conflict resolution. One important step in creating that vision—connecting peace issues with a more stable and just economy—is addressed in the next chapter.

Postscript: Comparison with (Former) West German Peace Movement

With respect to nuclear weapons, both the U.S. and West German peace movements of the 1980s were moderately effective. Their successes, while below the expectations generated during the height of the movement, were still greater than acknowledged by the prevailing orthodoxy, which held that their impact was minimal. With respect to overall influence, the two movements were similar in many ways. Each was internally diverse in terms of political goals and tactical orientation. Religious groups played a major role and the development of personal ethics was a significant component of both peace movements. While neither movement managed to impose its own preferred policy upon its political authority, each succeeded in making it impossible for conservative political forces to oppose a commitment to significant arms control once it emerged in the form of the INF Treaty. Even before the transformation of Eastern Europe and the Soviet Union, most of the population in both countries became tired of the Cold War, in no small measure due to the work of those who mobilized against nuclear weapons modernization. Explanations of the arms race focusing solely upon the responsibility of Moscow lost their appeal. In addition, in a way that is impossible to fix with precision but is nonetheless significant, both movements contributed to the growth of other reform movements. Finally, the activities of both movements encouraged millions of people to experience political life in a deeper, more profound fashion than merely voting for political candidates. In these respects, the antinuclear movements in both countries clearly embodied the themes of "new social movements" (Boggs 1986).

The most important difference between the U.S. and West German movements is the virtual absence in the United States of the Democratic party as either a participant or strategic focal point, and the deep involvement in West Germany of the Greens and the Social Democrats (SPD). The U.S. antinuclear movement developed quite apart from the Democratic party, except that occasionally, elected officials and their staff were the objects of lobbying efforts. Changes in the political platform of the Democratic party, including the eventual adoption of a pro-freeze plank, were not terribly significant. Party platforms are not very important in the American system, and there is little evidence that the Democratic party did anything to carry its new position to the electorate. The relative importance of political parties in Germany has important implications for the development of peace politics in the United States.

In West Germany, participation in the peace movement is correlated with post-materialist values (Rochon 1988; Mueller and Risse-Kappen 1987). However, post-materialist values did not by themselves determine the emergence of the peace movement. Ronald Inglehart points out that "the presence of postmaterialists would not automatically have generated the movement in the absence of those other [specifically political] factors. . . . But it does seem clear that the emergence of postmaterialism was one of the key conditions that facilitated the development of the peace movement and that enabled it to mobilize larger numbers of supporters than any of its various forerunners" (cited by Rochon 1988:37). Yet the role of party organization remains critical. Close to 50 percent of peace movement activists called themselves "fairly or very close to a party" while barely a quarter of those not joining the movement were close to a party (Rochon 1988:42).

The importance of party affiliation can be seen in two other areas. West German trade unions mobilized their constituents against INF deployments in the early 1980s within an organizational structure that was closely intertwined with the SPD. U.S. unions who encouraged their members to support the freeze campaign, including the Machinists, AFSCME, and the Hospital Workers, did so on their own (as opposed to in conjunction with either the AFL-CIO national organization or the Democratic party). In fact, the dissident elements that now exist within the AFL-CIO Executive Board, including those expressing a new desire to explore alternative concepts of security and to develop economic conversion, find themselves in opposition to precisely those elements of the AFL-CIO that are most closely associated with the core of the Democratic party.

Second, after the decline of the most visible features of the peace movement on both sides of the Atlantic, the strongest form of continued influence in Germany was the institutionalization of alternative policies within the Green and Social Democratic political parties. In fact, the official platform of the SPD changed dramatically in response to the pressures of the organized peace movement. Alternative policies were discussed in journals, newspapers, professional institutes and other forums affiliated with party structures; and the Greens and SPD have carried out extensive studies on alternative security and defense policies. Similar ideas were discussed in the United States, but the relevant forums were not affiliated with the Democratic party in any systematic way.

The greater importance of internal party politics in West Germany can be demonstrated with a brief history of the SPD's positions on nuclear weapons. Until the late 1950s, the SPD opposed the introduction of nuclear weapons to Europe. A resolution of May 1958 advocated the creation of a small professional army with no nuclear weapons. After the Bad Godesberg conference, however, the party moved toward the center of German politics, advocating a pro-West security policy which did rely upon nuclear weapons. Helmut Schmidt was among those instrumental in securing the change in policy. For the next twenty years, the SPD served as perhaps the most important political institution linking West Germany and NATO to Washington's nuclear policies (Blechman and Fisher 1988). The center and right factions of the SPD supported, despite the occasional quarrel, both the weapons systems that bolstered NATO's policy of flexible response, and efforts at regulating the arms race through arms control. Those supporting nuclear disarmament were marginalized. In the 1980s, the process was reversed. As public opposition to the deployment of Pershing II and GLCMs grew, the SPD, looking for new voters in the political territory between themselves and the Greens, moved to the left. At the Munich congress of April 1982, a majority of delegates, led by Erhard Eppler and Oskar Lafontaine, were convinced of the need to reject INF deployment. Party moderate Egon Bahr succeeded in delaying a decisive vote. But when the Free Democratic party left the governing coalition in favor of the Christian Democrats, and with the SPD no longer in office, long-standing opposition to deployment could not be denied any longer. Schmidt was forced from his leadership position. During the summer and fall of 1983, many SPD regional assemblies voted against deployment; overall party opposition to the European missiles was finally formalized in Cologne in November 1983. Policy was now determined by a coalition of the left and center factions of the political party.

In fact, the very concept of achieving arms control through the elimination of an entire category of weapons that was enshrined in the

INF Treaty can be traced back to political pressures operating in the SPD. Discontent within the party over the possible deployment of Pershing II and cruise missiles can be detected as early as 1979. At the SPD's special anti-missile congress in Cologne, the party leadership reacted critically to Schmidt's report of Carter's plans for new missile deployment in Europe. In response to these criticisms, Schmidt established the so-called double-track proposal which simultaneously called for deployment on the one hand, and arms control negotiations which in theory could prevent deployment on the other. Given the intransigence of Soviet diplomacy at that time, conservatives on both sides of the Atlantic felt confident that Moscow would never accept the West's formal offer in which the Soviet Union would have to remove its already deployed SS-20s in exchange for cancelation of still-to-be-deployed INF missiles. In the immediate sense, the conservatives were right and INF deployment proceeded. Later, the political will to engage in arms control emerged from the respective needs of the two superpowers, and culminated in the INF Treaty. The structure of that agreement, which removed all intermediate-range missiles (and short-range as well) can be traced back to internal SPD opposition to continued nuclear modernization by NATO (Risse-Kappen 1988). The peace movement forced Reagan to say yes to his own proposal. That proposal, in turn, emanated from arms control imperatives within the SPD. In contrast, the role of the Democratic party in the United States, either on its own or through interaction with the organized movement, was minimal.

Other contrasts exist between the United States and Germany, although they do not have as large an impact as political parties. With the exception of retired naval officers who staff the Center for Defense Information in Washington, D.C., military officers in the United States have not played a role in opposing nuclear orthodoxy. In Germany, the peace movement itself included former military officers such as General Gert Bastian, who in November 1980 joined in the Krefeld Appeal which gathered approximately two million signatures against missile deployment. Former Bundeswehr officers with extensive knowledge of NATO, including Alfred Mechtersheimer and Count von Baudissin, also contributed to the delegitimation of INF and to the credibility of alternative defense concepts. The development of "counter defense experts," or professionals capable of legitimating the positions of the peace movement, was also more extensive in West Germany. Peace research institutes played a more prominent role. Journalists, editors, and other media experts presented alternative views on defense in mainstream forums far more extensively than in the United States. Through these means, broader questions of alternative defense, alternative security, economic conversion, as well as the relationship between the arms race and Third World development were gradually brought more to the center of public discussion.

The general weakness of political parties as vehicles for policy debates in the United States has two consequences for the possible emergence of progressive politics. The first is the continued need for a social movement to advance new ideas and perspectives that will not, in the normal course of events, come from forums within the Democratic party. The second is the necessity of a presidential campaign to clearly articulate those new issues and present them to the public through the press and the media. The Democratic party is not the repository of the political will necessary to carry out this crucial function.[10]

10. This is not to exclude the Democratic party entirely. One might expect the policy forums that now exist in the national (and some local) party organizations to become more important if progressive politics do develop.

5

Developing a Peace Economy

We're not talking about a fundamental realignment of Government. Most of the money [the peace dividend] must go for deficit reduction.
—*Charles Schultze, former chairman of the Council of Economic Advisers*

I don't think the benefits from winning the Cold War should go to the Government. [We should reduce taxes instead.]
—*Senator Phil Gramm (R–Tex)*

It isn't communism that's threatening us. It's the problems of our cities.
—*Representative Charles Rangel (D–N.Y.)*

DOES THE near collapse of the state-dominated economies of Eastern Europe and the former Soviet Union reinforce the central role of market forces in determining a modern economy? To supporters of such a claim, state planning interferes with the more rational self-corrections that stem from the pursuit of self-interest. Decisions made without government interference provide for innovation, smoother resource allocation, greater efficiency, and a better standard of living. Preserving the freedom of the marketplace is the key element in any program of economic prosperity. Homilies invoking Adam Smith's "invisible hand" have accompanied the end of the Cold War. In fact, such rhetoric only reinforces the distortions in the U.S. economy and furthers the slow deterioration of economic security that characterizes the end of the old world order.

Understanding the implications of the breakdown of the Eastern bloc and deciding how best to build on the strengths of the U.S. economy are not simple, if only because a pure market economy has never existed. All economic systems contain some conscious coordination and planning. Even that of the United States, which lies at the minimalist end of the spectrum of state intervention, provides many adjustments to the decision making of the invisible hand. The federal government offers subsidies, preferential tax treatment, and other incentives that favor particular sectors of the economy including air lines, tobacco, agriculture, nuclear power, privately owned single-family houses, and those industries most directly connected with military production.[1] The federal government also encourages particular kinds of investments over others. During the 1980s, the combination of tax cuts for business and government deficit financing produced a wave of corporate mergers, a boom on Wall Street, speculation on rapidly rising international debt, disinvestment in key industries and regions of the country, and the acquisition of key economic assets and real estate by foreign buyers. Bond sellers benefited; basic manufacturers suffered. Condominium development and golf course construction grew, while the stock of affordable housing shrank and cities were forced to reduce many critical services including public education and recreation. The classic refrain "the rich got richer and the poor got poorer" applies more to the last ten years than to any other decade in recent history (Phillips 1990). These consequences flowed from specific government decisions even while the architects of this policy asserted a philosophy of economic noninterference. The thesis that the principal economic developments of the 1980s were the natural consequences of market forces is far from the truth.

Government subsidies and other forms of incentives are not inherently evil. The point is that they do exist—even in the United States. Once this fact is acknowledged, a key question becomes how to determine the goals of government intervention in the economy. The issue raised by the end of the Cold War has all too often been presented in the United States as a choice between command economies on one hand and free market forces on the other. In fact, because of the economic decay that accompanied the last twenty years of the Cold War, the issue should be determining the relative mix between market in-

1. A recent example of the Pentagon's de facto industrial policy was a $100 million annual commitment to an industrial research consortium called Sematech, which was designed to keep U.S. semiconductor manufacturers competitive. The Defense Department also provided $30 million a year to support the development of high-density television, and the Defense Manufacturing Technology Program provided $170 million a year to support the development of a range of industrial techniques including welding and automated inspection of engine parts.

centives and planning that can establish a stronger economic future. Are our priorities to be the accumulation of private wealth, the extension of social inequality, and the preservation of the sectors of the economy currently privileged by government largesse? Or are the priorities to be good jobs, greater equality, environmental protection, and a healthy mix of basic industry, high technology, and post-industrial services? Instead of focusing on the economic winner of the Cold War, we should decide what can be done to reverse the ongoing erosion of U.S. economic strength. The argument of this chapter is that a sizable peace dividend and the adoption of economic conversion are opportunities to address our social problems and to revitalize the economy in ways that meet the long-term interests of Americans.[2] The global transition from the old to the new world order should be matched by new ways to obtain economic security at home.

The Peace Dividend

The end of the Cold War has brought the prospect of a significant reduction in the military budget. In considering the size of the resulting "peace dividend" as well as the objectives to which the resulting savings might be applied, it is best to start with some basic facts. The current military budget is roughly $300 billion, or slightly more than 5 percent of the gross national product.[3] Military activity directly employs 6.5 million civilian and military personnel. Of these, 2 million are uniformed members of the armed forces, 1 million are civilians working on military bases, and 3.5 million are civilians working in military-supported industries. To determine the overall impact of military spending, economists usually assume a multiplier effect of one to one whereby each job in the defense sector indirectly supports another job in the rest of the economy. As a result, another 6.5 million are employed indirectly by military spending. The total of 13 million jobs in a work force of roughly 100 million is significant from any standpoint.

The debate accompanying the end of the Cold War has produced

---

2. Economic conversion means the "political, economic, and technical measures for assuring the orderly transformation of labor, machinery and other economic resources now being used for military purposes to alternative civilian uses" (Melman 1989).

3. In World War II, military spending reached 39 percent of the GNP. During the Korean War it was 13 percent, and during the height of the Vietnam War it was 10 percent. At the high point of the Reagan administration buildup, military spending was 7 percent of the GNP.

three positions on the future of military policy. The principal issues in this debate are: first, the size of the military budget; second, the extent to which we should overhaul our defense policies in response to changes in the post–Cold War era; third, to what use the savings from the military budget should be applied; and fourth, whether the United States should initiate a deliberate program of economic conversion. The first position, endorsing the status quo, covers a narrow range between the official position of the Bush administration, usually expressed by Secretary of Defense Richard Cheney, and that of moderate Democrats in Congress, often represented by Senator Sam Nunn or Representative Les Aspin. Essentially, this position continues to advocate as large a military budget as politically possible, rejecting significant readjustments in response to changes in the world situation.[4] In both the Republican and the Democratic versions of minor cuts, virtually every weapons system currently under production would continue. Instead, the focal point of reduction is manpower, with the number of active duty military personnel scheduled to decline to 1.65 million in 1995 (or roughly 20 percent from 1990) (Department of Defense projections in Defense Budget Project 1991). The Office of Management and Budget estimates defense outlays in fiscal year 1996 at $293 billion (in 1990 dollars), down only $6 billion from the $299 billion spent in 1990.[5] When inflation is taken into account, the administration's proposed defense budget will decline by only 14 percent over five years. No special action is contemplated to protect individuals and communities that would be hurt by whatever gradual reductions are made. The Economic Report of the President finds that "programs are in place to help workers and communities adjust to reductions in defense employment" (1991:153).

The second position calls for a cut in the defense budget by 50 percent over the rest of the decade. A *New York Times* editorial, based

---

4. Cheney has called for an annual decline in the Pentagon budget of 2 percent after adjustments for inflation. Most of Cheney's announced cuts, especially that of $180 billion between 1992 and 1994, are in fact only reductions from previously requested increases. Nunn and Aspin anticipate somewhat larger immediate cuts with slow reductions over the rest of the decade.

5. These figures do not include the cost of the Persian Gulf War, for which Congress voted a supplemental authorization of $17 billion. (Other countries have pledged payments toward a total cost estimated at between $45 billion and $70 billion.) Other costs that do not appear in the official Department of Defense budget, including veteran's benefits, the production of nuclear warheads (in the budget of the Department of Energy), the "black budget" for covert operations, and the military's share of interest on the federal debt, bring *actual* U.S. military spending in 1991 to $415 billion (Center for Defense Information 1991).

on the work of William Kaufmann (1990a), has gathered the most attention in elucidating this position. Kaufmann anticipates a three-stage reduction from the fiscal 1990 total of $300 billion: to $265 billion in 1994, to $251 billion in 1997, and to between $160 billion and $195 billion in 2000 (all figures are in 1990 dollars).[6] The two areas singled out for sizable cuts are nuclear forces, which according to Kaufmann are now costing $30 billion more than necessary, and those forces no longer required to defend Western Europe against an attack by the Warsaw Pact. Our military commitments to Western Europe currently cost about $125 billion, of which Kaufmann argues no more than $22 billion are necessary to maintain a significant presence (1990b). The Kaufmann plan would still provide for flexible, mobile forces capable of being deployed rapidly, and for continued research in new weapons technology. The cumulative savings are about $500 billion over the decade.

An additional feature of this second position is the need to develop new and explicit security requirements for the United States in the post–Cold War world. The existing pattern of incremental decision making should be jettisoned and replaced by a careful review of the new security requirements of the United States. The principal military threat is no longer the Soviet Union, and the main geographic area that needs defending is no longer Europe. Military policy should not reflect bureaucratic inertia but, instead, should respond to new forms of instability located primarily in developing countries. Finally, the *New York Times* calls for investing the peace dividend in two principal areas: human resources and public infrastructure, especially the deteriorating transportation system.[7] The need for economic conversion is not addressed.

The third position on defense policy and military spending supports the goal of building a genuinely new world order and revitalizing progressive politics in the United States. Two examples, the Quality of Life Budget of the Congressional Black Caucus (1990) and the

---

6. A 50 percent cut over the rest of decade has been supported by several other studies including that of the World Policy Institute (1989), and by a group headed by the former assistant secretary of defense, Lawrence Kolb, and former CIA director William Colby (Cain and Golding 1990).

7. The editorial noted that "a billion dollars would give comprehensive prenatal health care to an additional 1.5 million poor pregnant women. An additional billion would add 400,000 children to Head Start which, though widely successful, still reaches only one eligible child in five. . . . Urban areas now experience two billion hours a year of highway delays. Flight delays at 21 primary airports amount to 20,000 hours a year."

Economic Policy Institute (Faux and Sawicky 1990), call for cuts in the military budget that are even deeper than those proposed by the *New York Times*/Kaufmann plan.[8] But the distinguishing feature is the priority of developing a peace economy. The Congressional Black Caucus budget provides for an immediate defense budget cut of $27.4 billion, which would be devoted to education, health, employment projects, job training, and fighting drugs.[9] Cuts of significant magnitude raise the possibility of significant disruptions to key industries, regions, and communities. In response, peace activists have suggested a program of economic conversion that would ease the transition process (Dumas and Thee 1989; Gordon and McFadden 1984; Melman 1989, 1990). The proposed legislation that best captures the themes of economic conversion is the Defense Economic Adjustment Act (sponsored by Representative Ted Weiss, D–N.Y.). The act would require the establishment of labor-management alternative-use committees at large and medium-sized military facilities and would also mandate decentralized planning, training, and income support during a period of transition. The act is primarily defensive in the sense that it provides only for the protection of those communities that would be hurt by defense reductions. A more difficult, but also necessary, project is the identification of a peace dividend and economic conversion with a comprehensive program to revitalize U.S. society.

Projects Toward a Peace Economy

The United States must conduct a thorough reassessment of its future defense requirements. And the need to apply the peace dividend to specific domestic areas such as education and transportation is pressing. But it is unlikely that sufficient political will to enact drastic cuts in defense spending can be generated solely by the prospect of a rationally conceived post–Cold War defense policy. A politically useful

8. Jeff Faux and Max Sawicky of the Economic Policy Institute (1990) call for cutting the defense budget in half, not over the decade but in five years. This would produce, in contrast with the anticipated savings of $500 billion over the rest of the decade in the Kaufmann proposal, a savings of $1.5 trillion. The Center for Defense Information (1992) has proposed reducing military spending to $104 billion by the end of the century.

9. The National Commission for Economic Conversion and Disarmament (1990) proposed the following allocation from a peace dividend of $165 billion: $30 billion for housing and education; $26 billion for repair of roads, bridges, and water and sewer systems; $23 billion for educational needs; $17.5 billion for radioactive waste cleanup; $16 billion for toxic waste cleanup; $12.5 billion for health care costs; and $10 billion for electrification of the U.S. rail system.

vision of what Americans can expect from a new world order must be created before a significant peace dividend can be realized. Most U.S. citizens feel that improved relations between the United States and the Soviet Union can open the way for significant cuts in military spending. By a wide margin they want to apply this peace dividend to fighting problems at home (62 percent) rather than cutting taxes (10 percent) or reducing the federal budget deficit (21 percent) (*New York Times* 1990b). The strategy of mentioning specific projects to which the peace dividend could be applied, however, is by itself insufficient. Reducing the defense budget and adopting a program of economic conversion must do more than save particular communities. A clear identification of peace with rebuilding the economic strength of the United States is necessary if more than incremental cuts in the defense budget are to be achieved. At bottom, a true peace dividend will be not a certain number of dollars but a concerted strategy that will restore the vitality of the United States. Creating a new world order should be linked to creating a new domestic order.

U.S. citizens consistently identify the strength of the economy as the most important issue facing the country. We want to feel economically secure, and we want to think that the future holds at least as much promise for our children as it offers us. Peace politics cannot jeopardize the considerable accomplishments that our market-based society has already created. Proponents of economic and political change must be able to demonstrate that their specific proposals represent the best method of preserving those accomplishments, as well as the best path for extending them into the future. In blunt political terms: Polls consistently demonstrate that a majority of Americans are concerned most of all with better economic management. While the values of most Americans are consistent with a new world order and domestic reform, perceived pocketbook interests lead a significant proportion of the population to side with more conservative economic philosophies. A progressive political movement must be able to demonstrate that it represents fine values, and it must be able to demonstrate that its concrete programs will produce a sound economy that will best secure the future for Americans. In this respect, the possibility of a dramatic reduction in the defense budget raises the specter of disruption to businesses, employees, and local communities. For example, African Americans represent 12 percent of the population but form 21 percent of the armed forces and 28 percent of the army. Budget cuts and reductions in the armed forces without compensation through employment programs would only exacerbate an already difficult situation for many communities of color. At a minimum, economic conversion presents options for districts threatened by military base closings. Economic conversion can also address universal interests, not only by revitalizing the economy in such a way that all can benefit, but also by restoring the concept that it is possible to pursue the public good in public life.

The core issue raised by economic conversion is the relationship between democratic planning and markets. Most existing markets are either already saturated or, given foreign competition, simply not attractive from the standpoint of conventional profitability. What sense does it make to adopt a program of economic conversion if new enterprises are incapable of finding a profitable niche? The possibilities for exploiting current opportunities *are* limited, or they would already have been seized by existing aggressive and well-diversified companies. For example, there are currently only two factories where tanks are made in the United States. One is in Lima, Ohio, the other in Warren, Michigan; both are owned by General Dynamics. If nothing interferes with the army's plans to phase out tank production, General Dynamics will close a division that now employs 7,300 people. "What can you do with a tank factory?" asks Michel Wynne, a vice president of General Dynamics. "You can make tractors and heavy earth-moving equipment, but Caterpillar already has that market sewed up. If there is no defense work to support these factories, then we'll have no alternative but to give them up" (in Uchitelle 1990). Shipbuilding is another example. A virtual end to the construction of navy warships will bring dislocations. A logical substitute might be to build civilian freighters. But a competitive civilian shipbuilding industry is not easily achieved given the cost and productivity advantages of foreign shipyards. Most dedicated defense plants cannot be converted easily, as long as short-term profitability remains the criterion for performance. Exceptions may exist, of course. One of the most interesting possibilities is that of converting nuclear missiles for peaceful use rather than destroying them outright (Potter and Florini 1988). Existing tankers might be retrofitted with double hulls to provide stronger environmental protection. Diversification may enable some companies to develop new products for new markets. But overall, the process of conversion cannot be presented as simply taking advantage of existing market opportunities that otherwise are being ignored. For the most part, transformed defense plants will not fit easily into the current economy.

The size of the peace dividend, even in its most generous form, is also small relative to the demands that could be placed on it. The total cost of repairing the nation's roads, bridges, highways, waterways and sewer systems alone has been placed at between $3 trillion and $5 trillion, or more than twice the most optimistic estimate of a possible savings from the defense budget over the remainder of the decade. A peace dividend will not come close to providing the funds necessary to meet domestic needs. Instead, the peace dividend (a source of money) and economic conversion (a plan of what to do with it) should be devoted to specific projects that will promote a strategy for developing a more just and secure economy. The image of economic conversion should be one of deepening the public interest by laying the base for future areas of strength in the economy. Economic conversion could be used to explore the interaction between continued market incentives and the redirection of investment and other economic resources toward projects in the general public interest. The old order relies on the image of a market economy that sets winners up against losers and calls the result efficiency. Peace can become identified with specific projects that carry economic benefits while reestablishing working relationships that enable people to succeed with each other. Thus, conversion is not only about economics in a narrow sense. As a political symbol, the realization of a peace dividend becomes a method to counter the ongoing process of decay and enables Americans to pull together and to share a strong sense of mission.

Economic Conversion and Strengthening the Manufacturing Base

Economic conversion provides an opportunity to counter deindustrialization, or the relative decline in investment in the economy's basic production industries.[10] Deindustrialization has led not only to losses in employment and reduced wage scales but to the disruption of community life as well (Bluestone and Harrison 1982; Eitzen and Zinn 1989). The application of economic conversion and part of the peace dividend to efforts to reverse this process does not assume that we must restore an economy based fully on manufacturing. But the United States cannot afford to give up on manufacturing either. Economic conversion should not focus exclusively on the preservation of traditional industries—auto, steel, rubber, and glass—and preserving

10. As a percentage of gross national product, manufacturing output fell from 22 percent in 1977 to 18 percent in 1988 (Office of Technology Assessment 1988).

traditional levels of employment. This strategy would be too backward and might even invoke economic protectionism. The commitment to manufacturing cannot be all-encompassing. Thus, the process of determining priorities for economic conversion can also help balance the goals of preserving a strong manufacturing base and strengthening other forms of post-industrial economic activity.

Why is manufacturing such a critical component of a strong economy? Historically, manufacturing has provided wages at the center of the social stratification system.[11] Preservation of this employment base will counter the current trend toward polarization in both income levels and job skills. The service economy creates a few relatively well paid and skilled professional, technical, and managerial positions, but many more jobs demanding less skill and paying little money. Rather than providing economic security and leisure time for all, the service sector has reinforced existing social and economic inequities. A strategy of strengthening manufacturing industries in some communities will help counter the social bifurcation now taking place in the United States.

In addition, productivity gains from innovation in manufacturing have generated broad-based growth for the rest of the economy and are another reason to support programs that will strengthen the production of durable goods. A considerable proportion of employment in the service sector is created by developments in manufacturing (Cohen and Zysman 1987). Healthy manufacturing industries capable of exporting products also contribute to the country's balance of payments. It is extremely unlikely that the United States will be able to export services on a scale that will significantly reduce our currently large trade deficit.

Finally, economic conversion could sponsor efforts to better synthesize research and development with the actual industrial engineering of new products. Experts who have examined efforts to improve the productivity of the American economy often focus on the negative impact of the current practice of separating research and development from innovation in manufacturing (Brooks and Branscomb 1989; Reich 1989a, 1989b). In fact, it is in the integration of technical development with manufacturing that the Japanese have been able to demonstrate stronger strategies than the United States. Adeptness in producing durable goods continues to be critical for sustaining com-

11. In 1984, total compensation for manufacturing workers averaged $28,700 while total compensation for service workers was only $22,900 (Miller and Castellblanch 1988).

petitiveness in the world economy, improving our productivity, and maintaining social equity. Economic conversion provides an opportunity to strengthen this critical part of our economy.

Economic Conversion and Environmental Protection

The reduction of the defense budget also presents an opportunity to develop ecologically sustainable technologies. Equipment for monitoring pollution levels or enforcing new government standards could be developed and sold in newly created markets, thus providing additional employment. In both Japan and Sweden, new environmental programs created additional demand in the chemical and construction industries (Geiser 1984). But the potential for economic conversion goes well beyond the creation of new pollution-control technologies. As defense plants are reconfigured for civilian use, new technologies and methods of structuring work relations could be explored by promoting ecological sustainability within the production process itself.[12] The implications extend far beyond energy conservation or other measures that would improve the efficiency of the production process. At bottom, thinking through how work might be organized better in order to preserve the environmental security of future generations may also challenge the existing relationships between authority, the division of labor, and the concentration of knowledge. In this regard, economic conversion projects could also encourage greater worker initiative and enhanced productivity through worker democracy. In fact, environmentally conscious work designs may be dependent, ultimately, upon greater worker participation.

Investing in Education

Education is another important priority for the peace dividend. Our future security depends upon developing a more skilled and motivated work force. It is symbolically and politically important to rededicate ourselves to the importance of education for our citizens. This priority is likely to receive support from many segments of the political establishment. The National Governors' Association, for example, has called for a ten-year program to "set a new standard for an educated citizenry" while urging "the president and Congress to dedi-

12. Environmental sustainability can be defined as the development of economic and social practices that do not compromise the quality of life of future generations.

cate the peace dividend in a balanced manner among the federal budget deficit, education, and productive investments." It would take another $20 billion annually for the United States to spend as a proportion of our GNP what the average industrialized country allocates for primary and secondary education. In addition, some of the actual physical facilities now used by the Pentagon could be converted to use for adult education and job retraining.

Job Retraining

Supporters of economic conversion have often pointed to the need to retrain military engineers and managers, whose thinking about product development and cost strategies is entirely different from that of the civilian sector (Dumas 1986; Melman 1983, 1985). In military production, the government is the only customer. And that customer is guaranteed regardless of the eventual cost of the final product. The defense contractor is not in a competitive situation where product quality and price determine sales. Instead, the government's choice of defense contractors seems to be determined more by timing in the weapons acquisition cycle and by political positioning (Adams 1981; Rosen 1977). A defense contractor can always pass along additional costs to the government. Moreover, product quality is usually measured by optimum performance under optimum conditions. Simplicity and reliability are less important criteria in defense production than in the civilian sector. The Pentagon's acquisition system encourages a company to seek an additional 10 percent in performance even if this drives up the price by 50 percent. Because of these deeply ingrained practices, a substantial commitment may have to be made to enable engineers and management to work effectively in the civilian sector.[13]

While retraining white-collar, professional, and technical workers currently employed in the defense sector is an important goal, those cannot be the only occupational categories favored by economic conversion. Facilities and funds freed by the peace dividend should be applied to other job retraining efforts. The development of a peace economy must provide clear means of obtaining economic security for all citizens, not only for those already favored by their occupations in the defense sector. At a minimum, economic conversion must be at-

---

13. These goals for economic conversion can be linked. For example, retrained engineers could serve as consultants for efforts to configure economic activity aimed at pollution control or environmental enhancement.

tached to the goal of full employment. Unions should also perceive a clear stake in a program of economic conversion (Clark 1990; Gordon and McFadden 1984; Winpisinger 1982).

Urban Areas

Many feel that the central cities will play less and less of a role in our economic future. More people live in the suburbs, and new factories and other types of workplaces are more likely to be located on the periphery of the metropolis than at the core. New communications technologies make it no longer necessary for companies to be located close to each other. Schools, recreational facilities, and the overall quality of life seem to be better outside of the urban areas. Those who can move do so. What they leave behind is a concentration of poverty, crime and violence, an energetic drug trade, declining social services, and, in many places, a feeling of total cynicism regarding the chances of equal participation in the existing range of social opportunities. Cities are in decline.

Of the 335 metropolitan areas in the United States, 250, or roughly three-quarters, pay more in taxes to support military expenditures than they receive in return in the form of contracts, salaries, and facilities (Anderson 1991). The attempt to fulfill the national security requirements of the old world order has contributed to the economic decline of many of our cities as well as to the decline of living conditions for many of the people living in them. Banks have collected interest money from inner-city residents, sometimes through fraudulent secondary mortgage schemes. As with loans to Third World countries whose interest is being paid primarily by the poor, these same banks have failed to channel investment to those areas where the cycle of poverty could be broken. The application of part of the peace dividend to the renewal of the most stricken neighborhoods in our metropolitan areas raises the question of the relationship between peace politics and race and poverty. The current orientation of many Democratic candidates is to try to woo middle-class voters back from the Republican party, primarily by promising tax relief. Those in poverty, many of whom do not vote, and residents of inner cities are not the focus of these appeals. In many respects, inner cities and their residents have become the subjects of the same "enemy images" that are normally reserved for foreign threats. But large investments in cities are important both for their inhabitants and for the country as a whole. For example, if we are to overcome the environmental hazards that accompany the automobile, we must develop new light-rail transportation systems within cities, high-speed rail between cities, and employment patterns that do not require endless driving and time wasted in traffic jams. Cities are more energy efficient than suburbs. It is certainly less expensive to encourage the renewal of housing stock in cities and provide for new employment opportunities through federally directed investment than it is to pay the currently escalating costs of police, prisons, and other mechanisms of social control. We all suffer from the pervasive fear of crime and the deterioration of the quality of life in our cities. A report of the United States Conference of Mayors argues that, despite the revolution in information technologies, the face-to-face encounters provided by the physical density of cities are the basis for creativity and innovation that benefit all of us. A program of federal investment in our cities does not have to be centrally run and bureaucratically directed. Indeed, decentralization and reliance on community initiative is probably the only way to make a program of urban renewal work. Here as well, strengthening the sense of collective interest and the moral commitment to provide opportunities for everyone to better themselves is a essential part of peace politics.

International Development and Trade

In a global economy, prosperity is partly dependent on the ability to be competitive in the international market. Already, more than one-quarter of the manufactured goods that are consumed in the United States are produced abroad. It is not likely that this figure can be dramatically reduced, and it should not be a goal of economic conversion to reduce it. Indeed, protectionist measures designed to restore a larger share of manufacturing to the United States carry the danger of setting off trade wars. At the same time, economic conversion should be an important part of an overall strategy to regain strength in at least some industries that can export goods and help with current balance of trade problems.

In addition to supporting our export capabilities, the peace dividend should be allocated in part to developing countries. Despite the general lack of public support for international economic assistance, it is important to devote a modest number of economic conversion projects to strengthening local markets in developing countries. As argued in Chapter 1, our economic and ecological security can be enhanced by encouraging the kind of global development that will reduce poverty overseas and lead to added demand for our exports. A 1988 study by the Overseas Development Council found that a recovery of economic growth rates in less developed countries to the levels of the 1970s would produce an additional $32 billion a year in U.S. export earnings (*Boston Globe*, June 10, 1990). The result would be millions of jobs in the United States, many of which would be in the manufacturing sector. Under the right circumstances, improvements in wages, purchasing power, and living standards in developing countries are also in the ecological interest of the United States because they can provide an alternative to desperate—and destructive—methods of surviving. Many prevailing practices in developing countries, born of poverty, threaten our own long-term safety. Support for international development thus serves our own interests and helps concretize the connection between U.S. and global security.[14]

Public Investment and Productivity

For economists, the central issue in the allocation of resources is determining the four-way trade-off among consumption, investment, defense, and debt servicing. Suppose we decide that a larger commitment to investment is necessary. The question then becomes the source of the additional funds. In general, the preference of business would be to fund investment by lowering consumption (read: the standard of living) through reduced government spending and higher taxes on individuals. Economic conversion, however, is a way of explicitly linking reduced defense spending to increased public investment. As Robert Heilbroner recently pointed out: "The peace dividend is a once-in-a-lifetime opportunity to restore the nation's infrastructure to its level in the 1960s, without new taxes or new borrowing" (Uchitelle 1990).

Investment in public capital is strongly connected to increased investment in the private sector and increased productivity (Faux and Sawicky 1990; Heilbroner 1991). Yet, since 1970, the increase of public capital stock has averaged only 1.6 percent compared with a 4 percent annual growth rate between 1950 and 1970. Japan achieved a 5.1 percent growth rate in public investment between 1973 and 1985. Alicia Munnell, chief economist of the Federal Reserve Bank of Bos-

---

14. Obviously, debt relief for developing countries is also an important step, although the scale of the problem (now more than one trillion dollars) prohibits a solution stemming from the peace dividend in the United States.

ton, concludes that the "drop in labor productivity has not been due to a decline in the growth of some mystical concept of multifactor productivity or technical progress. Rather, it has been due to a decline in the growth of public infrastructure" (1990). The U.S. Department of Transportation has estimated that in 1985 total vehicle delays on the highways reached 772 million hours, and that this already alarming figure will rise further if a concerted program to improve our roads is not forthcoming. Air travel delays in 1986 resulted in $1.8 billion in additional operating expenses for the nation's airlines and $3.2 billion in lost time by travelers. In Los Angeles County alone, traffic congestion resulted in annual losses of $507 million of work time and 72 million gallons of fuel (Aschauer 1990). Part of the peace dividend and some economic conversion projects should be devoted to public infrastructure investment. At the same time, development funds might also be made available to the private sector as long as they were channeled into genuine investment (Rohatyn 1984). An example comes from Connecticut, whose quasi-public corporation, Connecticut Innovations, invests money in companies that intend to explore civilian applications of existing military technologies (the classic spin-off effect) but might not otherwise be able to afford developing new products.[15]

Business and Economic Conversion

The specific proposals outlined above will almost certainly clash with the ideology of the marketplace. In the opinion of the business community, and even many Americans, government should not interfere with whatever adjustments follow the reduction of the defense budget. The assumption is that workers, engineers, and managers will find substitute employment, and that planning, especially as carried out by a government bureaucracy, is not necessary. Advocates of economic conversion frequently stress the importance of decentralization and local planning groups, especially since successful conversion requires detailed knowledge of the local plant, its equipment, and the particular skills of its work force. Nonetheless, the emergence of a strong movement seeking to adopt progressive politics and establish a

15. Many states have elements of an industrial policy, even if their intervention in the economy does not carry that name. State-level industrial policies differ from each other. As a result, one important issue confronting a program of economic conversion is how to apply national priorities through an existing pattern of regional and state structures.

peace economy will raise questions, particularly from business leaders, regarding the need for a form of economic conversion that incorporates elements of an industrial policy (Gold 1984). It is already clear that the preference of business is to apply whatever savings result from a reduction in the military budget toward reduction of the federal deficit (Committee for Economic Development 1990). Business prefers monetary stability to social rejuvenation. Corporate leaders demonstrate no visible urgency to address pervasive social problems in the United States, apart from the argument that an economic climate that favors business will also produce trickle-down effects that will benefit all Americans. Certainly, business shows little desire to experiment with different forms of industrial policy as a means to restore manufacturing strength within the United States. For example, several years ago, 523 business executives were asked to answer the following question: "Regarding the development of our economy, which of these two statements comes closer to your own view?"

> The development of our national economy will work best if market forces are permitted to determine what direction business and industry should take and government plays a less interventionist role by removing some of the regulatory barriers.
>
> Because of dramatic structural changes in our economy and increased international competition, the U.S. needs to establish a coordinated long-range industrial policy, based upon intensified cooperation among business, labor and government. (Opinion Research Corporation, in Phillips 1984)

Sixty-three percent chose the first option, only 37 percent the second.[16]

Nonetheless, the strategy and priorities of economic conversion proposed above should fall short of provoking outright business hostility. Many in business should be able to recognize their own interest in creating a stronger manufacturing base, developing new technologies, and creating the increased demand that will emerge from a program of full employment. The international development programs should fuel new areas of future demand for U.S. exports. Business scholars and other students of U.S. commerce have argued that business would advance its own interests by developing perspectives that extend beyond short-term profitability. Peace economy projects could

16. While the question calls for a reaction to the prospect of an industrial policy rather than economic conversion, the poll taps a similar reservoir of hostility toward the prospect of planning that takes place outside the corporation itself.

be seen as a opportunity to insert this element of long-term stability into private decision making. Moreover, business would benefit from lower interest rates and technical innovations concentrated in the civilian sector.[17] Finally, economic conversion would not alter the fundamental role of the market in the U.S. economy.

Peace economy projects are not a disguised effort to install a command economy based on the discredited Soviet model. Economic conversion is only a recasting of the relationship between the market and more publicly determined social priorities. No substitute for the market is sought. Instead, we need to balance two objectives: to secure the advantages that the market economy has historically generated and to address the so-called externalities, or consequences generated by the market, including environmental decay and social inequities. And yet economic conversion presents a challenge, more ideological than material, to the prerogatives of business. Decisions would not be made exclusively in the boardrooms. The determination of investment priorities would be more public and democratic. To business, that is a threat.[18] The emergence of explicit options for the overall direction of the economy as subjects of public debate may bring about a challenge from business on these political and ideological grounds. In economic terms, however, business will benefit from economic conversion.

The key questions, then, are what sort of civilian economy we want to see emerge, and whether the planning and conversion projects

---

17. Even before the end of the Cold War, *Business Week* (1989b) estimated that substantial defense cuts would yield, with some near-term pain, a decline in interest rates to less than 5 percent, a surge in housing, a federal budget surplus, and accelerated growth throughout the economy (1989). *Fortune* (1989) also called for a 50 percent cut in the 300,000 U.S. troops now stationed in Europe, for a European-led NATO, and for restructured U.S.–European relations that go beyond the premises of containment. These optimistic business surveys were based on the macroeconomic effect deriving from the application of the peace dividend to deficit reduction rather than to structural changes that could be anticipated from investing in long-term projects.

18. Kevin Phillips (1984) has argued that even free market businessmen who oppose the adoption of industrial *policies* end up favoring milder interventionist elements of an industrial *strategy*. From the standpoint of business, an industrial policy raises the specter of too much interference in the market (and too much interference in their own decisions). However, according to Phillips, many business leaders accept the concept of a national industrial strategy in which the U.S. government plays a more active role in "leveling the playing field" for corporations facing competition from foreign companies whose own governments help subsidize their activities. Similarly, businessmen and many in the political mainstream like the idea of a "competitiveness" strategy, or one focused on restoring the national strength of the U.S. economy without adjusting social priorities. The goals of economic conversion outlined earlier in this chapter incorporate the objective of democratizing economic decision making and, hence, are closer to the traditional concerns of an industrial policy.

that stem from the reduction of the military budget over the 1990s can not only minimize local instability but encourage the development of a peace economy. Efforts to restore strength in manufacturing, improve our ability to export, reemphasize education and appropriate job training, revitalize our cities, encourage industrial democracy and public and private investment, and develop environmentally sound practices in our economic activities are all important steps in that direction.

6

Security, Democracy, and Nuclear Weapons Policy

DURING THE 1980s, the Reagan administration undertook an ambitious program of modernizing United States strategic forces. The new nuclear weapons included the land-based MX missile, the submarine-launched Trident II missile, air-launched cruise missiles, and two new bombers to carry them, the B-1 and B-2. Development was started on a new single-warhead missile, the Midgetman. New ground-launched cruise missiles were deployed in Europe along with a new intermediate-range land-based missile, the Pershing II. The Navy produced new sea-launched cruise missiles for attack submarines. All of the new weapons were counterforce—accurate enough to threaten Soviet retaliatory forces and military command centers. Thus they increased the feasibility of striking first by, in theory, limiting the damage that the Soviet Union would be able to inflict on the United States in response.

The Reagan administration also attempted to improve the defensive capabilities of the United States. Civil defense programs received more money, and the Strategic Defense Initiative accelerated development of space-based lasers and particle beam weapons designed to intercept Soviet missiles before they could strike the United States. New antisatellite weapons were tested and a coordinated military space program was created. The Pentagon launched an ambitious program to protect command, control and communication facilities against the effects of nuclear blast, radiation, and electromagnetic pulse. Administration documents defined as a goal for U.S. nuclear forces the ability "to prevail and be able to force the Soviet Union to seek earliest termination of hostilities on terms favorable to the United States" (Halloran 1982; Draper and Weinberger 1983).

Approximately ten years later, starting in the fall of 1991, the Bush administration offered a series of dramatic proposals for nuclear weapons that seemed to reverse the priorities of Bush's predecessor. The president ordered the unilateral destruction of land-based tactical nuclear weapons deployed in Europe and South Korea and the withdrawal of all tactical nuclear weapons from surface ships and submarines. Plans for a rail-based system for deploying the MX missile were scrapped, and Bush called for the reduction and eventual elimination of U.S. and Soviet ground-based missiles with multiple warheads. The Soviets were asked to destroy all of their nuclear artillery, short-range missiles, and nuclear land mines. Furthermore, in a step designed to move both sides away from the nuclear brink, the alert status of many U.S. strategic systems was downgraded. Armed, long-range bombers were no longer in flight continually.

Moscow was quick to respond. Within a week, Soviet leader Mikhail Gorbachev announced that he would meet the U.S. proposals by eliminating all land-based tactical weapons and removing all tactical nuclear warheads from surface ships and submarines. Moscow also reduced the alert status of its long-range bombers and many of its intercontinental ballistic missiles. In other details, the Soviet Union matched or went beyond what Washington proposed. By imposing a one-year moratorium on nuclear testing and asking other nations to follow suit, Gorbachev went one significant step further.

The pace of change continued to quicken. The Soviet Union had begun internal reform and in the process transformed its attitude toward the nuclear arms race in a way that held considerable promise for U.S. security. But then the Soviet Union itself ceased to exist. In its place was a loose confederation of states still in considerable flux—and thousands of nuclear warheads in four separate republics. Russia had the bomb, the Ukraine had the bomb, Kazakhstan and Belarus had the bomb. Rumors began to emerge—of possible sales of nuclear material to gain hard currency, and of the participation of former Soviet weapons technicians in the nuclear programs of other countries. The situation challenged U.S. nuclear strategy and raised the issue of proliferation with new urgency.

In June 1992, Russian President Boris Yeltsin visited the United States and signed an agreement with President George Bush that went even further than START. Instead of each country's reducing its arsenal from 12,000–13,000 to 8,000–9,000 warheads, Washington now pledged to reduce its strategic stockpile to 3,500 warheads by 2003; Moscow promised to lower its inventory to 3,000 by the same year. The United States promised to help Russia with the cost of dismantling its warheads and missiles. Even more important, each side agreed to remove all land-based missiles carrying multiple warheads—the weapons system that analysts feel is the most destabilizing. By this accord, Russia will have to destroy all its SS-18 and SS-24 missiles, each carrying 10 warheads that can be directed against targets hundreds of miles apart. On its part, the United States will have to give up 50 MX missiles, each of which also carries 10 warheads, and replace the 3 warheads now on its Minuteman III missile with only 1 warhead. Each of these systems had been the subject of intense scrutiny and concern: the Russian heavy missiles from U.S. conservatives and arms control negotiators, and the MX from the U.S. peace movement (as well as from Soviet arms negotiators).

By the time the June 1992 agreement was signed, the nuclear situation seemed to have been totally transformed from what it had been a decade earlier. Washington seemed finally to recognize the reciprocal nature of its security with respect to that of other countries holding nuclear weapons. Control and stability had become more important than adding more numbers or improving the performance of particular weapons. The arms control process itself seemed to be transformed as important leap-frogging initiatives were passed back and forth without waiting to secure specific agreements. Given the removal of major weapons systems and the dramatic reductions in numbers of strategic warheads, it now seemed that the nuclear genie, if not recapped entirely, was nonetheless well on the way to being shoved back into the bottle.

In other ways, however, little had changed. Critics of the Bush administration were quick to point out that the president's proposals left several important weapons systems intact, including the B-2 bomber and the Strategic Defense Initiative. Many of the cuts proposed by the United States, especially in MIRVed land-based missiles, were in areas of Soviet (Russian) strength, while American strong points such as sea-based ballistic missiles and cruise missiles were left untouched. Mutual elimination of land-based battlefield weapons was in the United States' interest because the threat of an invasion from the Warsaw Pact no longer existed. The principal fear remaining was that Soviet battlefield systems could become part of the ethnic and nationalist unrest accompanying that country's dissolution; thus it would be advantageous to either eliminate these systems or to strengthen central *Soviet* control over them. Moreover, these changes proposed by Washington would produce little in the way of dollar savings from the near-term defense budget. Even more tellingly, Bush refused to end nuclear testing, issue a pledge to not use nuclear weapons first, or take significant steps that could contribute to stronger international controls on proliferation.

The Reagan modernization program of the earlier 1980s sparked an important debate over nuclear strategy and the nature of U.S.–Soviet relations. Policy experts and an unprecedented proportion of the general public examined a series of important questions: Should the United States prepare to fight and win a nuclear war? Is it even possible to fight a nuclear war? Should nuclear weapons be used in the pursuit of foreign policy goals? Is a defense against nuclear attack technically feasible or politically desirable? The decade ended with the globe in a state of flux. Yet, no similar debate over the appropriate role for nuclear weapons in the post–Cold War world has emerged. Their dramatic impact aside, the Bush-Gorbachev and Bush-Yeltsin proposals still left the United States and the Soviet Union with thousands of nuclear weapons. Washington, in particular, continued to cling to the Cold War concept that nuclear weapons are politically useful. U.S. Defense Secretary Richard Cheney rejected Moscow's call for a joint nuclear test ban. Cheney also refused to issue a "no first use" agreement, arguing that "deterrence is stronger if you leave the element of uncertainty out there in the mind of an adversary" (*Boston Globe*, October 16, 1991:47). This rejection exemplified the essential old world order stance toward nuclear weapons. Given the nature of these weapons and the changes taking place in East-West relations, the failure to rethink the fundamentals of nuclear weapons policy seemed especially damaging.

In this chapter, I argue that the United States should reject its policy of extended deterrence and adopt instead a posture of basic deterrence (these terms are defined below). I identify three advantages of such a change. First, basic deterrence enhances our military security against any potential adversary who already possesses nuclear weapons. Whatever the outcome of the changes now taking place, the United States should change its strategic policy as a necessary step in the redefinition of its role as global leader. Adopting a new strategy for nuclear weapons is an essential component of a new world order and of the redefinition of U.S. security. Second, adopting basic deterrence is necessary to control nuclear proliferation, which may ultimately be more dangerous than the Cold War nuclear competition between the United States and Soviet Union. Third, carrying out such an important shift in nuclear policy will have a positive impact on the policy-making process itself. A growing number of critics are finding the federal government institutionally incapable of carrying out a concerted program of change (Ginsberg and Shefter 1990). In this view, the efforts of those who try to create a new policy direction are thwarted by generalized loss of faith in government among the public, congressional attempts at micromanagement, pressure from moneyed special interests, political resistance and bureaucratic inertia on the part of those charged with administering changes in policy, and subsequent legal challenges. Even when an alternative course has been chosen, actually getting there has become more and more difficult. The result is political impasse. At best we are left with incremental adjustments. Deliberate, positive policy departures to further agreed-upon goals seems less achievable. And yet the federal government must play a central role in any concerted effort to redirect national priorities. The concept that government can contribute to the public good must be rescued. The very political process of adopting basic deterrence will bolster that role for the federal government while simultaneously providing a concrete step toward a world without nuclear weapons.

The first step in developing my argument is to contrast existing U.S. nuclear policy (extended deterrence) with what most of the public thinks should be U.S. policy (basic deterrence), and to argue that the principal threat posed by the existing policy is not to the former Soviet Union, to Russia, or to any other presumed combatant, but to the United States itself.

Basic Deterrence, Extended Deterrence, and Nuclear War Fighting

Most Americans think that the main purpose of nuclear weapons is to prevent an attack against our physical territory (see Chapter 3). They are mistaken in this belief. In fact, since the very beginning of the nuclear era, Washington's strategic planning has rested on the premise that the United States could use nuclear weapons first and that by doing so Washington would retain the best chance of winning (Herken 1982, 1987; Rosenberg 1979, 1981/2, 1982). At the same time, most U.S. decisionmakers, including presidents, have been horrified at the prospect of nuclear war. The more we know of their behavior in actual crises, the more it appears that political leaders have been well aware of the dangers of crossing the nuclear threshold.[1] Nonetheless, the very same leaders have followed policies premised on the need to build the capability to win the nuclear war that their private thoughts rejected.[2]

Are our political leaders schizophrenic? How can we understand the Cold War pattern of holding simultaneously to two contradictory views about the nature of nuclear weapons—one recognizing the awfulness of nuclear war, the other approving weapons that sustain the possibility of just such a war? The answer resides not in psychology but in the two fundamentally different versions of deterrence that have been put forth in the nuclear debate over the past forty-five years. These alternative concepts of nuclear deterrence support, in turn, different perspectives on the role of the United States in global politics.

In his annual report to Congress for fiscal year 1984, Secretary of Defense Caspar Weinberger defined the national security goals of the United States in the following manner: "to deter military attack by the USSR and its allies against the United States, its allies, and other friendly nations, and to deter or to counter the use of Soviet military power to coerce or intimidate our friends and allies." Note that this statement applies deterrence to two distinct situations: preventing a direct military attack by the USSR against the United States; and preventing the use of Soviet military power to coerce or intimidate the United States and its allies. The first situation is called "basic deterrence"; the second, "extended deterrence." Basic deterrence is concerned with preventing a direct nuclear attack against the United States. Extended deterrence is concerned with preventing both nuclear and conventional military attack against either the United States

---

1. Recent research on the Cuban missile crisis indicates that the actions of political leaders were based not on calculations of the strategic balance or the capabilities of different weapons systems but on judgments about what was the appropriate balance of power between the United States and the Soviet Union, and deep-seated fear on the part of decisionmakers in both countries that they were about to enter something hideous (Blight 1987/88; Schwartz and Derber 1990; Trachtenberg 1985). It now appears that President Kennedy decided that he would not use nuclear weapons first, although he did not reassure Moscow on this point during his negotiations with Khrushchev.

2. Reagan's above-mentioned efforts to improve the credibility of the first use of nuclear weapons only paralleled previous efforts of the Truman, Eisenhower, Kennedy, Nixon, and Carter administrations. Even the Johnson administration, which did not initiate many new weapons systems or develop new plans to fight a nuclear war, did not break with the prevailing doctrine of threatened first use of nuclear weapons.

or its allies, *and* with using nuclear weapons to project political influence. The strategic logic and the weapons systems required under the two conceptions of deterrence are very different.

A policy of basic deterrence would try to create three conditions: first, that no country has an incentive to initiate the use of nuclear weapons; second, no country has the capacity to launch a disarming first strike; and third, there are no circumstances under which the accidental or unauthorized use of nuclear arms could occur. Under basic deterrence the only threat that warrants the use of nuclear weapons is a nuclear attack. By threatening devastation beyond any conceivable measure, nuclear capability prevents an opponent from attacking in the first place. No other military or political role is assigned to the arsenal.

Under extended deterrence, however, the range of threats that nuclear weapons are assigned to confront is far more diverse. Not only must our own territory be protected against nuclear attack, but Washington must be prepared to prevent both nuclear and conventional attacks against its allies. To better extend the protection of the nuclear umbrella, the United States has refused to rule out the first use of nuclear weapons. In strategic theory, this refusal enhances the political leverage of nuclear weapons. Paul Nitze, a member of the Reagan and several Democratic administrations, has compared this political use of nuclear weapons to a game of chess: "The atomic queens may never be brought into play; they may never actually take one of the opponent's pieces. But the position of the atomic queens may still have a decisive bearing on which side can safely advance a limited-war bishop or a cold-war pawn" (1956). Virtually every American decisionmaker has accepted the logic of extended deterrence (citing "global responsibilities"). The problem is that the implied threat of first use of nuclear weapons has to be made credible, and this can be accomplished only by building the very weapons systems that make fighting and winning a nuclear war at least somewhat plausible. The difference between extended deterrence, where Washington builds war-fighting systems that leaders believe are politically necessary but cannot be used militarily, and the nuclear war-fighting posture, where the United States intends to prevail in a nuclear war, is minimal. The threat to use nuclear weapons is present in both cases and tends to produce in an opponent a belligerent attitude and a determination to respond in kind. The continued pursuit of extended deterrence thus sustains both continued modernization on the part of other nuclear powers and proliferation among countries that do not yet possess nuclear weapons. In neither case is the security of U.S. citizens well served.

The principal tenets of basic deterrence, extended deterrence and the nuclear war–fighting posture are compared in Table 6-1. Extended deterrence poses a threat to the United States that is not significantly different from the dangers of nuclear war fighting. Neither conforms to

TABLE 6-1
Three Nuclear Weapons Postures

	Basic Deterrence	*Extended Deterrence*	*Nuclear War Fighting*
Nature of threats nuclear weapons are to confront	Nuclear strike against the U.S.	Nuclear and conventional attacks against the U.S. and its allies, and military-political influence of an opponent	
Is there a nuclear revolution?	Yes	In military terms, yes; in political terms, no	No
Can a nuclear war be won?	No	Probably not	Yes
Feasibility of limited nuclear war	None	Unlikely, but possible	Yes
Nature of deterrence	Inflict punishment	Not implausible first strike; prepare flexible response moving up ladder of escalation	Inflict defeat; denial of enemy objectives by war-winning capacity
Targeting	Countervalue	Counterforce	Counterforce
Possibility of defense	No	The effort to develop a defense may be politically important, even if it is militarily useless	Yes

TABLE 6-1 (*Cont.*)

	Basic Deterrence	*Extended Deterrence*	*Nuclear War fighting*
Expectation that nuclear weapons will really be used	No	No	Perhaps
Control of nuclear forces during nuclear attack	Sufficient to avoid decapitation and to stop a war if it starts; otherwise spasmodic	"Robust" to permit protracted nuclear war	
Nature of Soviet motives during Cold War	Defensive; security-minded	Expansionary	Aggressive, seeking empire
What Soviets valued	Cities/society	Communist party control over empire	
Soviet "strategic culture"	Also accepts basic deterrence	Respect military strength; will take advantage of perceived weakness	Believes in war-fighting doctrine
Declare no first use?	Yes	No	No
Arms control	Regulate competition between superpowers; in particular, remove destabilizing elements	Progress linked to compliant Soviet behavior in foreign policy	No
Examples of weapons systems	Submarines C^3I to permit delayed response Surveillance satellites Single warhead/ mobile ICBMs	MX SDI Cruise missiles Anti-satellite weapons Pershing II (now removed) Trident II (D-5) C^3I to fight actual nuclear war Anti-submarine warfare	

the realities of the current international situation. The recent changes and proposals announced by the Bush administration do not fundamentally alter the prevailing attitude toward nuclear weapons. Instead, progressive political leadership should push for a posture of basic deterrence and a renewed determination to control nuclear proliferation by starting at home. Some money will be saved by these changes, but the principal benefit will be to enhance the security of the United States.[3]

Nuclear Deterrence and the Nature of War

Advocates of basic deterrence recognize that nuclear weapons have changed the very nature of war. They believe that the awesome power of nuclear weapons makes it difficult, if not impossible, for societies to escape without suffering enormous damage. Once started, a nuclear war cannot be kept limited. In fact, nuclear weapons make the very concept of winning and losing war anachronistic. As Bernard Brodie argued shortly after two atomic bombs were used over Japan at the end of World War II: "Thus far the chief purpose of the military establishment has been to win wars. From now on its chief purpose must be to prevent them. It can have almost no other useful purpose" (1946). Hiroshima and Nagasaki represented a qualitative break in the history of war.

---

3. Those associated with extended deterrence include, while they were in government, Secretary of Defense Robert McNamara, National Security Advisor McGeorge Bundy, Secretary of Defense Harold Brown, and Secretary of State Henry Kissinger. Advocates of the war-fighting position during the Reagan administration included Assistant Secretary of Defense Richard Perle, National Security Council official Richard Pipes, and Reagan administration advisors Colin Gray, Scott Thompson, and William Van Cleave. Support for basic deterrence among top officials is quite rare. President Jimmy Carter may have believed in moving toward a basic deterrence position during the first year of his administration, but was eventually convinced by his national security advisor, Zbigniew Brzezinski, an advocate of extended deterrence, to return to the policy mainstream.

Over the course of their careers, several individuals have changed their position, sometimes more than once. Bernard Brodie, for example, outlined many of the premises of basic deterrence early in his career. Brodie later joined the RAND Corporation and became a proponent of some of the contrary tenets. Still later he switched again, this time back to his original arguments (Freedman 1981; Herken 1987; Kaplan 1983). Similarly, the support of McNamara, Bundy, George Kennan and Gerald Smith (expressed, significantly, by these prominent government officials only *after* leaving office) for a declaration of no first use is consistent with a basic deterrence position (Bundy et al. 1982). More recently, some of the former nuclear hawks of the Reagan administration have rejected the need for continued nuclear modernization. They have not, however, supported adoption of basic deterrence, and scaled-back versions of virtually every nuclear weapons program are continuing.

The advocates of the war-fighting position disagree.[4] In their view, nuclear weapons are more destructive than other weapons but are not qualitatively different. Our thinking about nuclear wars, they argue, should not be different from our thinking about previous wars. In the past, new instruments of war were introduced in combination with existing weapons. There is no reason to think that nuclear weapons are any different in this respect from the machine gun, the spear, the rifle, or the tank (Gray 1977). The bomb can be used alongside the existing arsenal. There is no great divide between nuclear and conventional weapons.

Nuclear Deterrence and Limited War

Supporters of basic deterrence are very skeptical about the possibility that nuclear war can be kept limited (in the sense that the conflict ends short of the virtual destruction of society). As Clausewitz noted long ago, the chaos and uncertainty of the battlefield, the "fog of war," makes it difficult to manage rationally the conflict between opposing military forces. Military commanders are not able to grasp fully what is going on around them and they may lose control over their forces. In nuclear war, the problems of maintaining the congruence between political intent and military actions are even more acute. Unique conditions make the critical tasks of assessing damage, determining the opposition's intentions, deciding on a proper response, communicating that decision reliably, and maintaining control extremely difficult to achieve (Ball 1981). One particularly important factor is the impact of electromagnetic pulse (EMP), a brief but intense electrical emission that accompanies a nuclear explosion. EMP could disrupt civilian and even military communication channels (Broad 1981). War games premised on a limited nuclear response to a Soviet conventional invasion of Western Europe have consistently shown that there would be little hope of maintaining restraint, and former secretary of defense Robert McNamara was led to conclude that "there is little chance of limiting a conflict that has already seen the use of

---

4. Here the comparison is between basic deterrence and nuclear war fighting. In general, supporters of extended deterrence recognize the qualitative difference of nuclear weapons from conventional ones—differences that preclude fighting a nuclear war rationally. On the other hand, a key premise of the extended deterrence position is that nuclear weapons have an important geopolitical influence that must be preserved, and this leads them to support war-fighting systems.

tactical nuclear weapons to tactical nuclear weapons" (in Mandelbaum 1979:19).

On the other hand, supporters of extended deterrence have endorsed the weapons systems and war planning that have been necessary to maintain the capability to fight a limited nuclear war. Their purpose is to retain the political leverage that nuclear weapons provide when such a capability exists. From this point of view, public statements by government officials expressing doubts about the possibility of keeping a nuclear war controlled are irresponsible and serve only to "undermine deterrence" (read: nuclear diplomacy).

Nuclear Deterrence and How Much Is Enough

Another contrast between the two positions is the way they view the nature of the damage inflicted by nuclear weapons, and the connection between this damage and the prevention of war. For the basic deterrence position, nuclear weapons can only inflict punishment on an aggressor. Traditionally, warfare, no matter how destructive, culminates in a settlement between the contending parties. But in the aftermath of the devastation of billions of people and the very institutions of society, it would no longer be possible for a national government to negotiate the end of hostilities. In this sense, the use of nuclear weapons means the end of warfare as normally conceived. Nuclear war signifies that Clausewitz's conception of war as the continuation of politics by other means has been transcended. Nuclear war can only mean the continuation of madness. By threatening unavoidable and "unacceptable damage" against whatever country strikes first, nuclear weapons are supposed to preserve stability. The near certainty of mutual destruction, sometimes called MAD, or mutually assured destruction, deters nuclear war in the first place.

The vast destruction that accompanies nuclear weapons leads to an important question central to the concept of mutual assured destruction: How does one fix the level of destruction beyond which an opponent finds the damage to be unacceptable and hence is deterred from striking first? The official definition, arrived at in a somewhat arbitrary manner during the Kennedy administration, is the loss of 25 percent of civilian population and more than 50 percent of the industrial capacity. Then secretary of defense Robert McNamara calculated that unacceptable damage could be delivered by perhaps as few as four hundred warheads (Ball 1980). More recent studies have found that the equivalent of fifty one-megaton warheads exploded over the urban areas of either the United States or the former Soviet Union could kill between 25 million and 50 million people and destroy the infrastructure (Daugherty, Levi, and von Hippel 1986; Levi, von Hippel, and Daugherty 1987/88). The United States is in possession of more than ten thousand strategic weapons.

An increasing number of strategists and former government officials feel that what might be called the "existential quality" of nuclear bombs is such that the prospect of an attack with only a dozen, or ten, or five, or even a single nuclear bomb on a single city may be sufficient to deter a nuclear war. As McGeorge Bundy has observed:

> Think-tank analysts can set levels of "acceptable" damage well up in the tens of millions of lives. They can assume that the loss of dozens of great cities is somehow a real choice for sane men. They are in an unreal world. In the real world of real political leaders—whether here or in the Soviet Union—a decision that would bring even one hydrogen bomb on one city of one's own country would be recognized in advance as a catastrophic blunder; ten bombs on ten cities would be a disaster beyond history; and a hundred bombs on a hundred cities are unthinkable. (1969:9–10)

McNamara has argued that the strategic balance holds little real meaning for decisionmakers:

> The "width" of the "band of parity" is very, very great. In 1962 [the Cuban missile crisis] it would have made no difference in our behavior whether the ratio had been seventeen to one, five to one, or two to one in our favor—or even two to one against us. In none of these cases would either we or the Soviets have felt we could use, or threaten to use, nuclear power to achieve a political end. (1986:45)

In addition, the very top leadership may decide privately that they will not use nuclear weapons, regardless of the operational capabilities and war plans of the defense bureaucracies. Robert McNamara recently maintained that Presidents Kennedy and Johnson followed a de facto no first use policy while he was secretary of defense: "In long private conversations with successive Presidents—Kennedy and Johnson—I recommended, without qualification, that they never initiate, under any circumstances, the use of nuclear weapons" (1986:79). Unfortunately, alongside this advice to his respective commanders in chief, McNamara continued the acquisition of nuclear war–fighting systems and plans to fight a limited nuclear war. McNamara did not find it wise to recommend the explicit adoption of no first use by the United States until long after he had left office.

Nuclear weapons involve such risks, and the possibility of losing control of events once a war starts is so great, that a country may "need" only relatively few weapons for deterrence. In fact, only the capacity "to get into trouble," to enter into actions without knowing where the resulting spiral will end, may be sufficient (Halperin 1987; McNamara 1986). Denying the need to go through a rationalist calculation of quantities and capabilities may be intellectually unsettling. But acknowledgment of the penetrating fear of entering into any form of nuclear war may be the most useful way of addressing the question of what constitutes "unacceptable damage."[5]

This existential element of nuclear weapons undermines the need for the elaborate weapons systems required by extended deterrence. In the actual world of foreign policy decisions, especially under crisis situations, the attention of political leaders is not drawn to such specifics as warhead numbers or missile accuracy. The details of the strategic balance matter far less than the simple fact that nuclear weapons exist and have become part of the power equation. Nuclear weapons are important, but only symbolically. It does not take many bombs to grab the attention of an opponent. The extra political impact of acquiring more bombs is not impressive. For example, the U.S. military would probably have been deterred from the extensive bombing of the Iraqi civilian infrastructure carried out in Operation Desert Storm if that country had possessed any level of nuclear capacity against the United States. The thought of Saddam Hussein acquiring even a small number of nuclear weapons is frightening. Iraq does not have to match the United States in order to be effective. Five or ten deliverable bombs count almost as much as five thousand. Thankfully, the prospect of nuclear war seems to create a powerful threshold that is difficult to cross. Unfortunately, this psychological barrier is by itself inadequate to insure security. Actual nuclear war–fighting weapons remain, and only an explicit restructuring of this arsenal will enable us to achieve more genuine stability and security. In the meantime, Washington's continued attempt to use nuclear weapons for influence

5. Both France and Great Britain possess nuclear arsenals of roughly five hundred nuclear warheads. Are these arsenals "small"? Is the size of Israel's unknown but certainly smaller nuclear arsenal also "small"? Is not the prospect of another tier of countries acquiring what will certainly be a "small" number of nuclear weapons still a massive threat to global security?

undermines U.S. security by encouraging other countries either to acquire atomic bombs, or to believe that it is necessary to modernize their arsenals in response. Proliferation and arms races are the result.

Neither supporters of extended deterrence nor advocates of the nuclear war–fighting posture can be content with mutually assured destruction, however it is defined, because such a situation undermines the credibility of first use and thus weakens the political leverage that nuclear weapons are supposed to confer. For the first twenty years of the postwar period, the United States possessed overwhelming nuclear superiority. But in the late 1960s, the Soviet Union acquired a secure second-strike capability against the United States. No matter how effective was a U.S. first strike, Moscow could now inflict enormous destruction. For those interested in using American nuclear power for political purposes, MAD presented an irresolvable problem. A nuclear war could not be fought—at least not rationally. Both sides would lose far more than they could ever hope to gain. Yet extended deterrence required the United States to maintain the possibility that nuclear weapons could be used first. MAD completely undercut the credibility of this threat. If Washington used nuclear weapons against the Soviet Union first, for example on behalf of West Germany following a Soviet land invasion, Moscow could now respond directly against the United States. As a result, a president could no longer make a realistic commitment to use nuclear weapons in support of an ally. Who in Moscow would believe that the United States would go to war on behalf of Bonn, or Tokyo, or interests in the Persian Gulf, when the almost certain result would be the destruction of Washington, New York and Los Angeles? To bolster the original foreign policy commitments, the credibility of the nuclear threat had to be maintained. This meant developing those weapons systems that made credible—or at least not incredible—the threat of going to war first. As Colin Gray, who was a consultant to the Reagan administration and in recent years has been most associated with the nuclear war–fighting position, has argued, "If American nuclear power is to support U.S. foreign policy objectives, the United States must possess the ability to wage nuclear war rationally" (1980). Gray's explicit advocacy of a position that many found frightening tended to isolate him. Yet the same argument can be attributed to the extended deterrence policy mainstream. Those U.S. decisionmakers who privately did not believe that a nuclear war could be fought, nonetheless refused to rule out the possibility that Washington would use nuclear weapons first. Strategic modernization programs were adopted that made the use of these weapons more plausible. In this manner, extended deterrence and its reliance on threatened first use created the need for nuclear war–fighting doctrines and for deployment of the necessary weapons hardware.[6]

The advocates of extended deterrence fear that any discussion of the inevitability of nuclear war ending in mutual destruction will undermine Washington's global influence. They believe that nuclear wars can be kept limited in the sense that they will end short of the complete destruction of state and society. The belief of the basic deterrence school, that a war involving nuclear weapons will inevitably escalate to an all-out exchange and lead to the destruction of both sides, is rejected. It is still considered possible to conduct warfare by traditional means. In this view, the link Clausewitz affirmed between war and politics has not been transcended by the nuclear revolution.

The need to harness nuclear weapons to the pursuit of foreign policy sustains the favorite question of nuclear-war fighters: what if deterrence fails? Their answer is that there will be war and the United States must be prepared to fight it. After the hostilities end, one side will be in a better position than the other to organize whatever remains. The victor will be in a position to issue orders to the loser. To maximize the possibility of winning, the United States should demon-

---

6. It may be helpful here to consider the distinctions between *declaratory policy*, or that which is stated publicly in the Annual Report of the Secretary of Defense and in speeches before general audiences; *action policy*, or how the United States actually plans to use its forces in a nuclear war; and *force deployment policy*, or what the existing weapons systems, and command, control and communications facilities are capable of carrying out.

The rhetoric of formal declarations of policy generally has supported basic deterrence. The Annual Posture Statements of the mid- and late sixties contained especially strong statements on the inevitably of mutually assured destruction. But there is another part of the public record. Each postwar administration has also refused to renounce the first use of nuclear weapons and has on occasion made that threat explicit (Blechman and Kaplan 1978; Ellsberg 1981). Every administration has accepted the premise of extended deterrence and the consequent need to threaten to use nuclear weapons in capacities other than strict retaliation. In this sense, a threat to use nuclear weapons first is as much part of declaratory policy as are the formal statements that such a war would only result in mutually assured destruction. Only the audience, Moscow instead of the U.S. public, is different.

The target list contained in the strategic integrated operating plan (SIOP) or action policy includes limited war options based on counterforce. Despite changes in declaratory policy, the SIOP continues to be based on counterforce and plans for limited nuclear war (Rosenberg 1981/82; Kaplan 1983; Pringle and Arkin 1983).

In general, force deployment policy—the policy that the existing weapons and command procedures are capable of carrying out—has been comparatively clumsy. With the Soviet acquisition of a secure second-strike capability, American forces can only carry out a policy of retaliation. It is impossible to argue with certainty that a successful first strike, or a controlled, limited nuclear war is possible (Ball 1981). Recent research indicating that the deto-

strate its superiority at every possible step in a "ladder of escalation." Political and military leaders should enjoy the flexibility of selecting from a "menu of options," both nuclear and conventional. In particular, the United States should never be in a position where it would be deterred from using nuclear weapons first. As noted by Richard Perle, former assistant secretary of defense for international security policy:

> I've always worried less about what would happen in an actual nuclear exchange than about the effect that the nuclear balance has on our willingness to take risks in local situations. It is not that I am worried about the Soviets' attacking the United States with nuclear weapons confident that they will win that nuclear war. It is that I worry about an American President's feeling he cannot afford to take action in a crisis because Soviet nuclear forces are such that, if escalating took place, they are better poised than we to move up the escalation ladder. (Scheer 1982:154)

Thus, the principal difference between the advocates of extended deterrence and of nuclear war fighting concerns not the weapons that are deployed but only the private belief whether a country can actually use these weapons in war. Ultimately, extended deterrence advocates do not think that it is possible to fight a nuclear war.[7] Yet they build the very weapons systems that make such a horrible outcome theoretically possible. They do so because they think the global manage-

---

nation of between five hundred and two thousand megatons may initiate a "nuclear winter" signifies that even a "successful" preemptive strike eventually will bring devastation to the attacking country as well (Turco et al. 1983; Simon 1984).

United States political leaders have generally been skeptical about the possibility of winning any form of nuclear war. Yet the same officials have sometimes felt that they must make more plausible the use of nuclear weapons in ways that do not ensure mutual destruction. Policymakers judge that the credibility of first use has been diminished and with it U.S. global influence. To compensate, they seek to restore the credibility of first use and regain the foreign policy leverage they feel is provided by the perception of nuclear superiority. A program of modernizing the existing force structure is approved so that capabilities are brought more into line with the requirements of action policy. What changes is not the premise of extended deterrence but the determination to carry out a modernization of the nuclear force structure that is required by extended deterrence. But the weapons systems mandated by extended deterrence are much the same as those required by nuclear war fighting. The result is that the attempt to restore the credibility of extended deterrence also permits advocates of nuclear war fighting to gain influence (Joseph 1985).

7. The contrast between desirability and feasibility helps us grasp the distinction between extended deterrence and nuclear war fighting. Believers in nuclear war fighting think that the capability to fight a nuclear war is both feasible and desirable. Most U.S. political leaders have thought that such a capability is desirable, probably not feasible, but that it is still important to try. Supporters of basic deterrence think it is neither desirable nor feasible.

rial role of the United States demands it.[8] At the end of the Cold War, Washington's official thinking on this point remains unchanged.

Nuclear Deterrence and Warhead Targeting

The two versions of deterrence also differ with respect to methods of targeting nuclear weapons. Under basic deterrence, the main purpose of nuclear forces is to prevent war by threatening unacceptable damage to the other side. To accomplish this, a country needs relatively few survivable warheads aimed at its opponent's cities and industrial base. This is called countercity targeting. Supporters of extended deterrence and war-fighting doctrines favor counterforce targeting, or aiming warheads at the military forces and command centers of the other side. Incredible accuracy is required to destroy these hardened targets in "surgical strikes" or "limited exchanges" involving only military forces.[9] The logical extension of counterforce is a first-strike capability, or the ability to strike at other side's retaliatory forces so that they are either unable to reply, or can reply only at a level that the attacking country considers "acceptable." Even short of preparing for a first strike, the development of counterforce involves conventionalized thinking in which nuclear weapons are treated in much the same way as other instruments of war (Utgoff 1982). Consider former secretary of defense Robert McNamara's June 1962 speech at Ann Arbor discussing nuclear strategy:

> The U.S. has come to the conclusion that to the extent feasible, basic military strategy in a possible general nuclear war should be approached

---

8. For example, those believing in extended deterrence supported the MX missile, not because they thought that it could actually be used rationally in war, but because it was important to preserve, in Moscow's thinking, the possibility that the United States would be able to conduct nuclear war rationally.

9. Many targets, especially missile silos and command bunkers, are "hardened" with steel and concrete. Destroying them requires accuracies, measured by CEP (circular error probable), at one-tenth of a mile or less over five or six thousand miles. Many of the new weapons systems are this accurate—at least in testing carried out under optimum conditions (MacKenzie 1988). Warheads on the MX missile, for example, have a CEP of one hundred yards, and a theoretical "kill probability" of well over 90 percent. However, accuracies achieved on test ranges are significantly different from those expected under the conditions of nuclear war (Bunn and Tsipis 1983; Fallows 1981). Variations in gravitational and magnetic fields and atmospheric density over the actual north-south flight path (missiles are tested east to west), reliability problems (some think that the actual readiness of operational missiles is below 80 percent), fratricide (the impact of one exploding bomb on the flight path of another warhead targeted nearby), errors in estimates of target locations, and weather combine to reduce the actual kill probability for even the most sophisticated missile to roughly 50 percent.

> in much the same way that the more conventional military options have been regarded in the past. That is to say, the principal military objectives, in the event of a nuclear war stemming from a major attack on the alliance, should be the destruction of the enemy's military forces, not his civilian population.

The development of counterforce and the hypothetical capacity to fight and win nuclear wars has been an important constant in Washington's policy. Nearly ten years later, in his 1971 State of the World speech, President Richard Nixon set out objectives for nuclear weapons in much the same way as did McNamara:

> I must not be—and my successors must not be—limited to the indiscriminate mass destruction of enemy civilians as the sole possible response to challenges. This is especially so when that response involves the likelihood of triggering nuclear attacks on our own population. It would be inconsistent with the political meaning of sufficiency [Nixon's term, an attempt to stamp his own mark on nuclear strategy] to base our force planning solely on some finite—and theoretical—capacity to inflict casualties presumed to be unacceptable to the other side. (in Greenwood 1975:72)

Targeting civilians also raises important ethical issues associated with deterrence. Supporters of extended deterrence and war fighting argue that targeting noncombatants is immoral (hence counterforce targeting is ethically superior). Supporters of basic deterrence argue that counterforce targeting is more likely to bring about a nuclear war in which civilians will inevitably die. The Office of Technology Assessment, for example, has estimated the number of American civilian deaths in a counterforce exchange at between two million and twenty million. Hence, civilian targeting is "more acceptable," or "less unacceptable," because it is more likely to deter any form of nuclear war. Even so, civilians are still held hostage in the name of peace. Therefore, the only permanent solution to the ethical issues of nuclear deterrence is full nuclear disarmament (National Conference of Catholic Bishops 1983; Kegley and Schwab 1991).

Nuclear Deterrence and Defense

Another comparison between the two versions of deterrence concerns the possibility of erecting an effective defense against nuclear attack. The basic deterrence position respects the weight of the scientific community which has argued that the difficulties associated with intercepting multiple warheads traveling at close to eighteen thousand miles an hour are virtually impossible to overcome. In general, supporters of extended deterrence agree that an effective defensive shield cannot be erected. Some, however, felt that the effort to do so would pressure the Soviet Union into concessions in arms control negotiations, or could be otherwise translated into political gain. On the other hand, many in the war-fighting camp believed in the possibility of erecting an effective defense. Two proponents of the war-fighting position argued that "no matter how flexible U.S. strategic deployment may be, if it is not matched by some very significant ability actually to defend North America, it would amount, in practice, to suicide on the installment plan" (Gray and Payne 1980). Currently, the United States is continuing to spend several billion dollars a year in the effort to acquire a defense against a limited nuclear attack from "any direction."

Nuclear Deterrence and Soviet Intentions

Before the end of the Cold War, the basic deterrence school argued that Moscow basically accepted the reality of mutually assured destruction, had no serious civil defense program, and wanted to reduce the risk of nuclear war through arms control measures. In this view the Soviet Union, reacting to a long history of invasion from the West, was essentially defense minded—almost obsessed with preserving its security—and its massing of nuclear arms should be seen in that light. The Soviet Union also valued its post-1917 achievements, including its cities and industrial base. The prospect of nuclear war was a threat to these achievements. As a result, Moscow's political leadership concluded that a nuclear war would produce no winner or loser (Garthoff 1978; Holloway 1984). Moscow's 1982 pledge before the United Nations to not use nuclear weapons first is evidence of this attitude.

The war-fighting camp argues that Soviet "strategic culture" did not reject the idea of fighting and winning a nuclear war, nor of striking first. Basing their analysis largely on military manuals, they argued that Moscow planned for nuclear war in much the same terms as previous wars. Moscow's strategic policy reflected a broader commitment to world domination and to an aggressive expansion that sought control over an empire (Pipes 1984). In this view, even in the aftermath of the Gorbachev reforms and the breakup of the Soviet Union, uncertainties regarding the traditional imperial designs of Russia, coupled with a huge remaining nuclear arsenal, are worrisome.

Nuclear Deterrence and Arms Control

Historically, different attitudes toward arms control have also divided the two deterrence positions. The logical result of basic deterrence was support for talks designed to regulate the competition between the two superpowers. Supporters of basic deterrence saw arms treaties as an important method of isolating nuclear weapons from the tension between Washington and Moscow that existed during the Cold War. Arms control negotiations were seen as fulfilling the national security interests of the United States.

Supporters of extended deterrence and nuclear war fighting did not see arms control in the same light. They recognized the fundamental incompatibility between stabilizing arms control measures and preserving the credibility of first use—and came down firmly on the side of the second priority. In their view, the arms control process was fundamentally flawed, and so arms negotiations were rejected entirely, especially if the process implicitly granted equal status to the Soviet Union. Arms control efforts that removed counterforce weapons or otherwise restricted the ability of the United States to project the credible threat of first use of nuclear weapons were also opposed.[10] As a result, arms control did not constrain the main strategic modernization programs (Myrdal 1982; Newhouse 1973; Talbott 1979).[11]

In the final analysis, extended deterrence threatens the security of the United States because it commits nuclear weapons to the goal of deterring conventional military attacks and unwarranted political influence against our allies. To make this commitment good, Washing-

---

10. In June 1992, President Bush agreed in principle to remove the MX missile, the most potent counterforce system, from the nuclear arsenal. (Washington will retain up to 1,750 Trident II sea-launched warheads, and air-launched cruise missiles, both of which are capable of some counterforce missions.) In return, the Russians agreed to dismantle their land-based MIRVed counterforce systems. By all accounts, the United States gained the most from the arrangement: arms control succeeded in preserving a somewhat reduced counterforce capability for the United States, while radically reducing that capability for Moscow. In addition, added control over the possibility of rogue nuclear warheads floating around the former Soviet Union will have been secured.

11. In the views predominating in the early 1980s, arms *races* were also seen as more stabilizing than arms *control*. Samuel Huntington, for example, asked, "Why have we been so successful in avoiding nuclear war for the past thirty years?" Not because of arms control. Huntington went on to argue: "It is totally wrong, just erroneous, to think that arms races inevitably lead to war. They don't. Quantitative arms races, those that involve the multiplication of the same weapons, usually do end in war. Qualitative arms races, for a variety of reasons, usually don't end in war. And I maintain that the nuclear arms race that the U.S. and Soviet Union have been engulfed in for the past thirty years has acted as a substitute for war" (1981).

ton has refused to rule out the first use of nuclear weapons.[12] In this thinking, the possibility of going nuclear first creates doubts among the political leaders of any potential aggressor, and thus prevents them from advancing military and political pressures in the first place. But the doctrine of plausible first use requires specific nuclear weapons to make that doctrine credible. These weapons themselves are destabilizing because they offer the illusion of being able to fight a nuclear war. In effect, counterforce and other war-fighting systems that are procured in the name of "making our commitment to our allies more credible," or "denying to the Soviets any capacity to achieve their objectives," cannot be distinguished from efforts to build a nuclear war–winning capability. War-fighting systems also introduce uncertainties in the political-military chain of command, particularly on the issue of who has the right to authorize the use of nuclear weapons.[13] Washington can claim that we do not contemplate a first strike. Indeed, most presidents and other political leaders would probably *not* use nuclear weapons first. Meanwhile, procuring nuclear weapons to "enhance deterrence," or to make more solid our global commitments and responsibilities, only sustains the argument by any potential enemy that the United States is preparing for a first strike. To Washington, the public explanation for counterforce is to protect our allies. To an opponent, U.S. counterforce capability is threatening. Thus, the logic of extended deterrence guarantees that at least some "enemy" decisionmakers will argue that the United States is seeking nuclear superiority and political leverage. In turn, these policymakers will conclude that their country should develop war-fighting systems, put their nuclear forces on higher stages of alert, or even on launch-on-warning status, in order to prevent them from being destroyed in a preemptive strike. This process is mutual. In the words of Thomas Schelling, the situation is underscored by the "reciprocal fear of surprise attack" (1960, 1966). The worst-case scenario of each side is that the other side is preparing to gain political and military advantage by striking first. Leaders on each side will argue that "we" should move closer to the nuclear trigger to avoid being caught unawares by "them." But in the circumstances of nuclear war there is no distinc-

---

12. President George Bush recently offered a partial revision of this long-standing doctrine. The "new" strategy is one of "no *early* first use" of nuclear weapons. The overall possibility of using nuclear weapons first has not been withdrawn.

13. Kohn and Harahan (1988) offer a frightening example from the 1950s involving Eisenhower, Curtis LeMay and the Strategic Air Command.

tion between "us" and "them." Like it or not, the potential for loss of control over nuclear forces, the prospect of nuclear winter, and the uncertainties of anger and revenge bind the fates of both sides. For a nuclear war to stop, we are dependent upon the decisions of those whom our leaders considered sufficiently dangerous that we had to go to nuclear war with them in the first place. In the final analysis, the development of counterforce mandated by extended deterrence poses as much of a threat to our own population as it does to an aggressor. Another way to achieve security against nuclear war must be sought.

Basic Deterrence in the 1990s

The weapons systems required by basic deterrence are more modest than those demanded by doctrines of nuclear war fighting, and the savings that could result from the adoption of such a policy are significant. The nuclear arsenal is a comparatively small component of the defense budget. Spending in fiscal year 1990 on strategic nuclear forces was $52 billion, or roughly 17 percent of the official budget of the Department of Defense (Kaufmann 1990a:9).[14] The START Treaty provides for reductions to as many as 6,000 (from more than 10,000) strategic warheads, with little dollar savings. On the other hand, William Kaufmann's more ambitious proposal for restructuring U.S. defense forces provides for reductions in strategic allocations to an annual outlay of $29.1 billion in fiscal 1994, or a decrease in the annual cost of more than 44 percent, even though his recommendations do not explicitly call for basic deterrence, and would retain the capability of delivering 2,400 warheads against Moscow even after a well-executed surprise attack (1990a:16).

The explicit adoption of basic deterrence, which would probably lead to still greater savings, relies on the following conditions, each of which becomes more important as the size of the nuclear arsenal decreases (Beckman et al. 1992:269–70):

1. The number of warheads per launcher must be reduced. Single-warhead missiles cannot destroy more than one enemy missile; their use

14. Because nuclear warhead production, which accounted for roughly another $10 billion, is formally part of the Department of Energy, the official figures understate the true cost of nuclear systems. Even after accounting for such hidden costs, the point concerning the comparatively low price of nuclear systems remains valid.

depletes the arsenal of the attacker faster than it depletes the weapons of the country being attacked.

2. Defensive systems must be contained, including antisubmarine warfare as well as ballistic missile defense.
3. Antisatellite and space-based weapons must be banned. Antisatellite systems threaten a country's capacity to respond to nuclear attack. In response, the country that feels itself vulnerable may move its own missiles closer to launch status.
4. Offensive systems with short warning times must be eliminated.
5. The survivability of command and communication systems, sometimes called C^3I, must be enhanced, so that war-fighting strategies based on the "decapitation" of the other side's leadership cannot be carried out.
6. Verification and other confidence building systems must be developed.[15]

Basic deterrence would rely heavily on submarine-launched ballistic missiles (SLBMs). The invulnerability and comparative lack of accuracy of these systems make them more stabilizing than land-based missiles. Ideally, a small number of single-warhead missiles based on submarines would guarantee a nuclear retaliatory capability without threatening an attack with accurate multiple warheads. On the other hand, continuing improvements in the Trident II (D-5) SLBM are strengthening that system's counterforce potential. Other legs of the strategic triad might be restructured with the goal of preserving an assured second strike. A small number of warheads could be placed on stand-off bombers (B-52s or the existing B-1s would be sufficient), and it may be prudent to deploy a land-based, single-warhead, mobile missile. Jettisoning the MX as a MIRVed counterforce system is a good step. Even allowing for redundancy, the United States and the former Soviet Union could reduce their current inventory of more than fifty thousand total warheads to one thousand or fewer.[16]

---

15. More detailed proposals for basic deterrence (also called "minimal" or "finite" deterrence) are provided in Kaufmann 1990; Feiveson and von Hippel 1990; and Bethe, Gottfried and McNamara 1991.

16. The exact method of deploying these warheads is not specified here, and might in fact differ from one country to another. Garwin (1988:10) has suggested a basing plan of 400 single-warhead small ICBMs, 400 warheads among 50 small submarines (8 single-warhead SLBMs on each ship), and 200 warheads carried on 100 aircraft (two air-launched cruise missiles on each aircraft). Versions of basic deterrence elaborated by Moscow just before the Soviet Union dissolved relied more on mobile land-based systems than either fixed silos or SLBMs. Moscow fears the accuracy of U.S. systems, thinks that communications are less reliable with submarines than with land-based systems, and considers, verification procedures to

Basic deterrence involves more than specific numbers and types of weapons. Stability would be enhanced by a series of political steps including the declaration of no first use of nuclear weapons and a comprehensive test ban treaty. Further stability could be acquired by strengthening verification using satellites and other technical means pertaining to individual nations, as well as by adopting so-called intrusive measures. Other confidence-building measures are possible, including creating crisis control centers, strengthening the ABM Treaty banning space-based weapons, and establishing more stringent proliferation controls. Indeed, genuine control of proliferation may depend ultimately on the drastic reduction of current arsenals by the nuclear powers. Finally, it may be necessary to improve command, control, and communication systems (C^3I) so that political authorities remain in constant contact with the retaliatory forces and do not feel any urgency to respond immediately to information of an impending attack (Steinbruner 1981/82).[17]

Basic Deterrence and Nonproliferation

The START Treaty will allow the United States nine thousand deployed strategic warheads and the former Soviet Union eight thousand. Recent proposals on both sides provide for still lower numbers. But even if agreement for further reductions are reached, each country will have thousands of bombs that cannot be deployed but are not destroyed either. Each side will also have thousands of tactical warheads. China, Britain, and France will together have approximately fifteen hundred warheads. India and Israel (and possibly South Africa) have still more. Furthermore, several other countries are actively pursuing nuclear status. Many observers feel that the spread of technology and material is the most pressing nuclear threat. From the standpoint of developing a genuinely new world order, the existence of so many atomic bombs and the continued proliferation of nuclear weapons capability is obviously unacceptable. What can Washington

---

be simpler if both sides deploy only nuclear-dedicated systems (Kokoshin 1988). Long-range bombers, for example, pose the problem of multiple (conventional and nuclear) use. Shenfield (1989) provides an important review of recent Soviet debates over basic deterrence. At this writing, a strategic concept for nuclear weapons has yet to emerge from Russia or the republics.

17. The ability to "wait out" an initial attack without fear of "decapitation," or be able to respond at one's own choosing, is stabilizing. It minimizes the chances of becoming the victim of a preemptive attack and significantly lowers the threshold of accidental war.

do to create more stability and enhance its security, not only in its military relations with Russia and the republics of the former Soviet Union, but also with respect to the proliferation of nuclear weapons?

One answer is still more ambitious arms control. On this issue, the best example is the Treaty on the Nonproliferation of Nuclear Weapons, signed in 1968 by 62 nations including the United States and the Soviet Union (Spector 1984). There are now 141 signatories. Unfortunately, France, China, India, Israel, and South Africa, all of whom have or are thought to possess nuclear explosives, have not signed the treaty. While our worst fears concerning nuclear weapons proliferation have not been realized, an additional concern is that a significant number of countries, including Pakistan, Brazil, Argentina, Iraq, North Korea, South Korea, Taiwan, and Libya, have improved their technical skills with regard to the possible manufacture and delivery of nuclear weapons. Other countries, especially in Europe, are capable of acquiring a nuclear capability, and the possibility also exists that bombs, weapons-grade materials, and nuclear experts will be exported from the former Soviet Union. Better global control of nuclear weapons is needed.

The explicit adoption of basic deterrence on the part of the United States will help secure a stronger commitment to the nonproliferation of nuclear weapons. Several nonaligned nations, particularly India, have argued that the Nonproliferation Treaty only ratifies the status quo and preserves a double standard under which between five and eight countries possess atomic bombs while the privilege is denied to the rest of the world. They point out that Article VI of the treaty commits all signatories to work toward universal nuclear disarmament. As the accomplishments of the major nuclear powers have not been impressive in this respect, little progress toward stricter control has been stimulated among the second tier of nuclear-capable and nearly nuclear-capable nations. Nations currently interested in acquiring nuclear weapons will be dissuaded from that intention only through the reassurance that nuclear weapons will not play a significant role in future global politics. As long as Washington continues to act as though nuclear weapons are useful, at least some other countries will also feel that their status and leverage are enhanced by a nuclear arsenal.[18]

---

18. Consider the extreme scenario in which terrorists smuggle a suitcase bomb into the United States and detonate it in a major urban area as support for the idea that genuine control can be secured only through political means. While such an act would likely be the product of deranged thinking, effective protection against this kind of threat requires not only

Hans Bethe, Kurt Gottfried, and Robert McNamara link reductions in the nuclear arsenal and nonproliferation as follows: "A very deep and swift cut in U.S. and Soviet forces, which should be reduced from their present total of approximately 50,000 warheads to something on the order of two thousand, is possible. To do so would, at one stroke, force the U.S. and the [former] USSR to adopt far less dangerous nuclear strategies and strengthen the global effort to halt the spread of nuclear weapons." The authors also connect changes in the nuclear arsenal with elements of the new world order: "These changes in nuclear policy [the adoption of basic deterrence] would be a major step toward a world in which relations among nations would be based on the rule of law, supported by a system of collective security, with the United Nations and regional organizations able to resolve conflicts and keep the peace" (1991:48).

Adopting a comprehensive test ban would be another important step in controlling proliferation (Doty 1987). During the mandated five-year Non Proliferation Treaty review proceedings, several nonaligned nations, especially Mexico, have pressed the nuclear powers to adopt a comprehensive test ban treaty. This step would help counter the dangerous argument among the tier of near nuclear-capable nations that an atomic arsenal enhances one's position in world politics. One implication of a CTB is that continued weapons modernization is not necessary and that our existing knowledge of nuclear explosions and warhead reliability is sufficient. The only reason to continue testing is to refine warheads so that they can carry out precise military missions (and hence convey a political message). A CTB would reject this example of conventionalized thinking about nuclear weapons and greatly assist the transformation of the old world order. Here as well, stronger control over proliferation will follow more easily after Washington explicitly acknowledges a reduced political and military role for its strategic arsenal.

Democracy and the Adoption of Basic Deterrence

Except for the few periods of active mobilization, U.S. policies concerning nuclear weapons have been made without significant citizen

---

strict control of the spread of nuclear technology, but an atmosphere in world politics where unresolved grievances are taken seriously. Marginalized and disaffected groups carry the seeds of potential terrorism. The security of United States citizens will be enhanced if such groups feel that there may be a just resolution to their legitimate grievances. The creation of such an atmosphere depends in part on a shift in nuclear strategy by the United States.

involvement. The conventional picture of democratic pluralism—the pull and tug of different interest groups, debate within the legislative branch, congressional checks upon the executive branch, expressed differences among agencies within the executive branch, and the formation of competing coalitions that reach down into the public to gain support—has corresponded less to the formation and development of nuclear weapons policy than any other issue in U.S. politics. Almost every other subject of government policy has seen stronger signs of citizen and interest group engagement. Some private interests, particularly in the defense sector, have profited from the continued emphasis on strategic modernization and have utilized a variety of lobbying and propaganda tactics to sustain it (Adams 1981; Bertsch and Shaw 1984). But businesses as a group, even those eager to expand their international markets, have not actively pushed for strategic modernization. During the Cold War, business has generally shared Washington's perception of the need to project offensive military force. However, business has not played a major role in the specific development of strategic doctrine, as it has in other policy areas. Even the most politically astute representatives of the business community probably consider the subject arcane or otherwise beyond their purview. Even the military itself, while it has benefited from extended deterrence, has not been nearly as involved as have certain key civilians in the development of the concepts that have guided strategic modernization (Herken 1987; Kaplan 1983). The various branches of the armed forces drew upon the presumed urgency of the Soviet threat as a rationale for selected programs and weapons systems. But these initiatives were based on assumptions regarding Soviet behavior that had been created and sustained by the intellectual class. Ideology, more than interest, has sustained extended deterrence. The political process in other areas such as health care, taxation, tariffs and trade, and environmental regulation may fall short of the pluralist ideal (Domhoff 1983; Lindblom 1977). But the range of alternatives within the established policy-making arena, and the engagement of different social actors in the policy process, has been far greater on these issues than on nuclear policy. Dahl (1985) has even asserted that the development of strategic weapons policy has not reflected any aspect of democratic politics except for occasional and limited disagreement within a small part of the policy elite.[19] In *Nuclear Weapons and*

---

19. My disagreement with this position, and my argument that the public, primarily

World Politics, David Gombert articulates the implications of nuclear weapons for democracy.

> In the long run, the existence of nuclear weapons could fundamentally alter government-citizen relations. If, over time, the need of government to field expensive deterrent forces is not appreciated by citizens who no longer sense a real nuclear threat, popular support for the maintenance of forces could fade—and governments might feel themselves compelled to provide for deterrence without the consent of the governed. (Quoted in Falk 1982:2)

In fact, nuclear issues are not beyond the reach of the public. Greater public involvement will speed the adoption of basic deterrence. A progressive coalition and presidential candidate can deepen this involvement, because much of the public already believes that basic deterrence should be our policy (see Chapter 3). The process of identifying a policy that has gone wrong (extended deterrence), rejecting the accompanying weapons that are no longer needed (counterforce systems, strategic defense, and continued warhead testing), and retooling the nuclear arsenal to provide greater stability, will reverse some of the more damaging trends that have compromised the quality of democratic life (Barber 1984).

The negative impact of nuclear weapons on democracy is partly cultural. We have sanitized and trivialized our references to nuclear weapons and the terror they represent. For example, during the Cold War, preserving the "balance of terror" became a good, a precious commodity that we did not want to upset. Measuring the impact of similar distorted reference points on our language and our sensibilities about violence is extremely difficult (Boyer 1985; Caldicott 1984; Cohn 1987; Lifton and Falk 1982; Mack 1982). Nuclear "peace" has been accompanied by such a strong threat of war that most of us accept the capacity for Armageddon as the natural course of human affairs. The threat of war appears permanent and we devote a significant part of our intellectual and material resources in preparation for it. Our capacity to consider alternatives is now very limited. Our learned helplessness before the nuclear threat is hastening the ongoing erosion of citizen rights and duties (Lifton and Falk 1982). Finally, the secrecy that must surround nuclear weapons has helped create

---

through the mobilization of social movements, has had an influence on nuclear weapons policy, was presented in Chapter 4. The issue here is somewhat different: the level of knowledge and involvement of the public as a whole during "normal" periods of policy formation.

political alienation and acceptance of the thesis that the modern human condition is one of vulnerability before bureaucratic and state structures. In this sense, extended deterrence and the Cold War has become an ideological form of social control that we must now attempt to dismantle (Falk 1982; Kaldor 1990).

Ironically, as the immediate dangers of the superpower confrontation begin to recede, it may become even more difficult to force ourselves to think about the unthinkable. We may become still more complacent, still more accepting of a false sense of security, still more willing to accept a "smaller" nuclear arsenal as consistent with the normal state of affairs. We may accept recent arms control developments as all that can be realistically achieved. The START process will cut the level of warheads and stop a few weapon systems. Other reductions may follow. But we run the considerable risk of accepting reduced numbers as a panacea rather than achieving true social and political control. The reduction of ten thousand weapons to five thousand or three thousand may appear to be sensible progress and a prudent hedge against the uncertainties of tomorrow. But the numbers have little meaning. Progress will come only with the transformation of the current conventionalized thinking whereby nuclear weapons are labeled useful for our security. The alternative of adopting basic deterrence is both a policy reversal and a component of democratic renewal that is central to the peace process.[20]

Manipulation of the public is an additional consequence of the continued reliance on nuclear weapons for political influence. Historically, when politicians and defense department officials have referred to the "need to bolster deterrence," the majority of the public has thought that they were speaking of the need for more nuclear

20. Adopting basic deterrence and a comprehensive test ban may be vital for preserving the fledgling democracy in Russia that must be nurtured for U.S. security in the long run. As George Perkovich observes: "The development of democracy in Russia will be significantly impaired if the Russian military-industrial complex is allowed to overcome popular and legislative demands for an end to nuclear testing. The environmental movement is perhaps the most important constituency in Russia, especially insofar as it unites conservative nationalist and liberal greens. This movement and its elected representatives strongly oppose the resumption of testing for environmental reasons and because continued testing will enable the nuclear weapons establishment to maintain its claims to large budgets, secrecy, and independence from democratic oversight.

"U.S. weapons tests play a role in this issue. U.S. testing is a strong lever for Russian nuclear officials, most of whom are anti-democratic carryovers from the Cold War. These Russians officials simply adopt the U.S. nuclear establishment's arguments for continued testing and translate them into Russia. If the United States must test, they say, Russia must test too" (1992:17).

weapons so that the United States could strike back if Moscow or some other country attacked first. The public may also have believed that we needed to redress a presumed gap in the overall strategic balance. These goals were considered legitimate and did not invoke opposition. But the actual meaning of the call to bolster deterrence has never been to insure our ability to retaliate after suffering a surprise attack. Instead, with this call political leaders seek public support for additional nuclear war–fighting systems. This devious use of the multiple meanings of deterrence also weakens the quality of democracy.

Extended deterrence and its attendant demand for modernization of nuclear weapons has also concentrated power in the executive branch of government, particularly in the presidency. Nuclear weapons enhance the interests of the national security apparatus as a whole. But presidents are also attracted to the special qualities of nuclear weapons and derive a considerable degree of political influence from their existence. Secrecy and special command procedures sustain presidential power and secure the president's role in defining the principal threats to the United States and what should be the appropriate response. Proposing new strategic systems can be a valuable way of managing internal Pentagon politics. And a president's virtual control over public pronouncements on strategic policy make it possible to influence the electorate. One of the best examples is President Jimmy Carter's use of Presidential Directive 59, which called for strategic modernization and new plans to fight a limited nuclear war, to protect his right political flank during the 1980 electoral campaign against Ronald Reagan. In this sense, presidents "like" nuclear weapons. They are politically useful even when presidents have no intention of using them militarily.[21]

Finally, the nearly universal adherence to extended deterrence helped secure a form of bipartisanship—that is, cooperation between the Democrats and Republicans in keeping the range of foreign and defense policy debate narrow. No national political campaign has argued that the use of nuclear weapons to gain political influence is dangerous and should be modified. Any progressive impulses that emerged during the Cold War stemmed from social movements on do-

---

21. This observation probably applies to executive authority in all countries that possess nuclear weapons. In France and Great Britain, nuclear weapons have furthered central political authority. The same was true for the Soviet Union during the Cold War era (Holloway 1984). During the breakup of the Soviet Union, one of the most important points of leverage left to Mikhail Gorbachev was the need for continued control of nuclear weapons. Boris Yeltsin seems to be using them in the same way.

mestic issues and from opposition to specific wars. Alternative foreign and defense policies have not been considered in the mainstream debate. The process of adopting basic deterrence will broaden the debate to include the goals of U.S. foreign policy and the meaning of national security in the new world order.

In the meantime, the search for another way, a search that carries us through the self-conscious adoption of basic deterrence and eventual nuclear disarmament, will not be carried out by the political elite alone. Some members of the elite will support such changes, but only in response to public mobilization. The Pentagon may not, in the post-Cold War world, pursue a concerted program of strategic modernization. Most existing nuclear weapons systems will either continue on their own inertia, or be scaled back only as far as budgetary constraints demand. Adopting basic deterrence is not an ultimate resolution—to the nuclear predicament as it now exists between the United States and the former Soviet Union, or to the threat posed by the possible spread of nuclear weapons over the next two decades. As many have pointed out, we cannot un-invent nuclear weapons. We must live with the fact that human beings can destroy themselves. Rather than accepting the orthodox conclusion that there is no substitute for the continuous task of managing inevitable nuclear tension, basic deterrence provides an opportunity to achieve the stability required to finally remove atomic bombs from the face of the earth. Achieving stable basic deterrence will permit us to discuss more realistically how we might create the global political conditions necessary to achieve full nuclear disarmament (Schell 1986; Schwartz and Derber 1990).

Basic deterrence is a necessary way station on the road to global nuclear disarmament. More immediately, basic deterrence can strengthen our security, help curb proliferation, and enhance the quality of democratic life within the United States. A presidential candidate can, through clear and careful articulation, offer a forceful explanation of the security benefits offered by a shift to basic deterrence, resurrect the optimism that is critical to political realignment, and counter the declining expectations that afflict much of the electorate. Most of the public wants the United States to continue to be a leader in world politics. A presidential candidate could present a shift to basic deterrence as the best way to preserve U.S. strength and security while beginning the transformation from a foreign policy premised on the need to project offensive military force to one based on the fulfillment of human rights and global justice. Basic deterrence reduces the risk of war, reduces the costs of preparing for war, and helps manage nuclear proliferation. The process of adopting this policy will help in a much-needed redefinition of the national interest and stimulate movement toward the creation of a new world order. By developing these themes, a presidential candidate could use nuclear weapons issues to develop among the public a sense of the universal interests that lie behind a shift in strategy, and thereby strengthen overall public support for the progressive political agenda. This role for presidential politics and other possibilities of progressive change are addressed directly in the concluding chapter.

7

Peace Politics: Obstacles and Possibilities

DRAMATIC CHANGES in global politics now offer an opportunity to strengthen the social foundations of the United States and to build a new world order. The definition of national security that prevailed during the Cold War rested ultimately on the projection of offensive military force and on the development of global economic interdependence guided by the principle of expanding market forces. The focus during the old world order upon external enemies helped create a national security state, which in turn configured domestic politics. A significant portion of the domestic economy was militarized. The public expected a war to occur and accepted as "natural" the commitment of between 5 and 10 percent of the gross national product to the acquisition of modern weapons and the training of personnel to use them. The political agenda narrowed as well. Constant preparations to fight the Soviet Union and Third World revolutionary forces made it more difficult to provide universal health care, rebuild our cities, improve public education, redress social inequalities, counter the spread of violence, and protect the environment.

What is the alternative? Currently, the war system in the United States is linked to alarming trends in the developing world including the destruction of rain forests, poverty, and the debt crisis. Among the results are violence, threats to democracy, global warming, and the drug trade. In building a new world order premised on common security, Washington should instead pursue human rights, environmental protection, stronger mechanisms of conflict resolution, and a form of international development that will strengthen our own economy while providing greater global justice. Achieving national security in concert with the rest of the world will require dramatic reductions in global militarization. Cutting arms expenditures and limiting the influence of military factors in global politics does not, in itself, constitute peace. But these measures form the threshold that must be crossed before the full range of world and domestic reforms can be effectively pursued. A new world order cannot be built around continued global military expenditures of $1 trillion a year. Nor can it be built around military expenditures in the U.S. of $250 billion to $300 billion a year.

Unfortunately, many features of the Gulf War, in which a U.S.–led coalition forced the Iraqi military to abandon its occupation of Kuwait, strengthened the old world order and the traditional concept of national security. Identifying a new enemy, the apparent success of military force, and the public celebration of the war—despite the rhetorical invocation of a "new world order"—seemed to preserve the status quo. At the same time, the Gulf War failed to resolve the underlying problems of the region. As in Vietnam, Lebanon, and Panama, Washington's use of military force created only human pain, local destabilization, and physical ruin. The only purpose served was to uphold the mistaken premise that military force should continue to be a central element of national policy. Never have the limits of armed conflict as an instrument of policy been more apparent. Though the Bush administration would deny this conclusion, it obliquely recognized the delicate status of the utility of war by the extraordinary attention it devoted to obtaining public support for the war. Washington also engaged in a protracted legitimation process in Congress and at the United Nations before committing its military forces. These actions will constrain the unilateral use of U.S. military force in the future. Thus, the paradox of the Gulf War is that it contains significant peace elements, or harbingers of a genuine new world order.

The public can be mobilized to support programs of common security and domestic renewal. Opinion polls demonstrate incipient support for policies based on alternative concepts of security—support that is all the more remarkable considering the virtual absence of an articulated alternative in the mainstream press and media and in other political forums. By itself, however, public opinion does not carry sufficient influence to enact a new political agenda. To achieve genuine change in our national and global priorities, social movements that mobilize opinion, bring new issues to the political arena, and create momentum for change are also necessary. A new coalition of social movements does not have to forge a single political identity. But it must create enough common ground among its participants that the connotations of peace reverberate positively among those concerned foremost with achieving full employment, reducing urban violence, protecting the environment, winning more clout for labor, and gaining equality for women and people of color.

Developing the concept of a "peace economy" is central to the emergence of this coalition. Given recent changes in the world situation, dramatic reductions of the military budget are both possible and necessary to support reordered domestic priorities. A significant "peace dividend" is possible, but only if the savings are to be applied to a variety of projects that are identified with the restoration of the economic strength of the United States. Other possible applications of the peace dividend, such as debt reduction, financial stabilization, and the preservation of local employment opportunities, are important. But it will be left to a progressive political movement to connect much lower military spending and economic conversion on the one hand, with the *universal* interest in restoring manufacturing strength, adopting more sound ecological practices, and investing in the public infrastructure on the other.

Adopting basic deterrence as a policy governing nuclear weapons is also critical. Despite the transformation of the Cold War and lower numbers of strategic warheads, modernization of many aspects of the nuclear arsenal continues. Moving toward basic deterrence will save money, be more consistent with the security interests of Americans, and ease the transformation of a global order dominated by one or two "policemen" to a more cooperative framework. Basic deterrence is also important because it will strengthen efforts to achieve global control over the proliferation of nuclear armaments and conventional, chemical and biological weapons. Adopting basic deterrence will also improve the ways we arrive at political outcomes. Currently, that process is dominated by money from lobbying groups and special interests, by congressional micromanagement, by undue attention to the self-interest of individual politicians, and by bureaucratic inertia stemming from the Cold War. Political decisions are not governed by deliberate, rational choice. Since it is in our interest to reform the ways in which ideology, interests, and inertia affect critical defense decisions, a conscious reordering of nuclear policy carries broader significance for the quality of our democratic institutions.

Since World War II the United States, particularly in its foreign and defense policies, has been a conservative nation. The changes outlined in this book would represent a significant departure from many current practices and can be achieved only through fundamental political realignment.

> Eras of critical realignment [as defined by Walter Dean Burnham] are marked by short, sharp reorganizations of the mass coalitional bases of the major parties which occur at periodic intervals on the national level; are often preceded by major third-party revolts which reveal the incapacity of "politics as usual" to integrate, much less aggregate, emergent political demand; are closely associated with abnormal stress in the socioeconomic system; are marked by ideological polarizations and issue-distances between the major parties which are exceptionally large by normal standards; and have durable consequences as constituent acts which determine the outer boundaries of policy in general, though not necessarily of politics in detail. (1970:10)

Realignment redefines what is politically possible. In the case of peace politics, the new priorities are a defense budget cut at least in half; a foreign policy predicated on the pursuit of democracy and human rights, global development, and environmental enhancement; full employment and greater equality at home; and the development of democratic mechanisms that would improve economic coordination while readjusting the balance between public good and private interests. Changes of the magnitude described here cannot be finessed within the existing orientation of the two-party system, although the possibility that they may be represented by a transformed Democratic party remains open.

Conditions for the Development of Progressive Politics

Obviously, one can only speculate as to the precise form in which policies geared toward establishing a new world order and achieving domestic renewal could be enacted by a progressive political coalition; but two components are critical. The first is a local base of social activism; the second is a series of presidential campaigns that would give national visibility to programs of common security. While each must be present for realignment to occur, it is useful to distinguish between a "bottom-up" approach resting upon the activities of local social movements and other political organizations, and a "top-down" process revolving around a national leader who catalyzes local activism. The main features of the bottom-up approach include the following:

- More citizens participate in local organizations, most of which continue to focus on single issues. This activity helps develop alternative policies and provides the momentum that enables these policies to enter the main political arena.
- Local political coalitions are formed. Organizational structures emerge that permit fuller appreciation of the links between issues, and awareness of shared interest in the reduction of the defense budget and the transformation of military policy. These discussions help reduce (but probably cannot eliminate) tensions among single-issue advocacy groups and their different constituencies. Political gravity begins to shift away from the single-issue focus and toward the coalitions and political formations that represent newly articulated shared interests.
- Revitalized single-issue groups and local coalitions engage in a broad range of activities. Wherever possible, more direct public involvement in educational efforts, lobbying, petition campaigns, and other forms of democratic activity is cultivated. In some cases, local coalitions run slates of candidates for urban and statewide political offices. Support for congressional campaigns supplements these activities.
- A presidential candidate emerges who is capable of presenting a vision of the new world order, domestic renewal, and the need to redefine security. The candidate is also capable of articulating the specific policies necessary to fulfill that vision. Initially, the campaign is aimed less at winning than at building a base of support within the Democratic party. The campaign gains press and media coverage and gives national exposure to progressive politics. Local political forces continue to gather strength. Indeed, the further development of local coalitions reflects the exposure that derives from the national campaign. Numerous tactical issues emerge, both between the presidential candidate and the local coalitions, and within the Democratic party itself.
- Progressive politics gains the attention of the national press who report on its developments in new, more favorable "frames": For example, greater visibility is given to the broad range of political *participation* at the local level, in much the same way as freeze politics were identified with the New England town meeting in press coverage in 1981 and 1982. Or the creation of a new world order and redefinition of national security are presented as fresh *alternatives* to the mainstream of the Democratic and Republican parties. More policy-linked frames include *equality*, *nonviolence*, or the possibilities of establishing a *mutuality* of interests. Circulation of existing progressive magazines increases and a new national daily newspaper is formed.
- Progressive think tanks become important arenas for the development of specific policies associated with the new world order and domestic

renewal. Academic work in universities becomes more relevant for the development of progressive politics.

- A new set of political symbols begins to emerge. The transition from spectator militarism to a civic culture that values peace is strengthened in diverse forms of popular culture including art, television, drama, and music. New symbolic understandings that counter the mythology of the old world order would be created. Examples of the themes to be communicated include appreciation of the costs of war, the value of conflict resolution, further environmental awareness, and acceptance of social activism as a more positive role for citizens. Rather than creating a radical break with the past, these symbols express and strengthen those elements of a positive civic culture that already exist.

Political realignment could also be focused more directly by a presidential campaign. Running for the presidency is especially important due to the weaknesses of political parties as forums for political debate and as vehicles for the development of policy-oriented platforms. A national leader could articulate the need for domestic renewal and the benefits for national security of moving toward a new world order. A presidential candidate could also legitimate the need for significant policy reform for the public and the media. The contradictions and ambiguities that now characterize the embryonic support for progressive politics within public opinion would change. While skepticism, hesitation, and even opposition would certainly continue, the overall contour of public attitudes would become more supportive of new alternatives. The debates and publicity that accompany a presidential campaign would also serve as an important vehicle for spreading progressive ideas. Local coalitions and social movements would continue to be important, but the impetus for their growth would derive as much from national developments as from local organizing efforts. At the same time, citizens participating in grass-roots activities would be important political assets for voter registration, fund-raising, influencing local and regional policies, and spreading ideas.

Will some form of progressive politics actually emerge over the 1990s? Certainly, there is nothing inevitable about this prospect. Intellectually, as the rest of this chapter will explore, there are good reasons to remain skeptical. Yet, the future cannot be predicted. The promise of common security and a new world order, popular participation in making history, the inclusion of the disenfranchised, and the development of a more vital and compelling political and social culture remains a vision. On one important level, progressive realignment is an act of faith; and the possibility that it will occur cannot be eliminated, simply because enough people may want it to happen and may get together to make it happen.

Naive? Hopelessly idealistic? Possibly. Yet we should remind ourselves that no one predicted the emergence of Mikhail Gorbachev and the possibilities of political democracy in Eastern Europe and the former Soviet Union. But that which was most unexpected came to pass. Similarly, any rational, empirically grounded assessment of the U.S. South during the mid-1950s would have predicted that a nonviolent movement for civil rights would fail. While the goal of racial equality remains unfulfilled, the civil rights movement brought about such fundamental transformations as black empowerment, greater acceptance of equality on the part of many whites, and a new legal role for the federal government in ending discrimination. The chance that the beginning of a new century will see the emergence of a progressive political coalition vying for national political power is certainly no more remote than the probability that neo-Stalinism and Jim Crow would be transformed by peaceful means.

The remainder of this chapter examines a range of obstacles to the political project of linking a new world order to domestic renewal. Much of this skepticism captures those aspects of the contemporary United States that solidify the status quo. My procedure is to temper each obstacle, or reason why political realignment will not occur, with counterarguments of my own. This exploration of the social space for progressive politics to develop does not conclude that the skeptics are wrong—only that the situation is more fluid than most realize. Mine is an exercise in what the innovative Italian theorist Antonio Gramsci called "pessimistic of the intellect, optimism of the will."

Can Progressive Politics Emerge?

The Problem of Popular Culture

Objection. The political culture prevailing in the United States may restrict the development of progressive politics. The United States has been described as essentially non-ideological, pragmatic, and suspicious of any political tendency that threatens to depart from the policies that have produced prosperity for a significant number of Americans. Even if a progressive movement starts to develop, it will flounder against the values that secure the center of the political spectrum.

This objection, perhaps the most critical of those to be considered, can be further developed in several steps. First, Americans may seem programmatically liberal. A majority support policies on defense, social spending, and the environment that are consistent with the new world order and a progressive agenda (see Chapter 3). In terms of overall ideology, however, individuals are more likely to label themselves conservative when asked by pollsters to locate themselves along the ideological spectrum. By this measure, over the past fifteen years, U.S. citizens have become even more conservative. A progressive coalition may invoke deeply held ideological hostility for the overall vision rather than the strong support foreshadowed by acceptance of particular policy options. In this case, the whole may actually be less than the sum of its parts.

Second, support for a new world order shown in public opinion polls may not reflect deep-seated values. Instead, poll results may be understood more as a moment in the ongoing oscillation within the existing political spectrum. Positions that seem to indicate an openness to significant change should be construed more as evidence of a desire to restore balance by moving away from what is now regarded as an overlong commitment to conservative positions during the 1980s. Public opinion should be interpreted more as a desire to return to the moderate center than as support for dramatic new ventures.

Third, a stronger role for progressive politics implies a critique of the current quality of life in the United States. The development of an alternative set of politics will require a more honest—and negative—assessment of prevailing strengths and weaknesses than has been offered by either of the two political parties. Yet the existing political culture may not tolerate such extensive criticism. As a people, we often want to be reassured that everything is fine. Much of President Reagan's popularity, and to a lesser degree that of Bush as well, is attributable to the subliminal message that nothing is fundamentally wrong with the country. To fix things up, all we have to do is go back to what has worked in the past. The cultural obstacle to reform is the fear of change itself (and its requirement that we look more honestly at ourselves as a society).

Fourth, popular culture is rife with hatred, anger, and violence. To take but one example: if a movement for significant realignment does develop, the chances of its presidential candidate being shot are remarkably high. A strong commitment to greater equality could be interpreted by some social groups as a threat to their social status, a reaction that in U.S. history has been associated with hate politics and scapegoating. Difficult times can easily reinforce simplistic "us" versus "them" dichotomies and obscure the need for universal programs premised on shared fate. The past decade has already seen numerous examples of coded messages from political leaders signaling that bigotry will be tolerated. When combined with the core of racial, ethnic, and religious prejudice that already exists in much of our popular culture, the result is significant interference in one of the essential projects of peace politics: identifying common interests among the elements of a heterogenous population. Many professional politicians, especially in the Republican party, think that thinly disguised racial appeals can be used to win elections. The pattern of some recent political campaigns have, unfortunately, supported this point of view.

Fifth, the new world order and domestic renewal may be identified as nothing more than an expensive form of liberalism. Voters are already reluctant to support higher taxes, even for universal programs such as public education. The public may fear that new social policies will cost large amounts of money, and that the middle class will be taxed to pay for them. Here as well, the prospect of a new political departure may invoke basic cultural values regarding the role of government that restrict the possibilities for development.

Response. Many aspects of U.S. political culture will restrict the possibilities of new politics. But the barriers that have just been outlined do not comprise the entirety of U.S. culture. Nor do they address the possibility that these tendencies can be transformed. From the standpoint of progressive politics, public attitudes contain both opportunities and constraints. Some elements secure existing social priorities. Other aspects support change. Political culture is not a universally shared, homogeneous entity. Tremendous variation exists and no easy description is possible. Political culture is contradictory and composed more of jagged edges than of the consensual aspects allegedly shared by the entire population. Elements of incipient change share space with elements that consolidate the status quo, often within the same individual. Culturally, the United States is more contested than the formal political system is able to capture.[1] A few illustrations will help convey this point.

A progressive political movement can nurture two alternatives that already exist within our value system. The first is a richer concept of citizenship, one rooted more deeply in participation in public life. The second is an ethical code for individual behavior that calls for a strong respect for others and restores the social values celebrating human decency that are now eroding. Much of our existing social culture has left us indifferent to the suffering of others. Usually, we don't feel an urgency to counter violence, homelessness, poverty, abuse of public property, rising infant mortality, and other social pathologies that are quite possible to correct. We shrug our shoulders and tell each other that these things are terrible. A few people are capable of tossing an individual gesture against the onslaught. But all too frequently, it is hard to see the impact of such acts against the social tide of indifference. Our sense that we can do something to improve our future quality of life is becoming lost.

We do not want it to be this way. The desire for a just society and a more secure feeling for all of its members does not have to be imposed in any way. But our usual experience of the rights and obligations of citizenship is passive. We are supposed to vote (although only half the population thinks that it is worth their while to do so), keep up with the news, and avoid blatant criminal activity. Those who are especially dedicated participate in a local civic association or charitable organization. Unfortunately, no matter how many "points of light" these activities create, the root causes of our social problems are not addressed.

---

1. Culture is a tricky term and a few more words of explanation are in order. A stronger "culture of peace" does not imply a sea change in the core values that have characterized the United States over the course of its existence. In this, more fundamental, sense of culture, the United States is often described as favoring individualist values over collectivism, and pragmatism over ideology. In addition, U.S. culture demonstrates faith in scientific and technical solutions, optimism, and more focus upon the present and future than the past. History and tradition hold comparatively little meaning for the population. Changes in this cultural bedrock may occur, but usually quite slowly. But such descriptions are problematic. The internal contradictions and paradoxes of any culture defy easy characterization. Americans, for example, are said to be highly individualistic. Yet there are many examples of communal behavior, along with evidence of a strong desire for a society with a more developed sense of community. Fortunately, we can pass over the difficulty of developing an adequate description of the American value system. Creating a new world order is not oriented toward this level of cultural change; rather, change refers here to alteration of the symbols that carry political meaning and help orient political behavior.

Citizenship has come to mean only the exercise of individual rights. Liberty has been similarly restricted to the protection of these rights against a possibly repressive state. This negative concept of citizenship has become so dominant that it has become difficult to think of any other model of citizen participation. Peace politics can restore those values capable of guiding human life and social activity beyond the marketplace. A new world order would certainly reinforce individual rights, but would also give these rights new meaning by creating a more active, informed, and democratic citizenry. This more participatory, or positive, concept of citizenship is already present, albeit dimly. But contemporary society systematically undercuts the possibilities. It is hard to identify elements that comprise the "common good"—and harder still to point to places where our political culture encourages us to look. In fact, many would say that virtually any effort to define and pursue any collective set of interests smacks of the tyranny of the majority. Yet, without attention to the development and expression of individual rights in the pursuit of the common good, the exercise of even the more limited concept of citizenship is becoming ritualistic. A progressive movement can appeal to people's need to do a job well and to their desire to mark their lives with stronger social and individual commitments. These feelings lie close to the surface of our culture but are frustrated by the quality of contemporary life. Daily life can become more peaceful if we recapture the sense of moral obligation to others that is both necessary for a decent society and a source of satisfaction for the individuals living within it. By connecting with the deep impulse toward democracy, and the capacity for energy and innovation that is such a strong part of U.S. tradition, a civic culture of peace can move beyond the constant repetition of negative views to offer positive cultural benefits and a compelling vision of change.

For realignment to occur, the public must feel that it is actually possible to create a stronger structure of national and global security in which they will benefit. A progressive movement can serve as the lightning rod for the more positive inclinations in our current behaviors. Take as an example the claim that U.S. citizens are overtaxed and that progressive politics will be just another form of liberalism that will end up costing the public still more. The objective facts are clear: we pay a lower proportion of our income for taxes any other industrialized nation (Ferleger and Mandle 1991). Furthermore, our tax structure is the most regressive. The wealthy pay less of their income to the government than do the middle class. But these are not the political facts. United States citizens feel that the government plunders their hard-earned pay and that their tax dollars are essentially wasted. Is there an effective response? While it is already clear that the new world order and progressive politics are not conservative, a movement to redefine security must establish an identity beyond the commonly understood concept of liberalism as a federal, centrally administered, bureaucratically run series of expensive social programs. A key component of new approaches to security is retrieval of the lost sense that government can actually do some good.

Take the current anger of many voters as another example of how progressive politics must wend its way through existing cultural contradictions. Much of the population does not like politicians and holds them responsible for the deteriorating ability of government to do anything to improve the quality of life in the country. Many opinion surveys find increased political alienation, economic worries, and a personal sense of hopelessness. These discontents have increased political volatility whereby voters shift drastically in their pattern of participation and choice of candidates. In 1992, Ross Perot's run for the presidency drew on these feelings. Voters are less likely than ever to vote *for* someone. Instead they vote *against*, often in disgust. While a political movement cannot be based on this dynamic, the unpredictable cauldron that is the result could conceivably produce additional support for progressive politics. Voters now switching parties and candidates out of disgruntlement could, fortuitously, combine with those making a more explicit political choice to produce additional support for progressive candidates. Recent elections in Minnesota and Ontario, for example, saw progressive politicians and parties voted into office partly because of the slow, patient building of political support, and partly because of "accidental" factors such as voters siding with new alternatives out of anger at the tactics employed by the more established candidates. Political disenchantment does not guarantee support for progressive politics. Anger is more like a wild card—a catalyst whose dimensions and impact are unpredictable. But the crisis of legitimacy left by the failure of the Democrats to offer an alternative to Republicans, and by citizen recoil from the thinness of our democratic life, has left the door open to new ideas and political alternatives.

It is especially important for a movement centered on a new definition of national security to be reassuring. A new world order and political realignment must not feel threatening. The perception must be that programs of common security and the domestic progressive agenda represent the most practical strategy of providing good jobs and enhancing our standard of living without demanding a dramatic tax increase. In a new world order, people will still be able to have cars, own single-family homes, go on vacation, shop in malls, watch television, and own VCRs. Redefining security rests on traditional beliefs: hard work brings just rewards; flexibility and innovation are important assets; bureaucracy gets in the way of creativity; giving to others is fine but the best system is one that enables people to help themselves; everyone has a right to equal opportunity; we should want the best for our children and expect that our children's future will be better than our own. In these respects, the basic aspects of alternative social policies are already familiar. At the same time, it is crucial that progressive politics not be equated with expensive handouts that will continue to subsidize alleged dependency on government bureaucracies. This false perception fuels the current anger, hostility to taxes, and scapegoating along racial lines that is so prevalent in our political system. The best answer is the development of policies premised on universal entitlements such as full employment, quality public education, health coverage, and social security. Economic justice is a tremendous unifier.

The cultural component of domestic renewal also brings us to the relationship between peace politics and ethnic diversity. Peace politics projects a common interest in reconceptualizing security, creating a new world order, and using a peace dividend to support a variety of projects that will strengthen our future. Multiculturalism advances a vision of a more heterogeneous society in which more specific identities are cultivated. Can the two projects be brought together?

Peace politics rests on the possibility of forming working coalitions that reflect shared interests and creating a stronger community in which all can participate. Individuals and social groups come to recognize that their fate is intertwined with that of others. People come together in a collective project. But a progressive movement must also recognize the importance of the politics of identity now emanating from diverse communities. For many participants in this form of social activism, the call to join together could be heard as just another chapter in a long history in which their own interests have been subordinated to others in the name of the common good. Peace politics must avoid the pitfall of becoming a false universality that only recasts existing privileges in new form. The social groups who have been culturally disenfranchised are already more disposed to support progressive realignment. But narrowly conceived issues of war and peace will not bring together all of the social movements that are necessary to form an effective coalition. To achieve this goal, peace politics must renovate itself and respect the specific interests of different groups. A common core of human identity still must be established, on which rests any chance of successful transformation. At the same time, different voices expressing different perspectives are also needed. A movement seeking political realignment must establish a concept of peace and a political process that celebrates cultural diversity and supports a broad range of personal identities. Can progressive politics mature to the point where the search for common interests and respect for differences exist side by side? Can we develop a concept of peace sufficiently powerful that human universality and particular identity form two aspects of a multi dimensional project rather than opposite poles along a single spectrum? Everyone should feel that they have a place—and that they do not have to sacrifice themselves in order to be admitted. There are no simple answers to this dilemma of social change. Peace, as Gandhi reminded us, is a path to be traveled, not an end result.

The Influence of Money on the Political Process

Objection. The dominant role of money in politics is another obstacle to the emergence of a progressive movement. Finances are a critical factor in the outcome of elections, and help define the spectrum of what is considered legitimate political debate. Without access to significant financial resources, progressive candidates will have an extremely difficult time getting elected and their ideas will be marginalized.

Members of Congress think that access to money determines their chances for reelection, and they spend one-half to three-quarters of their time raising funds (Smith 1989). The functions that most think of as comprising the job of an elected public official—developing informed opinions on issues, drafting legislation, and "constituent work" (addressing problems of individuals in their district)—take a backseat to preparing for the next election. In many respects, politicians are actually involved in a permanent campaign. The business of government is less important than retaining one's office. Most officials do not approve of this situation. Yet they devote a large proportion of their time to raising funds so that they will be able to defend themselves against an opponent's negative campaign. Politicians think that negative campaigning will work against them—unless they have the financial resources to mount an effective rebuttal or a negative campaign of their own. The process of continually raising money and spending it on ad hominem attacks excludes progressive ideas.

Money also plays an important role beyond the arena of political campaigns. Political access is aided and sometimes guaranteed by sizable contributions to political action committees. Politicians are reluctant to take stands that may jeopardize funding sources. In the 1980s, the especially lavish contributions of defense contractors helped structure a pattern in which many congressmen voted in favor of a nuclear freeze (thus responding to the sentiments of the majority of their constituents), and for the very nuclear weapons systems the freeze was supposed to block (thus protecting themselves from retribution from a valuable source of funding). The proliferation of PACs has the additional impact of limiting the coherence of the policy formation process. Instead of an attempt to match legislation with clearly established goals, the political process has become more of a jury-rigged, fragmented affair in which key decisions reflect bargaining *among only those with the resources to command attention*. The result is frustration and inertia on the one hand, and the systematic exclusion of important social groups and interests on the other. As a result, the possibilities of progressive politics are restricted. It is unlikely that such a movement will be in a position to raise funds that rival those of the well-heeled contributors to the present political system. Without such funds, those seeking political realignment will be marginalized.

Response. The argument that the dominant role of campaign finances constrains progressive politics is certainly true. At issue is whether anything can be done about it. Ample funding certainly helps run a campaign, but the public resents the dominance of money in politics. Several recent political campaigns have demonstrated that it is possible to overcome financial handicaps by using volunteers and mobilizing all potential supporters to actually come out and vote. In fact, the absence of traditional sources of money seemed to help these campaigns. Near the top of any new political agenda should be legislation to secure the public financing of elections. This step would help reduce the distortions imposed by the existing structure of funding. The public already understands that private funds play too large a role in determining who is elected. But the reforms debated in Washington, such as caps on campaign spending, ending all political action committees, and less expensive television advertising, do not go to the heart of the matter. Private funds are so unequally distributed that reliance upon them almost inevitably distorts the quality of political democracy. Transforming public sentiment into effective reform of the electoral system, especially in the context of a concerted effort to reorder national priorities, is possible.

The Limits of Presidential Campaigning

Objection. A strong presidential campaign is a key element in the emergence of progressive politics and the creation of a new world order. Such an effort can help focus attention on the need to redefine national security and on the new policies that will be necessary to achieve that security. But presidential candidates tend to be self-interested. Surviving the primaries, winning the election, and preparing the ground for reelection become more important than the promotion of a particular program. Candidates run on abstract themes calculated to avoid alienating voters rather than on issues that may challenge vested interests. A candidate may initially regard local coalitions as a base of support. But the process of securing the nomination and winning the presidency may encourage a more personal view of the political map. Instead of a broad-based movement intent upon social renewal, we will be presented with an attractive candidate who tries everything possible to gain the largest possible share of the vote. Meanwhile, the press and media will reinforce the prevailing tendency to focus more upon personality rather than issues. Presidential campaigns may substitute for the more painstaking process of strengthening the social forces necessary to embark upon genuine reform. Can the core of a presidential campaign be a concerted program of change rather than the advancement of personal interests?

Response. The argument that presidential candidates must project image over political substance is simply not true. While political style plays a distressingly high role, presidents remain identified with substantive issues and concrete programs. For example, Ronald Reagan was a successful president in the sense that he was able to enact a significant portion of an explicit political agenda. His personal popularity and the public relations capacities of his administration were important tools. But Reagan remained foremost an "ideological president" who was able to follow a deliberate program of change. The fact that the U.S. economy and its citizens are now paying for it should not obscure the point that a president can provide leadership for programmatic change. The fact that a progressive presidential candidate will "stand for something" does not preclude defeat, and may even be a point of attraction.

Public mobilization and enacting an alternative security program will take at least a decade. In this respect, a presidential campaign is also necessary to explain both the possibilities and the problems of social change that may take years to achieve full fruition. Expectations of what can ultimately be accomplished should be high; but expectations of immediate results must be kept realistic. But virtually everything in our current political system demands the opposite. Lowi (1985) argues that modern U.S. presidents who seek change experience only partial success. Their capacity to implement change is far less than the promises they made in order to be elected had implied. The virtual certainty of public disappointment in presidential performance creates a need for a huge public relations staff to exercise "spin control." Presidents also compensate for the failure to live up to initial expectations by controlling information, inflating their rhetoric, and manipulating both the press and the electorate through claims of success. Democracy is not served well by this situation.

On the other hand, unique aspects of running as a progressive secure the mutual dependency of a presidential candidate and a popular base, and thus limit the possibility that a presidential candidate will become entirely self-interested. A movement seeking political realignment must demonstrate credibility. And the presentation of the need for a new world order by a presidential candidate is the easiest way to legitimate new ways to secure the national interest. But a candidate cannot win office and remain true to the base of progressive principles without mobilizing the significant part of the electorate now marginalized from the current system. The Democratic party has largely turned its back on the constituency that brought it to power earlier in the century. Those who are not now registered to vote are also those most likely to support a movement that ties peace issues to economic justice. But those feeling disenfranchised will not register and vote unless they hear a candidate represent their interests. Effective voter registration also requires mobilization by activist networks. And these networks will also require a variety of assurances from a presidential candidate that will minimize the candidate's opportunities to pursue a more individualist quest for power. The process of running for the presidency thus creates obligations to the activist base. Both the candidate and coalition activists could appreciate that alternative politics cannot be implemented by either a top-down presidential campaign or a grass-roots movement operating on its own. But the tension between a presidential campaign and a local popular base is an inescapable dilemma for a progressive movement.

The Role of Substitute Enemies

Objection. The end of the Cold War raises the possibility of a new world order and domestic reform. Using peace issues to develop programs of common security requires new perceptions of the national interest. In particular, foreign policy must move from a model that relies on domineering forms of strength toward one that recognizes shared fate between the United States and the rest of the planet. The political possibilities of developing such a perspective could be limited by the emergence of new enemies to take the role performed by the "Soviet threat" of the old world order. International terrorism, economic competition with Japan and Europe, and the dangers emanating from regional conflicts are all possible candidates for reinforcing the fundamental dynamic of "us" versus "them." The Gulf crisis is a perfect illustration: Iraq's occupation of Kuwait and the portrayal of Saddam Hussein as "another Hitler" enabled the Bush administration to argue that the United States continues to face enemies. Public opinion may indicate incipient support for the development of alternative politics. But the development of new weapons and the use of the military overseas are still possible. Economic competition from our allies may also provoke narrow-minded protectionism. In short, the ideological dynamic of the Cold War, which seems to require a hostile response to a threatening "other," is still very much present.

Response. Blaming others for our problems enjoys a long history in U.S. politics, especially during difficult economic conditions. The temptation to blame foreign workers or the Japanese for a variety of social problems within the United States can be easily detected, and may even deepen if little is done to counter U.S. decline. Unhappiness and frustration usually find ugly outlets. Creating an alternative strategy to protect national security so that people can identify their interests with a positive plan is the most effective response. Anger politics will not have a significant impact where the expectation exists that conditions will improve. Steady employment and hope undercut xenophobia. A systematic effort at domestic renewal can bolster the latent peace sentiment that already exists in contemporary popular culture.

Peace politics can catch the imagination of people rather than play to their fear. In particular, it is possible to establish a non-belligerent form of patriotism that holds a special affection for one's country. A progressive movement should identify strongly with the well-being of the United States and its citizens, and should not shy away from presenting its programs in that light. For example, establishing a new world order is not just a foreign aid giveaway that benefits international consultants and corrupt leaders in the Third World. Nurturing global development that is environmentally sustainable is consistent with the national interest. A progressive movement might even consider a program of national service and the establishment of other civic duties that contribute to social cohesion. A program that provided subsistence wages for youth service "performed at the state, local, and community levels for government and nonprofit organizations" could sustain a sense of the civic whole, of obligation, and the opportunity to serve social goals (Moskos 1988). An international set of programs oriented toward sustainable development would be important as well. As long as national service did not take other people's jobs, the result could be a systematic and concrete commitment to a better country and globe. A nonbelligerent patriotism of this type is fully compatible with respect for other people, and can accompany a critical attitude toward the particular policies followed by one's national leaders (Nathanson 1989).

The Role of the Media

Objection. The media plays a critical role in framing political options and determining which alternatives are legitimate and which should be marginalized. Preference for intriguing personalities and individual flair over political substance and nuance creates significant distortions in the coverage of oppositional politics. Social movements, in particular, have been victimized by the media inclination to focus on the dramatic. A vast majority of the public has not been exposed to the newer ideas and overall perspective of progressive politics. Yet it is difficult to compress a complex description of the threats and opportunities presented by the end of the Cold War into usable sound bites. Like most industries, ownership of the media is concentrated in a few powerful centers that are not favorably disposed toward alternative ideas. In addition, advertisers may threaten to withdraw their support of programming or news coverage that contains a powerful critique of contemporary conditions. As a result, the mass media will not be a good conduit for progressive politics. And yet the movement for domestic renewal needs the publicity and legitimation that could be conferred by the industry.

Response. Four possible developments can enable a progressive movement to break out of its current marginalization in the media. First, social activism can influence the media to broaden its coverage of events by adopting new frames of analysis that focus attention on parts of the story that established coverage tends to ignore. For example, movements against the Vietnam War and U.S. intervention in Central America influenced the media to introduce material that broke the hegemonic presentation of Washington's point of view. Information about corruption, human rights abuses, and private profiteering by political and military elites supported by the United States, found their way into the mainstream media—after these facts had been pressed by oppositional movements (Hallin 1987; Ryan 1991). Similarly, environmental and anti–nuclear power movements modified the media's initial tendency to portray these issues in ways preferred by powerful corporate and political actors (Gamson 1988). It may even be possible to strengthen social mobilization directed at the media itself. Focusing pressure so that opinion forums become more open to a broader range of views is one important step. Creating alliances with journalists to examine questions of censorship, self-censorship, and media complicity with government is another (Hoynes 1992). In these ways, the strength of movement mobilization can affect the manner in which critical social issues are presented to the public.

Second, new political challengers can give more visibility to, and redefine the significance of, progressive themes that already exist in popular television. A significant number of screenwriters, actors, directors, and producers already favor an alternative direction for national policy and present some of these themes in shows viewed by millions of people. Embedded in the miasma that generally characterizes commercial television are a few shows that are remarkable for their more honest confrontation with difficult social issues, their representation of more democratic values, and their exploration of what personal integrity means in the midst of a contradictory and distorted social world.[2] The emergence of a visible alternative movement could give added meaning and explicit political impetus to the interesting experiments now occurring within the boundaries of commercial television.

Third, the deepening of a social movement over the 1990s could strengthen alternative media outlets. Many cities in the United States already feature a local newspaper freed from the constraints of corporate ownership and advertisers. A small national press and a series of important magazines open to progressive ideas also exists. Other possibilities, some resting on new communications technologies, include establishing a national newspaper, disseminating ideas using the flexibility and submarkets offered by cable TV, and gaining more permanent or institutionalized slots in local radio and television programming. These opportunities could be enhanced by legislation and federal regulations aimed at creating more competition and openness to alternative points of view. New ways of funding public television, which could help to free it from potentially limiting corporate sponsorship, are also important (Herman 1992).

Fourth, public representatives of the effort to redefine national security can examine how they might express their positions in shorthand forms that can be used by the media and grasped by the population. In general, oppositional movements have been slow to take advantage of the opportunities offered by mainstream outlets. They have no media strategy. It has been noted that the first thing social activists will do with newly acquired funds is write up a long leaflet and hand it out on the street corner, while the first thing the Republican party will do is hire a public relations expert. That reality is changing as a new discussion emerges to weigh the pros and cons of becoming a sophisticated player of the media game. Learning the details of how to become a good source and how a story is put together can be especially useful for those seeking exposure for new points of view. On the other hand, an unthinking strategy of pursuing media coverage can centralize authority within a broad movement, create celebrities, and accelerate the pace of activism in a superficial way that substitutes coverage and spectacle for genuine citizen mobilization. At any rate, the creation of progressive sound bites and other ways of encapsuling relevant information in attractive and accessible ways is

2. Examples have included "M*A*S*H," "All in the Family," "Hill Street Blues," "L.A. Law," "Northern Exposure," "Civil Wars," some of the programs by Phil Donahue, and, on PBS, individual presentations by Bill Moyers and on "Frontline."

both necessary and possible. The electoral campaign of Paul Wellstone in Minnesota, and the promotional literature of the environmental organization Greenpeace, are evidence that progressives are becoming more sophisticated in their use of the media.

Development of Policy Alternatives

Objection. The difficulty of translating the broad goals of the new world order and domestic renewal into concrete policies is an additional constraint on the possibilities of political realignment over the 1990s. A vision of change, no matter how necessary, is no substitute for the pragmatic steps required to reassure voters and create the confidence that a new world order can be attained. Without a collection of sustaining think tanks, professional networks, and other policy forums, the public may remain skeptical. Voters cannot be sure that progressive politics will produce more security and a higher quality of life unless they acquire a "feel" for what alternative policies would actually accomplish.

Response. This objection is comparatively weak. Alternative policies exist for virtually every issue area including foreign policy (Hoffmann 1989; Klare and Thomas 1991), defense (Cain and Golding 1990; Kaufmann 1990a), housing (Appelbaum 1988; Dreier and Appelbaum 1992; Dreier and Atlas 1992), health care (Grumbach et al. 1991; Noble 1992), environmental protection (Brown et al. 1991), education (Orfield 1992), investment policies (Anderson 1991; Aschauer 1990) and human services (Green and Pinsky 1990). No progressive policy consensus exists—one would, at any rate, be undesirable. Nonetheless, the evolution of an alternative set of social policies is further developed than most realize. Indeed, one consequence of a generation of opposition to the Vietnam War has been the formation of a core of professionals whose careers have focused on the elaboration of policies not offered by the current political system. Public appreciation of these alternatives has been restricted by three factors: First, they are virtually absent in the press and media whose prevailing frames legitimate some policy options while excluding others. Progressive policies are generally articulated only in occasional op-ed pieces. Second, most established politicians have not sponsored alternative policies, much less built support for them. Visibility comes with political influence. And third, the proponents of these alternatives have not felt the sense of urgency that comes with the knowledge that the specifics of their proposals will soon enter the caldron of the legislative process. The main point is that other policy mechanisms capable of providing security and meeting human needs are known. The relative lack of public discussion is more an indication of the comparative weakness of the social forces necessary to bring these social programs into the political mainstream than it is a statement about the existence of alternative policies.

Economic Circumstances

Objection. While peace issues are important, the strength of the economy remains the single most pressing issue to the electorate. Many argue that economic conditions will have to change dramatically before substantial support for progressive politics can emerge. In the meantime, the prospect of a progressive movement may raise the specter of economic dislocations. As long as the majority are living relatively comfortably, the perception that we have more to lose than to gain by a dramatic change in policies will persist. Despite an inclination to favor new politics, many will vote their pocketbooks by supporting orthodox political positions.

Response. The relationship between economic conditions and social change cannot be reduced to a set of simple axioms. Severe dislocations may in fact be necessary before the population is willing to entertain progressive politics. The 1990s may in fact see such dislocations. On the other hand, economic downturns do not automatically generate support for alternative positions. No formula links economic crisis with a particular type of change. In some cases, new policies have been accepted only in the context of a recession or depression. The New Deal legislation of the 1930s is an example. But change can also arise from the higher expectations generated by an *improvement* in economic conditions. The concept of a new world order used in this book addresses both sides of the issue: protection against economic stagnation and social erosion; and the cultivation of citizenship, democracy, and environmental sensibilities that derive from a positive vision of what is possible.

Our economy no longer meets the needs of many Americans. Things do not have to get worse before people will consider the need for reform. The main issue is whether the public will identify a progressive movement with a brighter economic future. Advocates of a peace economy can make a case for realignment based partly on the failures of the existing economy. The costs of continuing our current policies include polarization, deteriorating health care for many, lack of access to quality education, increased housing costs, more crime, and the slow grinding away at the public infrastructure. But this critique is not sufficient. To be politically successful, the specific policies attached to the concept of a peace economy must be perceived as efficient and competitive as well as compassionate and caring. The progressive movement must be identified with a sound economy that provides good jobs to a vast majority of the population. A peace economy must work.

A peace economy must also rest upon existing social values. Domestic renewal can respect the traditional value system favoring individual initiative, hard work, self-reliance, and entrepreneurship by situating these attributes within the values of community, democracy, and giving that are also firmly embedded in our culture. For example, progressive politics will not be attractive if it means only more taxes to support a welfare system. A peace economy must reflect the universal interest in creating full employment and removing the barriers that prevent many from succeeding. Many economic values already are deeply rooted in the popular ethic—we value manufacturing over financial manipulation, employment over paper entrepreneurship, and stability over maximizing short-term profits. A progressive movement, using the concept of the peace economy, can easily represent these values more fully than the current ideology of the unchecked marketplace and the invisible hand, which only weakens the fabric of local community. Locating market incentives within a framework of meeting the common good is a difficult intellectual and political challenge. But it is one with which redefining security must be identified.

The Constraints of Our Political System

Objection. The U.S. political system may be exceptional among Western market democracies in the centrist pull it exerts against movements seeking new alternatives. Constitutional factors have been invoked to explain this moderation. Electoral rules reinforce the two-party system. The separation of powers provides checks and balances against efforts to initiate sweeping programs. And federalism tends to diffuse the power necessary to coordinate change through a multiplicity of state and local governments. Each element makes it more difficult for a new movement and president bent upon domestic realignment to carry out a long-term program of change.

Democracies with electoral systems based upon proportional representation have a better chance of preserving smaller political parties. Under the winner-take-all system in the United States, votes for a third political party seem wasted. The electoral college system discourages candidates outside the two major parties and exaggerates the margin of victory. It is difficult for third-party candidates to play even a spoiler role or otherwise influence the balance of power between the Democrats and Republicans. Constitutional provisions separate responsibilities into three branches of government. Pushing and later implementing legislation through a complex, fragmented system favors politicians who are skilled at bargaining and making pragmatic trade-offs. The emphasis on short-term effectiveness splits one issue off from another and prevents a more coherent vision of change from crystallizing. Progress is only incremental and the patient building of a constituency for policy-oriented change is extremely difficult to achieve. The U.S. Constitution also tends to splinter government power at all levels: within the national government itself, and between the national and state governments. An important role for city governments is preserved as well. The result is political balkanization, a so-called weak state that makes it possible for popular pressures to be expressed but simultaneously robs these views of sustained political impact. The diffusion of political power also contributes to regionalism which, in some accounts, makes it difficult to characterize a common experience that cuts across the entire United States. In this view, progressive politics will flounder against the priority of the Democratic party to win the next election, the loss of coherence imposed by localism, and the need to preserve short-term tactical advantage over long-range strategic development.

Response. First, it is not at all clear that the United States has been more successful in containing alternative politics than the other Western democracies. Explicitly left-wing political parties and social movements may have been smaller than their European counterparts (but larger than most histories and the popular memory acknowledge). But other types of oppositional movements reflecting labor, ethnic, gender, and antiwar issues, as well as more broad-based populist currents have played a significant role in shaping U.S. history. The proportion of the population mobilized by these movements is probably equal to that achieved in Europe. A critical aspect of a progressive political movement is recapturing that memory. Nor is it clear that the United States can be characterized as a "weak state" crosscut with fissures and hampered by divided responsibilities. In foreign affairs, certainly, a president commands tremendous power. And significant military, economic, and cultural resources have been concentrated in the national security state.

Much of this book rests on the promise of a unifying theme. Redefining security rather than class, inequality, tax reform, "America first," or populism, is identified as the principle to cohere a common democratic project. Transcending the constitutional obstacles outlined above will require substantial mobilization. Yet many people do not even participate in elections. Is this a natural consequence of our political system? Or is such behavior a reflection of the fact that we are no longer presented with a viable political alternative? Only half the public bothers to vote, the lowest rate of participation of any advanced capitalist nation. While registration rules partly explain this failure of democracy, a more powerful reason can be found in the absence of genuine debate that gives the public a clear choice. Campaigns based upon television, expert consultants, and the images cultivated by individual candidates have corrupted the quality of democracy. We could raise voter registration and participation rates by making it easier to register and by presenting coherent political alternatives rather than packaged candidate images (Cloward and Piven 1988). Instabilities would be introduced into the electoral system, especially within the Democratic party. Money and business interests would play less of a role.

U.S. history contains a significant record of popular opposition. But mobilization is not the same as institutionalizing change, creating a genuinely oppositional political party, and making progress toward a new world order. Can the many forms of citizen mobilization that now exist in the United States be focused in way that results in political realignment, either by transforming the Democratic party or by forming a third party? Voters are increasingly inclined to view Democrats and Republicans as existing along a single continuum—and to be disenchanted with the quality of leadership provided by each. Democrats are seen by the public as better protectors of the environment, and better providers of educational programs and critical social services. Republicans are viewed as stronger on foreign affairs and, at least until recently, as better economic managers. But there is no reason why this split should remain. Democrats are wasting an important opportunity to appeal to the public by developing new ideas on foreign policy that could provide more security for less money. Abdication to the Republicans on half the issues is not necessary. For the moment, however, the key point is that the public no longer has the confidence in the ability of either party to perform its respective function. A stronger concept of national security should be introduced within the Democratic party. Efforts to form a third party before a sizable political base is created will encounter great difficulties. By serving as an arena for building ideas and coalitions capable of pushing those ideas, primaries can serve some of the purposes of third parties without diverting votes to a candidate who is unlikely to win in a general election. Thus, the question of whether the development of grass-roots and electorial coalitions will produce a transformation or a split in the Democratic party is left open.

Finally, the meaning of federalism is now undergoing significant change. Regional differences remain, but appreciation of the vast influence of national and even global developments upon local conditions has become nearly universal. Most large cities, for example, have established offices to sustain contacts and establish working connections with the world economy. Many U.S. cities have also created sister city relations in other countries. The motivations for these arrangements range from commercial to political. Whatever the reason, it is no longer possible for local political authorities to ignore the impact of global developments on their immediate surroundings. The political advantage of a movement to redefine national security is that it rests fundamentally on this recognition. The democratic component of domestic renewal would strengthen the power of local decision-making bodies at the expense of federal bureaucracies in Washington, but not in a way that is isolationist. A genuinely new world order rests on an appreciation of global interdependence that does not obliterate local differences.

Conclusion

In many ways, the possibilities of significant reform in the United States are remote. There is no shortage of problems, and it is no longer possible to be unreservedly optimistic about our future. Cynicism and fatalism prevail. The current political leadership exhibits little awareness of the pace of social erosion. The world continues to be a dangerous place, but the actual threats to U.S. and global security have not been acknowledged by our policymakers in a meaningful way. The Cold War has ended. While that is a benefit, it sometimes appears that little has changed. Foreign policy continues to revolve around the perceived need to confront enemies with military force, while nuclear and conventional weapons modernization proceeds. Soon after the Berlin Wall fell, the United States went to war in the Persian Gulf. Domestically and internationally, economic priorities remain focused on the extension of market forces. In the United States, the commitment to civilian research and development and rebuilding the civilian infrastructure remains stunted. In many ways, U.S. citizens seem open to new ideas. But the obstacles to change are enormous. Neither the Democratic nor the Republican party seems capable of offering a plan of domestic renewal. Many of the political instincts characteristic of the national security state and the Cold War persist. And we are quite capable of generating enemies from within: women, people of color, gays and lesbians, and the poor are objects of attack. Movements for social change face enormous concentrations of political and economic power. Capital is concentrated in the hands of a few banks and corporations whose decisions do not come under the jurisdiction of any government. Multinational corporations see the world in global terms. Yet their decisions determine the vitality of communities throughout the United States. Our political culture does not encourage social activism, or even substantial involvement in the central issues facing the country. Most people are aware of these problems in a general way yet feel resigned or incapable of responding to such threats to our security. The old world order certainly seems tenacious.

Peace Politics has presented a coherent alternative of a new world order. The fate of U.S. citizens is fully intertwined with the fate of the rest of the world, and self-interest requires that we encourage global development aimed at the reduction of poverty, sustainable development, and local democracy. Within the United States, a significant base of social activism has been created. Despite the concentration of political and economic power in the United States, social movements have had considerable impact. In public opinion, incipient support exists for common security policies and domestic renewal. A vital discussion has also emerged about how virtually every institutional area could be reformed to make its organizations and programs more responsive to human needs. A framework of ideas—the beginnings of how we might achieve a firmer grasp on national security—has been created at the policy level. Models of more active and democratic citizenship that draw on U.S. traditions are also present. The movement toward a new world order could also revitalize our democratic institutions. The public is looking for an alternative, and we can say with confidence that a politics infused with ethics would be attractive. Cultivating shared fate, reducing the impact of enemy images, and renewing the social contract between society and the individual involves both interests and morality. An imaginative presidential campaign could bring all of these pieces together and encourage the public mobilization that is necessary to extend peace and the new world order through a program of domestic renewal that will bring greater equality, community, and democracy. I do not know whether resignation or social inspiration will turn out to be stronger. But the possibilities are more promising than we appreciate.

References

Adams, Gordon. 1981. *The Iron Triangle: The Politics of Defense Contracting*. New York: Council on Economic Priorities.

Albright, David, Tom Zamora, and David Lewis. 1990. Turn off Rocky Flats. *The Bulletin of the Atomic Scientists*, June, 12–19.

Almond, Gabriel. 1950. *The American People and Foreign Policy*. New York: Praeger Publishers.

Americans Talk Security (ATS). 1987–91. 17 vols. Winchester, Mass.

Anderson, James. 1991. *Bankrupting American Cities*. Lansing, Mich.: Employment Research Associates.

Anderson, Marion. 1991. *Converting the American Economy*. Lansing, Mich.: Employment Research Associates.

Appelbaum, Richard. 1988. *Rethinking Rental Housing*. Phildelphia: Temple University Press.

Applebome, Peter. 1991. At home, war healed several wounds. *New York Times*, March 4.

Aschauer, David. 1990. *Public Investment and Private Sector Growth*. Washington, D.C.: Economic Policy Institute.

Ball, Desmond. 1980. *Politics and Force Structure: The Strategic and Missile Policy of the Kennedy Administration*. Berkeley: University of California Press.

———. 1981. Can nuclear war be controlled? Adelphi Papers no. 169, Institute for Strategic Studies, London.

———. 1982/83. U.S. strategic forces: How would they be used? *International Security* 7, no. 3:31–60.

Ball, George. 1990. The Gulf crisis. *New York Review of Books*, December 6.

Ball, Nicole. 1988. *Security and Economy in the Third World*. Princeton: Princeton University Press.

Barber, Benjamin. 1984. *Strong Democracy: Participatory Politics for a New Age*. Berkeley: University of California Press.

Bard, Mitchell. 1987. Strategic thoughts about SDI. *Public Opinion*, March/April.

Barnet, Richard. 1991. The uses of force. *New Yorker*, April 29.

Beckman, Peter, Larry Campbell, Paul Crumlish, Michael Dobklowski, and Steven Lee. 1992. *The Nuclear Predicament: Nuclear Weapons in the Cold War and Beyond*. Englewood Cliffs, N.J.: Prentice-Hall.

Benford, Robert. 1988. The nuclear disarmament movement. In Lester Kurtz, *The Nuclear Cage*. Englewood Cliffs, N.J.: Prentice-Hall.

Berger, John. 1991. Science of the scams. *In These Times*, April 24–30.

Berger, Suzanne, Michael Dertouzos, Richard Lester, Robert Solow, and Lester Thurow. 1989. Toward a new industrial America. *Scientific American* 260, no. 6 (June): 39–47.

Bertsch, Kenneth, and Linda Shaw. 1984. *The Nuclear Weapons Industry*. Washington, D.C.: Investor Responsibility Research Center.

Bethe, Hans, Kurt Gottfried, and Robert McNamara. 1991. The nuclear threat: A proposal. *New York Review of Books*, June 27.

Blake, David, and Robert Walters. 1987. *The Politics of Global Economic Relations*. Englewood Cliffs, N.J.: Prentice-Hall.

Blechman, Barry, and Cathleen Fisher. 1988. *The Silent Partner: West Germany and Arms Control*. Cambridge, Mass.: Ballinger Publishing.

Blechman, Barry, and Stephen Kaplan. 1978. *Force Without War*. Washington, D.C.: Brookings Institution.

Blight, James. 1987/88. October 27, 1962: Transcripts of the meeting of the ExCom. *International Security* 12, no. 3. (Winter): 30–92.

Bluestone, Barry, and Bennet Harrison. 1982. *The Deindustrialization of America*. New York: Basic Books.

Boggs, Carl. 1986. *Social Movements and Political Power*. Philadelphia: Temple University Press.

Bosso, Christopher. 1989. Setting the agenda: Mass media and the discovery of famine in Ethiopia. In Michael Margolis and Gary Mauser, eds., *Manipulating Public Opinion: Essays on Public Opinion as a Dependent Variable*. Belmont, Calif.: Wadsworth.

Boulding, Elise. 1988. *Building a Global Civic Culture*. New York: Teachers College Press.

Boyer, Paul. 1984. From activism to apathy: The American people and nuclear weapons, 1963–1980. *Journal of American History* 70, no. 4 (March): 821–44.

———. 1985. *By the Bomb's Early Light*. New York: Pantheon Books.

Brandes, Lisa. 1992. The gender gap and attitudes toward war. Paper delivered at the annual meeting of the Midwest Political Science Association, Chicago, Ill., April 9–12.

Broad, William. 1981. Nuclear pulse: Awakening to the chaos factor. *Science* 212 (May 29): 1009–12.

———. 1990. A mountain of trouble. *New York Times Magazine*, November 18.

Brock-Utne, Birgit. 1985. *Educating for Peace: A Feminist Perspective*. New York: Pergamon Press.

Brodie, Bernard. 1946. *The Absolute Weapon: Atomic Power and World Order*. New York: Harcourt, Brace.

Bronner, Ethan. 1991. Former envoy to Iraq has yet to tell her story. *The Boston Globe*, March 14.

Brooke, James. 1989. Peruvian farmers razing rain forest to sow drug crops. *New York Times*, August 13.

———. 1990. Harvesting exotic crops to save Brazil's forest. *New York Times*, April 30.

Brooks, Harvey, and Lewis Branscomb. 1989. Rethinking the military's role in the economy. *Technology Review*, August/September, 55–64.

Brown, Lester. 1987. Analyzing the demographic trap. In Lester Brown et al., *State of the World 1987*. New York: Norton.

Brown, Lester, et al., 1991. *State of the World 1991*. New York: Norton.

Brundtland, Gro. 1987. *Our Common Future*. New York: Oxford University Press.

Bulletin of the Atomic Scientists. 1990. Special issue on arms trade. May.

Bundy, McGeorge. 1969. To cap the volcano. *Foreign Affairs* 48, no. 1 (October).

Bundy, McGeorge, George Kennan, Robert McNamara, and Gerald Smith. 1982. Nuclear weapons and the Atlantic alliance. *Foreign Affairs* 60, no. 4 (Spring): 753–68.

Bunn, Matthew, and Kosta Tsipis. 1983. The uncertainties of a preemptive nuclear attack. *Scientific American* 249, no. 5 (November): 38–47.

Bunyard, Peter. 1989. Guardians of the forest. *New Scientist*, December.

Burnham, Walter Dean. 1970. *Critical Elections and the Mainsprings of American Politics*. New York: Norton.

Business Week. 1989a. The peace economy. December 11.

———. 1989b. Fewer guns could mean a whole lot more butter. June 12.

———. 1990. Who pays for peace? July 2.

Cain, Stephen Alexis, and Natalie Golding. 1990. Restructuring the U.S. military: Defense needs in the 21st century. A report by the Committee for National Security and Defense Budget Project, Washington, D.C.

Caldicott, Helen. 1984. *Missile Envy*. New York: Bantam.

Canham-Clyne, John. 1991. Gun-control bills shoot blanks at U.S. violence. *In These Times*, May 22–28.

Carlsson-Paige, Nancy, and Diane Levin. 1987. *The War-Play Dilemma*. New York: Teachers College Press.

Carter, Luther. 1987. *Nuclear Imperatives and the Public Trust: Dealing with Radioactive Waste*. Washington, D.C.: Resources for the Future.

CBS News/*New York Times*. 1982. May 19–23.

Center for Defense Information. 1989. Defending the environment? The record of the U.S. military. *The Defense Monitor* 18, no. 6.

———. 1991. A new military budget for a new world. *The Defense Monitor* 20, no. 2.

———. 1992. Defending America: CDI options for military spending. *The Defense Monitor* 21, no. 4.

Chan, Steve. 1985. The impact of defense spending on economic performance: A survey of evidence and problems. *Orbis*, Summer, 403–34.

Chang, Gordon. 1988. To the nuclear brink: Eisenhower, Dulles, and the Quemoy-Matsu crisis. *International Security* 12, no. 4 (Spring): 96–123.

Chatfield, Charles. 1973. *Peace Movements in America*. New York: Shocken.

Children's Defense Fund. 1991. The state of America's children 1991. Washington, D.C.

Chomsky, Noam, and Edward Herman. 1988. *Manufacturing Consent*. New York: Pantheon.

Churchill, Ward, and Winona LaDuke. 1985. Radioactive colonization and the Native American. *Socialist Review* 81 (May/June): 95–119.

Clark, Jack. 1990. Unions organize for industrial renewal. *In These Times*, August 1–14.

Cloward, Richard, and Frances Piven. 1988. *Democrary Thwarted*. New York: Pantheon.

Cohen, Bernard. 1973. *The Public's Impact on Foreign Policy*. Boston: Little, Brown.

Cohen, Muriel. 1990. Survey finds teachers less satisfied than in 1987. *Boston Globe*, September 4.

Cohen, Stephen, and John Zysman. 1987. *Manufacturing Matters: The Myth of the Post-Industrial Economy*. New York: Basic Books.

Cohn, Carol. 1987. Nuclear language and how we learned to pat the bomb. *Bulletin of the Atomic Scientists*, June, 17–24.

Coles, Robert. 1985a. The freeze: Crusade of the leisure class. *Harper's*, March.

———. 1985b. Children and the bomb. *Time Magazine*, December 8.

Coll, Steve, and William Branigin. 1991. U.S. road raid: Were Iraqis needlessly slaughtered? *Boston Globe*, March 14.

Committee for Economic Development. 1990. *Battling America's Budget Deficits*. Washington, D.C.

Conetta, Carl. 1988. *Peace Resource Book*. Institute for Defense and Disarmament Studies. Cambridge, Mass.: Ballinger.

Congressional Black Caucus. 1990. Quality of life budget: FY 1991. Washington, D.C.

Congressional Budget Office. 1983. Defense spending and the economy. Washington, D.C. February.

Constable, Pamela. 1990. Latin drug effort revives old fears. *Boston Globe*, June 16.

———. 1991. Peace bid viewed as test of post–cold war ties. *Boston Globe*, February 23.

Cooper, Sandi. 1991. *Patriotic Pacifism*. New York: Oxford University Press.

Cortright, David. 1982. Forum. *Nuclear Times*, October.

———. 1991. Assessing peace movement effectiveness in the 1980s. *Peace and Change* 16, no. 1 (January): 46–63.

Dahl, Robert. 1985. *Controlling Nuclear Weapons.* Syracuse: Syracuse University Press.

Daugherty, William, Barbara Levi, and Frank von Hippel. 1986. The consequences of "limited" nuclear attacks on the United States. *International Security* 10, no. 4 (Spring): 3–45.

Davis, M. Scott, and Christopher Kline. 1988. The role of the public in foreign policy making: An overview of the literature. A report by the Roosevelt Center for American Policy Studies, Washington, D.C., January.

Deadline. 1991. Covering the gulf crisis. Vol. 6, no. 1 (January/February).

DeBenedetti, Charles. 1973. On the significance of citizens' peace activism, 1961–1975. *Peace and Change* 9 (Summer).

———. 1980. *The Peace Reform in American History.* Bloomington, Indiana: University Press.

Defense Budget Project. 1991. *Responding to Changing Threats.* Washington, D.C.

DeGrasse, Robert. 1983. *Military Spending, Economic Decline.* New York: Council on Economic Priorities.

DeParle, Jason. 1991. Long series of military decisions led to Gulf war news censorship. *New York Times,* May 5.

Devine, Robert. 1978. *Blowing on the Wind: The Nuclear Test Ban Debate, 1954–1960.* New York: Oxford University Press.

Domhoff, William. 1983. *Who Rules America Now?* Englewood Cliffs, N.J.: Prentice-Hall.

Domke, William, Richard Eichenberg, and Catherine Kelleher. 1987. Consensus lost? Domestic politics and the "crisis" in NATO. *World Politics* 34, no. 3 (April): 382–407.

Donner, Frank. 1982. But will they come? The campaign to smear the nuclear freeze movement. *The Nation,* November 6.

Dornbusch, Rudiger. 1987. International debt and economic instability. *Economic Review,* January, 15–32.

Doty, Paul. 1987. A nuclear test ban. *Foreign Affairs,* Spring.

Dowd, Maureen. 1989. U.S. giving Bogota $65 million in aid to fight drug war. *New York Times,* August 26.

Draper, Theodore. 1992a. The Gulf War reconsidered. *New York Review of Books,* January 16.

———. 1992b. The true history of the Gulf War. *New York Review of Books,* January 30.

Draper, Theodore, and Caspar Weinberger. 1983. On nuclear war: An exchange with the secretary of defense. *New York Review of Books,* August 18–30, 27–33.

Dreier, Peter, and Richard Appelbaum. 1992. The housing crisis enters the 1990s. *New England Journal of Public Policy,* Spring.

Dreier, Peter, and John Atlas. 1992. How to promote homeownership for middle Americans: Step one—Replace the mansion subsidy with a progressive tax credit. *Challenge,* March.

Drew, Elizabeth. 1985. *Campaign Journal*. New York: Macmillan.

Dumanoski, Dianne. 1990. Huge bird declines reported. *Boston Globe*, January 15.

———. 1991. Poll says 50 percent of Americans believe troops in Gulf to protect oil. *Boston Globe*, January 13.

Dumas, Lloyd. 1982. Military spending and economic decay. In Dumas, ed., *The Political Economy of Arms Reduction: Reversing Economic Decay*. AAAS Selected Symposium Series 80. Boulder, Colo.: Westview Press.

———. 1986. *The Overburdened Economy*. Berkeley: University of California Press.

Dumas, Lloyd, and Marek Thee, eds. 1989. *Making Peace Possible: The Promise of Economic Conversion*. Oxford: Pergamon Press.

Durning, Alan. 1990. Ending poverty. In Lester Brown et al., *State of the World 1990*. New York: Norton.

Economic Report of the President. 1991. Washington, D.C.

Eichenberg, Richard. 1988. *Society and Security in Western Europe: A Study of Public Opinion in Four Countries*. London: Macmillan.

Eitzen, D. Stanley, and Maxine Baca Zinn. 1989. *The Reshaping of America: Social Consequences of the Changing Economy*. Englewood Cliffs, N.J.: Prentice-Hall.

Ellsberg, Daniel. 1981. Call to mutiny. In Dan Smith and E. P. Thompson, eds., *Protest and Survive*. New York: Monthly Review Press.

Ennis, Jim. 1987. Mobilizing weak support for social movements: The role of grievance, efficacy, and cost. *Social Forces* 66:390–409.

Epstein, Barbara. 1991. *Political Protest and Cultural Revolution: Nonviolent Direct Action in the 1970s and 1980s*. Berkeley: University of California Press.

Etzold, Thomas, and John Gaddis, eds. 1979. *Containment Documents on American Policy and Strategy: 1945–1950*. New York: Columbia University Press.

Everts, Philip. 1989. Where the movement goes when it disappears. *Bulletin of the Atomic Scientists* 43, no. 9 (November): 26–30.

Fagan, Shannon. 1991. The wasteland: Environmental devastation in the wake of the Gulf War. *In These Times*, March 27–April 2, 12–13.

Falk, Richard. 1982. Nuclear weapons and the end of democracy. *Praxis International* 2:1–11.

Fallows, James. 1981. *National Defense*. New York: Random House.

Farrell, John. 1991. War distracted but not for long. *Boston Globe*, August 2.

———. 1992a. Iraq exploited Bush's bid to woo it. *Boston Globe*, June 15.

———. 1992b. "Iraqgate": The search for a coverup. *Boston Globe*, June 16.

———. 1992c. Memos: U.S. knew by '85 about Iraqi diversions. *Boston Globe*, July 4.

Faux, Jeff, and Max Sawicky. 1990. *Investing the Peace Dividend*. Washington, D.C.: Economic Policy Institute.

Fearnside, Philip. 1989. Deforestation in Brazilian Amazonia: The rates and causes. *The Ecologist* 19, no. 6 (November/December): 214–18.

Federation of American Scientists. 1991. FAS hearing of options in the Persian Gulf. *FAS Public Interest Report* 44, no. 1 (January/February).

Feiveson, Harold, and Frank von Hippel. 1990. Beyond START: How to make much deeper cuts. *International Security* 15, no. 1:154–80.

Ferguson, Thomas. 1991. The economic incentives for war. *The Nation*, January 28.

Ferleger, Lou, and Jay Mandle. 1989. The savings shortfall. *Challenge*, March/April.

———. 1991. Americans' hostility to taxes. *Challenge*, July/August.

Ferraro, Vincent. 1991. Global debt and Third World development. In Michael Klare and Daniel Thomas, eds., *World Security: Trends and Challenges at Century's End*. New York: St. Martin's Press.

Fialka, John. 1992. *The Hotel Warriors: Covering the Gulf*. Washington, D.C.: Media Studies Project, Woodrow Wilson Center.

Fisher, Roger. 1991. Saddam Hussein's currently perceived choices. Mimeo distributed at Tufts University, January 23.

Fisher, Roger, Andrea Kupfer, and Douglas Stone. 1991. How do you end a war? *Boston Globe*, February 8.

Flavin, Christopher. 1991. Conquering U.S. oil dependence. *World Watch*, January/February, 28–35.

Fortune. 1989. So the Cold War is won. Now what? September 11.

Fotion, Nicholas. 1991. Cleanly fought. *Bulletin of the Atomic Scientists* 47, no. 7 (September): 24–29.

Frank, Andre Gunder. 1984. Can the debt bomb be defused? *World Policy Journal* 1, no. 4 (Summer): 723–43.

Freedman, Lawrence. 1981. *The Evolution of Nuclear Strategy*. New York: St. Martin's Press.

———. 1988. I exist; therefore I deter. *International Security* 13, no. 1 (Summer): 177–95.

Friedberg, Aaron. 1989. The political economy of American strategy. *World Politics* 41, no. 3 (April): 381–406.

Friedman, Thomas. 1990a. Confrontation in the Gulf: U.S. Gulf policy—Vague "vital interest." *New York Times*, August 12.

———. 1990b. How U.S. won support to use Mideast forces. *New York Times*, October 17.

Frisby, Michael. 1991. Rich got richer, poor poorer, another study on taxes finds. *Boston Globe*, September 13.

Fukuyama, Francis. 1989. The end of history. *The National Interest*, Summer.

Gallup Organization. 1985. March.

———. 1987. July.

———. 1989. Survey for *Times Mirror*. People, press, and politics series, January 27 to February 5, 1989. As cited by *Commonwealth Report*, no. 2 (April).

Galtung, Johan. 1969. Violence, peace, and peace research. *Journal of Peace Research* 6, no. 3:167–91.

Gamson, William. 1988. Political discourse and collective action. In B. Klandermans et al., eds., *From Structure to Action: Social Movement Participation Across Cultures*. Greenwich, Conn.: JAI Press.

———. 1990. *The Strategy of Protest*. 2d ed. Belmont, Calif.: Wadsworth.

Gamson, William, David Croteau, William Hoynes, and Theodore Sasson. 1992. Media images and the social construction of reality. *Annual Review of Sociology*.

Gansler, Jacques. 1980. *The Defense Industry*. Cambridge, Mass.: MIT Press.

———. 1989. *Affording Defense*. Cambridge, Mass.: MIT Press.

Garthoff, Raymond. 1978. Mutual deterrence and strategic arms limitations in Soviet policy. *International Security* 3 (Summer).

Garwin, Richard. 1988. A blueprint for radical weapons cuts. *Bulletin of the Atomic Scientists* 44, no. 2 (March).

Gault, Michael. 1989. Navajos inherit a legacy of radiation. *In These Times*, September 13–19.

Geiser, Ken. 1984. Converting economic conversion: An argument for building broader coalitions. In Suzanne Gordon and Dave McFadden, eds., *Economic Conversion: Revitalizing America's Economy*. Cambridge, Mass.: Ballinger.

Ginsberg, Benjamin. 1986. *The Captive Public: How Mass Opinion Promotes State Power*. New York: Basic Books.

———. 1989. How polling transforms public opinion. In Michael Margolis and Gary Mauser, eds., *Manipulating Public Opinion: Essays on Public Opinion as a Dependent Variable*. Belmont, Calif.: Wadsworth.

Ginsberg, Benjamin, and Martin Shefter. 1990. *Politics by Other Means: The Declining Importance of Elections in America*. New York: Basic Books.

Gitlin, Todd. 1980. *The Whole World is Watching*. Berkeley: University of California Press.

Glaspie, April. 1991. The Glaspie transcript: Saddam meets the U.S. ambassador. In Micah Sifry and Christopher Cerf, eds., *The Gulf War Reader: History, Documents, Opinions*. New York: Random House.

Gold, David. 1984. Conversion and industrial policy. In Suzanne Gordon and Dave McFadden, eds., *Economic Conversion: Revitalizing America's Economy*. Cambridge, Mass.: Ballinger.

———. 1990. *The Impact of Defense Spending on Investment, Productivity, and Economic Growth*. Washington, D.C.: Defense Budget Project.

Gordon, Suzanne, and Dave McFadden, eds. 1984. *Economic Conversion: Revitalizing America's Economy*. Cambridge, Mass.: Ballinger.

Graham, Thomas. 1989. American public opinion of NATO, extended deterrence, and use of nuclear weapons. Center for Science and International Affairs, Occasional Paper no. 4, May.

Gray, Colin. 1977. Across the nuclear divide: Strategic studies, past and present. *International Security* 2, no. 1 (Summer).

———. 1979. Nuclear strategy: The case for a theory of victory. *International Security* 4, no. 1 (Summer).

———. 1980. Targeting problems for central war. *Naval War College Review* 33, no. 1 (February).

Gray, Colin S., and Keith Payne. 1980. Victory is possible. *Foreign Policy* 39 (Summer): 14–27.

Green, Mark, and Mark Pinsky. 1990. *America's Transition: Blueprints for the 1990s.* Washington, D.C.: University Press of America.

Greenberg, Stanley. 1988. Looking toward '88: The politics of American identity. *World Policy Journal* 5, no. 4 (Fall): 695–722.

Greenberg, Stanley, and Melinda Lake. 1989. *Defining American Priorities.* Poll conducted for World Policy Institute, May 18–23.

Greenwood, Ted. 1975. *Making the MIRV.* Cambridge, Mass.: Ballinger.

Grobar, Lisa, and Richard Porter. 1989. Benoit revisited: Defense spending and economic growth in LDCs. *Journal of Conflict Resolution* 33, no. 2 (June): 318–45.

Grumbach, K., T. Bodenheimer, D. Himmelstein, and S. Woolhandler. 1991. Liberal benefits, conservative spending: The Physicians for a National Health Program Proposal. *Journal of the American Medical Association* 265:2549–54.

Hall, Welling. 1984. The antinuclear peace movement: Toward an evaluation of effectiveness. *Alternatives* 9 (Spring): 475–517.

Hallin, Daniel. 1986. *The Uncensored War: The Media and Vietnam.* New York: Oxford University Press.

———. 1987. Hegemony: The American news media from Vietnam to El Salvador. In D. Paletz, ed., *Political Communication Research.* Norwood, N.J.: Ablex.

———. 1991. TV's clean little war. *Bulletin of the Atomic Scientists* 47, no. 4 (May): 16–19.

Halloran, Richard. 1982. Pentagon draws up first strategy for fighting a long nuclear war. *New York Times*, May 30.

Halperin, Morton. 1987. *Nuclear Fallacy: Dispelling the Myth of Nuclear Strategy.* Cambridge, Mass.: Ballinger.

Harris, Louis. 1990. The gender gulf. *New York Times.*

Hart, Gary, et al. 1986. World policy forum: On debt and solvency. *World Policy Journal* 3, no. 2 (Spring): 347–67.

Hart Research Associates. 1984. June. In *Public Opinion Index* 1988.

Hartung, William. 1991. The boom at the arms bazaar. *Bulletin of the Atomic Scientists* 47, no. 8 (October).

Hecht, Susanna. 1989. The sacred cow in the green hell. *The Ecologist* 19, no. 6 (November/December).

Hecht, Susanna, and Alexander Cockburn. 1989. *The Fate of the Forest.* London: Verso.

Heilbroner, Robert. 1991. Lifting the silent depression. *New York Review of Books*, October 24.

Herken, Gregg. 1982. *The Winning Weapon: The Atomic Bomb and the Cold War, 1945–1950*. New York: Vintage.

———. 1987. *Counsels of War*. New York: Oxford University Press.

Herman, Edward. 1992. Democratic media. *Z Papers* 1 (January/March).

Hertsgaard, Mark. 1989. *On Bended Knee: The Press and the Reagan Presidency*. New York: Schocken.

Higgins, Richard. 1991a. U.S. foreign religious leaders declare moral opposition to Gulf war. *Boston Globe*, February 14.

———. 1991b. Protestant panel offers videotape on war questions. *Boston Globe*, February 24.

Hildyard, Nicolas. 1989a. Adios Amazonia? *The Ecologist* 19, no. 2 (March/April).

———. 1989b. Amazonia: The future in the balance. *The Ecologist* 19, no. 6 (November/December).

Hitchens, Christopher. 1991. Why we are stuck in the sand? *Harper's* 282, no. 1688 (January).

Hoffmann, Stanley. 1989. What should we do in the world? *The Atlantic*, October.

Holloway, David. 1984. *The Soviet Union and the Arms Race*. New Haven: Yale University Press.

Homer-Dixon, Thomas. 1991. On the threshold: Environmental changes as causes of acute conflict. *International Security* 16, no. 2 (Fall): 76–116.

Hoynes, William. 1992. Media, the market, and democracy: A study of public television. Ph.D. dissertation, Boston College.

Huntington, Samuel. 1981. *Boston Globe*, November 15.

———. 1988/89. The U.S.—Decline or renewal? *Foreign Affairs* 67, no. 2 (Winter): 76–96.

Hussein, King of Jordan. 1991. Interview: In the middle of the Middle East. *Village Voice*, March 5.

Inglehart, Ronald. 1977. *The Silent Revolution*. Princeton: Princeton University Press.

Institute for Peace and International Security. 1988. Call to common security. Cambridge, Mass. November.

Isaac, Rael Jean, and Erich Isaac. 1982. The counterfeit peacemakers: Atomic freeze. *American Spectator*, June.

James, Carol. 1988. *Strengthening People-to-People Development in the 1990s*. Washington, D.C.: U.S. Agency for International Development.

Jeffords, Susan. 1991. Protection racket. *The Women's Review of Books* 8, nos. 10–11 (July): 10.

Jervis, Robert. 1982/83. Deterrence and perception. *International Security* 7, no. 3 (Winter): 3–30.

———. 1988. The political effects of nuclear weapons: A comment. *International Security* 13, no. 2:80–90.

———. 1984. *The Illogic of American Nuclear Strategy*. Ithaca, N.Y.: Cornell University Press.

———. 1989. *The Meaning of the Nuclear Revolution: Statecraft and the Prospect of Armageddon.* Ithaca, N.Y.: Cornell University Press.

———. 1990. Arms control, stability and causes of war. *Daedalus*, Fall.

Johansen, Robert. 1991. A policy framework for world security. In Michael Klare and Daniel Thomas, eds., *World Security: Trends and Challenges at Century's End.* New York: St. Martin's Press.

Johnstone, Diana. 1992. The Greens in Rio de Janeiro: The missing political link? *In These Times*, July 8–21.

Jones, Dorothy. 1991. *Code of Peace.* Chicago: University of Chicago Press.

Joseph, Joe. 1984. The economic impact of military spending. In Paul Joseph and Simon Rosenblum, eds., *Search for Sanity: The Politics of Nuclear Weapons and Disarmament.* Boston: South End Press.

Joseph, Paul. 1982. From MAD to NUTs: The growing danger of nuclear war. *Socialist Review* 61:13–56.

———. 1983. Nuclear strategies and American foreign policy. *Socialist Register*, 202–18.

———. 1985. Making threats: Minimal deterrence, extended deterrence, and nuclear warfighting. *Sociological Quarterly* 26, no 3:293–310.

———. 1987. *Cracks in the Empire: State Politics in the Vietnam War.* New York: Columbia University Press.

———. 1992. Direct and indirect effects of the movement against the Vietnam war. In Jayne Werner and Luu Doan Huyhn, eds., *Essays in the History of the Vietnam War.* Armonk, N.Y.: M. E. Sharpe.

Kaldor, Mary. 1990. *The Imaginary War: Understanding the East-West Conflict.* Oxford: Basil Blackwell.

Kaplan, Fred. 1991a. Laser bombs hit targets 60 percent of time, officials say. *Boston Globe*, January 29.

———. 1991b. Specialists debate the value of Patriot. *Boston Globe*, May 5.

———. 1991c. Should U.S. retreat from Pacific? *Boston Globe*, July 14.

———. 1983. *The Wizards of Armageddon.* New York: Simon and Schuster.

Karns, Margaret, and Karen Mingst. 1991. Multilateral institutions and international security. In Michael Klare and Daniel Thomas, eds., *World Security: Trends and Challenges at Century's End.* New York: St. Martin's Press.

Katz, Milton. 1986. *Ban the Bomb: A History of SANE, the Committee for a Sane Nuclear Policy, 1957–1985.* New York: Greenwood Press.

Kaufmann, William. 1990a. *Glasnost, Perestroika, and U.S. Defense Spending.* Washington, D.C.: Brookings.

———. 1990b. A plan to cut military spending in half. *Bulletin of the Atomic Scientists* 46, no. 2 (March).

Kaysen, Carl. 1990. Is war obsolete? *International Security* 14, no. 4 (Spring): 42–64.

Keeny, Spurgeon, and Wolfgang Panofsky. 1982. MAD versus NUTs. *Foreign Affairs* 60:287–304.

Kegley, Charles, and Kenneth Schwab, eds. 1991. *After the Cold War: Questioning the Morality of Nuclear Deterrence.* Boulder, Colo.: Westview Press.

Kennedy, Paul. 1987. *The Rise and Fall of the Great Powers.* New York: Random House.

Kirk, Robin. 1991. Oh! What a lovely drug war in Peru. *The Nation,* September 30.

Klare, Michael. 1988. The interventionist impulse: U.S. military doctrine for low-intensity warfare. In Michael Klare and Peter Kornbluh, eds., *Low Intensity Warfare.* New York: Pantheon.

———. 1991a. Fighting drugs with the military. *The Nation,* January 1.

———. 1991b. Fueling the fire: How we armed the Middle East. *Bulletin of the Atomic Scientists* 47, no. 1 (January/February).

———. 1991c. Deadly convergence: The arms trade, nuclear/chemical/missile proliferation, and regional conflict in the 1990s. In Michael Klare and Daniel Thomas, eds., *World Security: Trends and Challenges at Century's End.* New York: St. Martin's Press.

Klare, Michael, and Daniel Thomas, eds. 1991. *World Security: Trends and Challenges at Century's End.* New York: St. Martin's Press.

Kohn, Richard, and Joseph Harahan, eds. 1988. U.S. strategic air power, 1948–1962: Excerpts from an interview with Generals Curtis E. LeMay, Leon W. Johnson, David A. Burchinal, and Jack J. Catton. *International Security* 12, no. 4 (Spring): 78–95.

Kokoshin, Andrei A. 1988. A Soviet view on radical weapons cuts. *Bulletin of the Atomic Scientists* 44, no. 2 (March).

Kotz, David, and Mehrene Larudee. 1991. Settling accounts: Who gets what in the postwar grab for contracts and oil. *In These Times,* March 27–April 2.

Kovel, Joel. 1983. *Against the State of Nuclear Terror.* Boston: South End Press.

Kramer, Bernard, S. Michael Kalick, and Michael Milburn. 1983. Attitudes towards nuclear weapons and nuclear war: 1945–1982. *Journal of Social Issues* 39, no. 1:7–24.

Kranish, Michael. 1991. Conservationists decry Bush oil plan. *Boston Globe,* February 18.

Krauthammer, Charles. 1989. Universal dominion: Towards a unipolar world. *The National Interest,* Winter, 46–49.

Kriesberg, Louis. 1992. *International Conflict Resolution.* New Haven: Yale University Press.

Kriesberg, Louis, and Stuart Thorson. 1991. Epilogue: War in the Persian Gulf. In Kriesberg and Thorson, eds., *Timing the De-escalation of International Conflicts.* Syracuse, N.Y.: Syracuse University Press.

Kupchan, Charles. 1989. Empire, military power, and economic decline. *International Security* 13, no. 4 (Spring): 36–53.

Kurkjian, Stephen. 1991. U.S. sent Iraq technology last summer. *Boston Globe,* March 12.

Ladd, Everett Carll. 1982. The freeze framework. *Public Opinion*, August/September.

Lakoff, George. 1991. Metaphor and war: The metaphor system used to justify war in the Gulf. Manuscript. January.

Lamare, James. 1989. Gender and public opinion: Defense and nuclear issues in New Zealand. *Journal of Peace Research* 26, no. 3: 285–96.

Levi, Barbara, Frank von Hippel, and William Daugherty. 1987/88. Civilian casualties from "limited" nuclear attacks on the Soviet Union. *International Security* 12, no. 3 (Winter): 168–89.

Levy, Jack. 1989. The causes of war: A review of theories and evidence. In Philip Tetlock et al., eds., *Behavior, Society, and Nuclear War*. New York: Oxford University Press.

Lifton, Robert, and Richard Falk. 1982. *Indefensible Weapons: The Political and Psychological Case Against Nuclearism*. New York: Basic Books.

Lindblom, Charles. 1977. *Politics and Markets*. New York: Basic Books.

Lindeman, Mark. 1989. U.S. public opinion findings and implications for mutual security. Manuscript.

Linden, Eugene. 1991. Getting blacker every day. *Time*, May 27, 50–51.

Little, David. 1991. The role of international norms in governing war. Lecture at the annual meeting of the Peace Studies Association, Washington, D.C., April 12.

Lopez, George. 1990. Why the generals wage war on the people. *Bulletin of the Atomic Scientists* 46, no. 4 (May): 30–33.

———. 1991. Not so clean. *Bulletin of the Atomic Scientists* 47, no. 7 (September): 30–35.

Lowi, Theodore. 1985. *The Personal President: Power Invested, Promise Unfulfilled*. Ithaca, N.Y.: Cornell University Press.

McCrea, Frances, and Gerald Markle. 1989. *Minutes to Midnight*. Newbury Park, Calif.: Sage.

MacDougall, John. 1990. Congress and the campaign to stop the MX missile. In Sam Marullo and John Lofland, eds., *Peace Action in the Eighties*. New Brunswick, N.J.: Rutgers University Press.

———. 1991a. Congress, the grassroots, and the comprehensive nuclear test ban. *Research in Social Movements, Conflicts and Change* 13:173–97.

———. 1991b. The freeze movement, Congress, and the MX missile. *International Social Movement Research* 3:263–82.

MacEwan, Arthur, and William Tabb. 1989. The economy in crisis: National power and international instability. *Socialist Review* 89, no. 3:67–91.

Mack, John. 1982. The perception of U.S.–Soviet intentions and other psychological dimensions of the nuclear arms race. *American Journal of Orthopsychiatry* 52, no. 4 (October): 590–99.

———. 1983. The psychological impact of the nuclear arms competition on children and adolescents. Testimony to Select Committee on Children, Youth and Families, U.S. House of Representatives, September 20.

MacKenzie, Donald. 1988. The Soviet Union and strategic missile guidance. *International Security* 13, no. 2:5–54.
McNamara, Robert. 1962. Untitled. *Newsweek*, June 9.
———. 1983. The military role of nuclear weapons: Perceptions and misperceptions. *Foreign Affairs* 62, no. 1 (Fall).
———. 1986. *Blundering into Disaster: Surviving the First Century of the Nuclear Age*. New York: Pantheon.
MacNeill, Jim, Pieter Winsemius, and Taizo Yakushiji. 1991. *Beyond Interdependence*. New York: Oxford University Press.
Mandelbaum, Michael. 1979. *The Nuclear Question*. Cambridge: Cambridge University Press.
Mann, Michael. 1987. The roots and contradictions of modern militarism. *The New Left Review*, no. 162 (March/April): 77–96.
Margolis, Michael, and Gary Mauser, eds. 1989. *Manipulating Public Opinion: Essays on Public Opinion as a Dependent Variable*. Belmont, Calif.: Wadsworth.
Markusen, Ann. 1986. The Militarized Economy. *World Policy Journal*, Summer, 495–516.
Marullo, Sam, and David Meyer. 1991. Grassroots mobilization and international politics: Peace protest and the end of the cold war. In Louis Kriesberg, ed., *Research in Social Movements*. Newbury Park, Calif.: Sage.
Massing, Michael. 1991. The way to war. *New York Review of Books*, March 28.
Mathews, Jessica Tuchman. 1989. Redefining Security. *Foreign Affairs* 68, no. 2 (Spring): 162–77.
Maxwell, Kenneth. 1991a. The tragedy of the Amazon. *New York Review of Books*, March 7.
———. 1991b. The mystery of Chico Mendes. *New York Review of Books*, March 28.
Mead, Walter Russell. 1987. *Mortal Splendor*. New York: Basic Books.
———. 1988/89. The United States and the world economy. 2 parts. *World Policy*, Winter 1988/89 and Summer 1989.
Mearsheimer, John. 1990. Back to the future: Instability in Europe after the Cold War. *International Security* 15, no. 1 (Summer).
Melman, Seymour. 1970. *Pentagon Capitalism: The Political Economy of War*. New York: McGraw Hill.
———. 1983. *Profits Without Production*. New York: Knopf.
———. 1985. Problems of conversion from military to civilian economy: An agenda of topics, questions, and hypotheses. *Bulletin of Peace Proposals* 16, no. 1.
———. 1989. *The Demilitarized Economy: Disarmament and Conversion*. Montreal: Horizon Press.
———. 1990. Planning for economic conversion. *The Nation*, April 16.

Meyer, David. 1990. *A Winter of Discontent: The Nuclear Freeze and American Politics*. New York: Praeger.

———. 1991a. Peace movements and national security policy: A research agenda. *Peace and Change* 16, no. 2:131–61.

———. 1991b. Peace protest and policy: Explaining the rise and decline (and rise and decline) of antinuclear movements in post-war America. Paper delivered at the annual meeting of the American Political Science Association, Washington, D.C., August.

Migone, Gian Giacomo. 1989. The decline of the bipolar system, or a second look at the history of the Cold War. In Mary Kaldor, Gerald Holden, and Richard Falk, eds., *The New Detente: Rethinking East-West Relations*. London: Verso.

Milburn, Michael, Paul Watanabe, and Bernard Kramer. 1986. The nature and sources of attitudes towards a nuclear freeze. *Political Psychology* 7, no. 4:661–74.

Miller, John, and Ramon Castellblanch. 1988. Does manufacturing matter? *Dollars and Sense*, October.

Miller, S. M. 1989. Latent liberalism? *The Commonwealth Report*, no. 2 (April).

Miller, William. 1991. Slaughter of Iraqis called factor in war's halt. *Boston Globe*, August 4.

Moberg, David. 1991. Can public rescue the infrastructure in a tale of three deficits? *In These Times*, February 13–19.

———. 1992. Decline and inequality often the great U-turn. *In These Times*, May 27–June 9.

Molander, Earl, and Roger Molander. 1990. The anti–nuclear war movement of the 1980s. In Francesca Cancian and James Gibson, eds., *Making War/Making Peace*. Belmont, Calif.: Wadsworth.

Moomaw, William. 1990. Policy responses to global climate change. *Fletcher Forum* 14, no. 2 (Summer): 249–61.

Morales, Waltraud Queiser. 1989. The war on drugs: A new U.S. national security doctrine? *Third World Quarterly*, July, 147–69.

Morgenthau, Hans. 1967. *Politics Among Nations*. New York: Knopf.

Moskos, Charles. 1988. *A Call to Civic Service: National Service for Country and Community*. New York: Free Press.

Mueller, Carol. 1988. *The Politics of the Gender Gap: The Social Construction of Political Influence*. Newbury Park, Calif.: Sage.

Mueller, Harald, and Thomas Risse-Kappen. 1987. Origins of estrangement: The peace movement and the changed image of America in West Germany. *International Security* 12, no. 1 (Summer): 52–88.

Mueller, John. 1988. The essential irrelevance of nuclear weapons: Stability in the postwar world. *International Security* 13, no. 2 (Fall): 55–79.

———. 1989. *Retreat from Doomsday: The Obsolescence of Major War*. New York: Basic Books.

Munnell, Alicia. 1990. Why has productivity growth declined? Productivity and public investment. *New England Economic Review*, January/February, 3–22.

Myrdal, Alva. 1982. *The Game of Disarmament: How the United States and Russia Run the Arms Race*. New York: Pantheon.

Nathanson, Stephen. 1989. In defense of moderate patriotism. *Ethics* 99:535–52.

National Center for Health Care Statistics. 1990. *Health United States 1989*. U.S. Department of Health and Human Services. Washington, D.C.: Government Printing Office.

National Commission for Economic Conversion and Disarmament. 1990. *A Peaceful Way to Spend $165 Billion*. Pamphlet.

National Conference of Catholic Bishops. 1983. *The Challenge of Peace: God's Promise and Our Response*. Washington, D.C.: USCC.

NBC News/Associated Press. 1982. March 29–30.

Neuffer, Elizabeth. 1991. Report sees crisis in health of Iraqis. *Boston Globe*, October 23.

Newhouse, John. 1973. *Cold Dawn: The Story of SALT*. New York: Holt, Rinehart and Winston.

New York Times. 1990a. $150 billion a year. Editorial. March 9, 10.

———. 1990b. Polls finds U.S. expects peace dividend. January 25.

Nickerson, Colin, and Elizabeth Neuffer. 1991. Press losing war on curbs. *Boston Globe*, February 17.

Nitze, Paul. 1956. Atoms, strategy and policy. *Foreign Affairs* 34:187–98.

Noble, Laura. 1992. Healthcare reform stews in congressional pressure cooker. *Healthcare Financial Management*, January, 21–39.

Nolan, Martin. 1991. A victory for the psyche. *Boston Globe*, March 10.

Nusbaumer, Michael. 1990. Effects on scholarship and higher education. In Sam Marullo and John Lofland, eds., *Peace Action in the Eighties*. New Brunswick, N.J.: Rutgers University Press.

Office of Technology Assessment. 1988. *Paying the Bill: Manufacturing and America's Trade Deficit*. Washington, D.C. June.

Opinion Roundup. 1988. *Public Opinion*, March/April.

Orfield, Gary. 1992. *Choice and Control*. Stanford: Stanford University Press.

Page, Benjamin, and Robert Shapiro. 1983. Effects of public opinion on policy. *American Political Science Review* 77, no. 2: 175–90.

———. 1989. Educating and manipulating the public. In Margolis and Mauser, eds., *Manipulating Public Opinion*. Belmont, Calif.: Wadsworth.

Palme, Olof. 1982. *Common Security: The Report of the Independent Commission on Disarmament and Security Issues*. London: Pan Books.

Panayotou, Theodore. 1990. Counting the cost: Resource degradation in the developing world. *Fletcher Forum* 14, no. 2 (Summer): 270–83.

Parenti, Michael. 1986. *Inventing Reality: The Politics of the Mass Media*. New York: St. Martin's Press.

———. 1989. Mass media bias and class control. In Michael Margolis and Gary Mauser, eds., *Manipulating Public Opinion: Essays on Public Opinion as a Dependent Variable*. Belmont, Calif.: Wadsworth.

Parkin, Frank. 1968. *Middle Class Radicalism: The Social Basis of the British Campaign for Nuclear Disarmament*. New York: Praeger.

Parsons, Talcott. 1968. Social systems. In *International Encyclopedia of the Social Sciences*. New York: Macmillan.

Peace, Roger. 1991. *A Just and Lasting Peace*. Chicago: Noble Press.

Peach, J. Dexter. 1989. GAO's views on modernizing and cleaning up DOE's nuclear weapons complex. Testimony before the Subcommittee on Procurement and Military Nuclear Systems, Committee on Armed Services, House of Representatives. February 21.

Perkovich, George. 1992. Weapons complexes v. democracy. *Bulletin of the Atomic Scientists* 48, no. 5 (June).

Pertman, Adam. 1991. Most residents favor continued sanctions. *Boston Globe*, January 17.

Phillips, Kevin. 1984. *Staying on Top: The Business Case for a National Industrial Strategy*. New York: Random House.

———. 1990. *The Politics of Rich and Poor*. New York: Random House.

Pipes, Richard. 1980. Militarism and the Soviet state. *Daedalus*, Fall.

———. 1984. Can the Soviet Union reform? *Foreign Affairs* 63, no. 1 (Fall).

Pollen, Robert. 1989. Debt dependent growth and financial innovation: Pathways to instability in the U.S. and Latin America. In Arthur MacEwan and William Tabb, eds., *Instability and Change in the World Economy*. New York: Monthly Review Press.

Porter, Gareth. 1990. Post–Cold War global environment and security. *Fletcher Forum* 14, no. 2 (Summer): 332–44.

Posey, Darrell. 1989. Alternatives to forest destruction: Lessons from the Mebengokre Indians. *The Ecologist* 19, no. 6 (November/December).

Postel, Sandra, and Chrisopher Flavin. 1991. Reshaping the global economy. In Lester Brown et al., *State of the World 1991*. New York: Norton.

Postol, Theodore. 1991/92. Lessons of the Gulf War experience with Patriot. *International Security* 16, no. 3 (Winter).

Potter, William, and Ann Fliorini. 1988. Converting nuclear missiles for peaceful use. Foreign Policy Institute, Johns Hopkins University.

Powers, Thomas. 1982. Choosing a strategy for World War III. *Atlantic Monthly*, November.

Pringle, Peter, and William Arkin. 1983. *SIOP*. New York: Norton.

Public Agenda Foundation. 1984. Voter options on nuclear arms policy. Paper prepared for the Center for Foreign Policy Development, Brown University.

———. 1988. The public, the Soviets, and nuclear arms. Paper prepared for the Center for Foreign Policy Development, Brown University.

Public Opinion. 1988. Dealing with the Soviets. March/April.

Qualter, Terence. 1989. The role of the mass media in limiting the public agenda. In Mark Margolis and Gary Mauser, eds., *Manipulating Public Opinion: Essays on Public Opinion as a Dependent Variable*. Belmont, Calif.: Wadsworth.

Radosh, Ronald. 1983. The "peace council" and peace. *New Republic*, January 31.

Reich, Robert. 1989a. *Made in America*. Cambridge, Mass.: MIT Press.

———. 1989b. The quiet path to technological preeminence. *Scientific American* 261, no. 4 (October): 41–47.

———. 1989c. Why the rich are getting richer and the poor poorer. *New Republic*, May 1.

Renner, Michael. 1989. National security: The economic and environmental dimensions. Worldwatch Paper no. 89. Worldwatch Institute, Washington, D.C.

———. 1990. Converting to a peaceful econony. In Lester Brown et al., *State of the World 1990*. New York: Norton.

———. 1991. Assessing the military's war on the environment. In Lester Brown et al., *State of the World 1991*. New York: Norton.

Repetto, Robert. 1990. Deforestation in the tropics. *Scientific American* 262, no. 4 (April): 30–42.

Repetto, Robert, and William Magrath, Michael Wells, Christine Beer, and Fabrizio Rossini. 1989. *Wasting Assets: Natural Resources in the National Income Accounts*. Washington, D.C.: World Resources Institute.

Rich, Bruce. 1989. The "greening" of the development banks: Rhetoric and reality. *The Ecologist* 19, no. 2.

Rielly, John. 1992. Public opinion: The pulse of the nineties. In Charles Kegley and Eugene Wittkopf, eds., *The Future of American Foreign Policy*. New York: St. Martin's Press.

Risse-Kappen, Thomas. 1988. Zero option: The global elimination of ground-launched intermediate-range missiles: A political assessment. Peace Research Institute of Frankfurt Report no. 2, June.

———. 1990. Public opinion, domestic structure, and security policy: The cases of France, West Germany, Japan and the United States. ECPR Workshop Paper, Bochum, April 2–7.

Rochon, Thomas. 1988. *Mobilizing for Peace: the Antinuclear Movements in Western Europe*. Princeton: Princeton University Press.

Rogne, Leah, and Bradley Harper. 1990. The meaning of civil disobedience: The case of the Honeywell project. In Sam Marullo and John Lofland, eds., *Peace Action in the Eighties*. New Brunswick, N.J.: Rutgers University Press.

Rohatyn, Felix. 1984. *The Twenty-Year Century*. New York: Random House.

Romm, Joseph. 1991. Needed: A no-regrets energy policy. *Bulletin of the Atomic Scientists* 47, no. 6 (July/August): 31–36.

Roper Organization. 1988. Report 88-2, January, 9–23.

Rosen, Stephen. 1977. *Testing the Theory of the Military-Industrial Complex*. Lexington, Mass.: Heath Publishers.

Rosenbaum, David. 1989. Pentagon savings unlikely to be spent elsewhere. *New York Times*, November 11.

Rosenberg, David Alan. 1979. American atomic strategy and the hydrogen bomb decision. *Journal of American History* 66:62–87.

———. 1981/82. A smoking radiating ruin at the end of two hours. *International Security* 6, no. 3 (Winter).

———. 1982. U.S. nuclear stockpile, 1945 to 1950. *Bulletin of Atomic Scientists* 38, no. 4 (May): 25–30.

Rostow, Eugene. 1981. *Aviation Week and Space Technology*, June 29, 24.

Russett, Bruce. 1972. The revolt of the masses: The effect of public opinion on military expenditures. In Bruce Russett, ed., *War, Peace, and Numbers*. Beverly Hills, Calif.: Sage.

———. 1989. Democracy, public opinion and nuclear weapons. In Philip Tedlock, Jo Husbands, Robert Jervis, Paul Stern, and Charles Tilly, eds., *Behavior, Society, and Nuclear War*. New York: Oxford University Press.

———. 1990. *Controlling the Sword: The Democratic Governance of National Security*. Cambridge, Mass.: Harvard University Press.

Russett, Bruce, and H. Starr. 1985. *World Politics: The Menu for Choice*. New York: Freeman.

Ryan, Charlotte. 1991. *Prime Time Activism*. Boston: South End Press.

Sagan, Scott. 1987. SIOP-62: The nuclear war plan briefing to President Kennedy. *International Security* 12, no. 1 (Summer): 22–51.

Said, Edward. 1991. Ignorant armies clash by night. *The Nation*, February 11.

Sanders, Jerry. 1982. *Peddlers of Crisis*. Boston: South End Press.

———. 1989. Peace and political economy: Is there a strategy for activists in U.S. economic turmoil? *Annual Review of Peace Activism*.

Schauffler, David. 1988. Citizen diplomacy. *Nuclear Times*, May/June.

Scheer, Robert. 1982. With enough shovels. *Playboy*, December.

Schell, Jonathan. 1986. *The Abolition*. New York: Avon Books.

Schelling, Thomas. 1960. *The Strategy of Conflict*. New York: Oxford University Press.

———. 1966. *Arms and Influence*. New Haven: Yale University Press.

Schwartz, Tanya. 1989. The Brazilian forest people's movement. *The Ecologist* 19, no. 6 (November/December).

Schwartz, William, and Charles Derber. 1990. *The Nuclear Seduction*. Berkeley: University of California Press.

Sciolino, Elaine, and Michael Wines. 1992. Bush's greatest glory fades as questions on Iraq persist. *New York Times*, June 27.

Serrano, Alfonso. 1991/92. Fighting cocaine in Peru. *Nuclear Times*, Winter.

Shabecoff, Philip. 1990. Loss of tropical forests is found much worse than was thought. *New York Times*, June 8.

Shapiro, Robert, and Benjamin Page. 1988. Foreign policy and the rational public. *Journal of Conflict Resolution* 32, no. 2:211–47.

Shaw, Martin. 1988. *Dialectics of War*. London: Pluto Press.

Shenfield, Stephen. 1989. Minimum nuclear deterrence: The debate among civilian analysts. Paper prepared for the Center for Foreign Policy Development, Brown University.

Shulman, Seth. 1990. Toxic travels: Inside the military's environmental nightmare. *Nuclear Times*, Autumn.

Simon, Herbert. 1984. Mutual deterrence or nuclear suicide. *Science* 223:775–76.

Sivard, Ruth Leger. 1989. *World Military and Social Expenditures 1989*. Washington, D.C.: World Priorities.

Small, Melvin. 1988. *Johnson, Nixon, and the Doves*. New Brunswick, N.J.: Rutgers University Press.

Smith, Hedrick. 1989. *The Power Game: How Washington Works*. New York: Ballantine Books.

Smith, Philip. 1991. Codes and conflict: Towards a theory of war as ritual. *Theory and Society* 20:103–38.

Smuckler, Ralph, and Robert Berg, with David Gordon. 1988. New challenges, new opportunities: U.S. cooperation for international growth and development in the 1990s. Center for Advanced Study of International Development, East Lansing, Mich.

Solo, Pam. 1988. *From Protest to Policy: Beyond the Freeze to Common Security*. Cambridge, Mass.: Ballinger.

———. 1989. The Reagan era: The freeze campaign and political power. *Annual Review of Peace Activism*, 1–10.

Solo, Pam, Ted Sasson, and Rob Leavitt. 1989. *Principles of Common Security*. Cambridge, Mass.: Institute for Peace and International Security.

Southgate, Douglas. 1990. The causes of land degradation along "spontaneously" expanding agricultural frontiers in the Third World. *Land Economics* 66, no. 1 (February).

Spector, Leonard. 1984. *Nuclear Proliferation Today*. New York: Random House.

Speth, James Gustave. 1989. Coming to terms: Toward a North-South bargain for the environment. *World Resources Institute: Issues and Ideas*, June, 1–4.

Steele, Karen Dorn. 1989. Hanford: America's nuclear graveyard. *Bulletin of Atomic Scientists*, October, 15–23.

Steinbruner, John. 1981/82. Nuclear decapitation. *Foreign Policy*, Winter.

Stone, Jeremy. 1982. Forum. *Nuclear Times*, October.

Stowsky, Jay. 1986. The future of high-tech R and D. *World Policy Journal*, Fall, 697–722.

Strong, Susan. 1991. Militarism and/or third world development. *The New Economy*, February.

Stucky, Bill. N.d. More security for less money, strength through balance. Mimeo.

Talbott, Strobe. 1979. *Endgame: The Inside Story of SALT II*. New York: Harper and Row.

———. 1984. *Deadly Gambits*. New York: Knopf.

Tarrow, Sidney. 1989. Struggle, politics and reform: Collective action, social movements, and cycles of protest. Occasional Paper no. 21, Center for International Studies, Cornell University.

Taylor, Richard, and Nigel Young. 1987. *Campaigns for Peace*. Manchester: Manchester University Press.

Terbough, John. 1989. *Where Have all the Birds Gone?* Princeton: Princeton University Press.

Thompson, Edward. 1990. History turns on a new hinge. *The Nation*, January 29.

Thompson, Koy, and Nigel Dudley. 1989. Transnationals and oil in Amazonia. *The Ecologist* 19, no. 6 (November/December).

Thurow, Lester. 1985. America among equals. In Sanford Ungar, ed., *Estrangement*. New York: Oxford University Press.

Tilly, Charles. 1978. *From Mobilization to Revolution*. Reading, Mass.: Addison-Wesley.

Tirman, John. 1991. Shifting balances point to new spurs for war. *Boston Globe*, December 22.

Tonelson, Alan. 1991. What is the national interest? *The Atlantic*, July.

Trachtenberg, Marc. 1985. The influence of nuclear weapons in the Cuban missile crisis. *International Security* 10, no. 1 (Summer).

Treece, Dave. 1989. The militarization and industrialization of Amazonia. *The Ecologist* 19, no 6 (November/December).

Turco, R. P. et al. 1983. Nuclear winter: Global consequences of multiple nuclear explosions. *Science* 222:1283–92.

Tye, Larry. 1990. "Gender gap" grows on backing for war. *Boston Globe*, November 22.

———. 1991a. Kinder light on U.S. image. *Boston Globe*, January 22.

———. 1991b. All-volunteer force no mirror of society. *Boston Globe*, February 2.

Tyler, Patrick. 1992. Pentagon imagines new enemies to fight in post-Cold-War era. *New York Times*, February 17.

Uchitelle, Louis. 1990. Economy expected to absorb effects of military cuts. *New York Times*, April 15.

Ullmann, John. 1984. Can business become a participant? In Suzanne Gordon and Dave McFadden, eds., *Economic Conversion: Revitalizing America's Economy*. Cambridge, Mass.: Ballinger.

———. 1989. Economic conversion: Indispensable for America's economic recovery. National Commission for Economic Conversion and Disarmament Briefing Paper no. 3, April.

Union of Concerned Scientists. 1989. Poll on U.S. role on global warming. Cited in *Boston Globe*, November.

United Nations Development Program. 1991. *Human Development Report 1991*. New York: Oxford University Press.

Urquhart, Brian. 1991. Learning from the Gulf. *New York Review of Books*, March 7: 34–37.

Utgoff, Victor. 1982. In defense of counterforce. *International Security* 6, no. 4 (Spring): 44–60.

Viorst, Milton. 1991a. The house of Hashem. *New Yorker*, January 7.

———. 1991b. Letter from Baghdad. *New Yorker*, June 24.

———. 1991c. After the Liberation. *New Yorker*, September 30.

Walker, Paul, and Eric Stambler. 1991. Dirty weapons in the Gulf war. *Bulletin of the Atomic Scientists* 47, no. 4 (May): 20–24.

Waller, Douglas. 1987. *Congress and the Nuclear Freeze*. Amherst: University of Massachusetts Press.

Wallerstein, Immanuel. 1989. Peace and war in the modern world-system. In Linda Forcey, ed., *Peace: Meanings, Politics, Strategies*. New York: Praeger.

Waltz, Kenneth. 1967. International structure, national force, and the balance of world power. *Journal of International Affairs* 21:220–28.

———. 1979. *Theory of International Politics*. New York: McGraw-Hill.

Weinberger, Caspar. 1990. *Fighting for Peace: Seven Critical Years in the Pentagon*. New York: Warner.

Winpisinger, William. 1982. Organized labor and economic conversion. In Lloyd Dumas, ed., *The Political Economy of Arms Reduction*. Boulder, Colo.: Westview Press.

Wirth, David. 1991. Catastrophic climate change. In Michael Klare and Daniel Thomas, eds., *World Security: Trends and Challenges at Century's End*. New York: St. Martin's Press.

Wittkopf, Eugene. 1990. *Faces of Internationalism: Public Opinion and American Foreign Policy*. Durham, N.C.: Duke University Press.

Wittner, Lawrence. 1984. *Rebels Against War: The American Peace Movement, 1933–1983*. Philadelphia: Temple University Press.

Wolf, Edward. 1988. Avoiding a mass extinction of species. In Lester Brown et al., *State of the World 1988*. New York: Norton.

Wood, Robert. 1988. Debt crisis update: 1988. *Socialist Review* 3:103–15.

Woodward, Bob. 1991. *The Commanders*. New York: Simon and Schuster.

World Bank. 1991. World debt tables 1990–91: External debt of developing countries. Supplement. Washington, D.C.

World Federalist Association. 1991. *A New World Order? Essays on Restructuring the United Nations*. Washington, D.C.

World Policy Institute. 1989. American priorities in the new world era. Statement prepared by Richard Barnet, Lester Brown, and Robert Browne. New York.

World Resources Institute. 1990. *World Resources 1990–91*. Washington, D.C.

Worldwatch. 1988. Reclaiming the future. In Lester Brown et al., *State of the World 1988*. New York: Norton.

Yankelovich, Daniel, and John Doble. 1984. The public mood: Nuclear weapons and the USSR. *Foreign Affairs*, Fall, 33–46.

Yankelovich, Daniel, and Richard Smoke. 1988. America's "new thinking." *Foreign Affairs*, Fall, 1–17.

Young, Nigel. 1986. The peace movement: A comparative and analytical survey. *Alternatives* 11:185–217.

Yudkin, Marcia. 1984. When kids think the unthinkable. *Psychology Today*, April, 18–25.

Zald, Mayer. 1987. The future of social movements. In Mayer Zald and John McCarthy, eds., *Social Movements in an Organized Society*. New Brunswick, N.J.: Transaction Books.

Index